The Early Childhood Educator

Feminist Thought in Childhood Research

Series editors: Jayne Osgood and Veronica Pacini-Ketchabaw

Drawing on feminist scholarship, this boundary-pushing series explores the use of creative, experimental, new materialist and post-humanist research methodologies that address various aspects of childhood. *Feminist Thought in Childhood Research* foregrounds examples of research practices within feminist childhood studies that engage with post-humanism, science studies, affect theory, animal studies, new materialisms and other post-foundational perspectives that seek to decentre human experience. Books in the series offer lived examples of feminist research praxis and politics in childhood studies. The series includes authored and edited collections – from early career and established scholars – addressing past, present and future childhood research issues from a global context.

Also available in the series:
Feminist Research for 21st-Century Childhoods: Common Worlds Methods,
edited by B. Denise Hodgins
Feminists Researching Gendered Childhoods: Generative Entanglements,
edited by Jayne Osgood and Kerry H. Robinson
Theorizing Feminist Ethics of Care in Early Childhood Practice,
edited by Rachel Langford
More-Than-Human Literacies in Early Childhood,
Abigail Hackett

The Early Childhood Educator

Critical Conversations in Feminist Theory

Edited by
Rachel Langford and Brooke Richardson

BLOOMSBURY ACADEMIC
LONDON • NEW YORK • OXFORD • NEW DELHI • SYDNEY

BLOOMSBURY ACADEMIC
Bloomsbury Publishing Plc
50 Bedford Square, London, WC1B 3DP, UK
1385 Broadway, New York, NY 10018, USA
29 Earlsfort Terrace, Dublin 2, Ireland

BLOOMSBURY, BLOOMSBURY ACADEMIC and the Diana logo are
trademarks of Bloomsbury Publishing Plc

First published in Great Britain 2023
This paperback edition published 2024

Copyright © Rachel Langford and Brooke Richardson and contributors, 2023

Rachel Langford and Brooke Richardson and contributors have asserted their right under
the Copyright, Designs and Patents Act, 1988, to be identified as Author of this work.

For legal purposes the Acknowledgements on p. xv constitute an
extension of this copyright page.

Series design by Anna Berzovan
Cover image: © Vizerskaya /Getty Image

All rights reserved. No part of this publication may be reproduced or transmitted
in any form or by any means, electronic or mechanical, including photocopying,
recording, or any information storage or retrieval system, without prior
permission in writing from the publishers.

Bloomsbury Publishing Plc does not have any control over, or responsibility for,
any third-party websites referred to or in this book. All internet addresses given in this
book were correct at the time of going to press. The author and publisher regret any
inconvenience caused if addresses have changed or sites have ceased to exist,
but can accept no responsibility for any such changes.

A catalogue record for this book is available from the British Library.

A catalog record for this book is available from the Library of Congress.

ISBN: HB: 978-1-3502-6719-0
        PB: 978-1-3502-6723-7
        ePDF: 978-1-3502-6720-6
        eBook: 978-1-3502-6721-3

Series: Feminist Thought in Childhood Research

Typeset by Integra Software Services Pvt. Ltd.

To find out more about our authors and books visit www.bloomsbury.com
and sign up for our newsletters.

Contents

List of Contributors	vii
Series Editors' Foreword	xiii
Acknowledgements	xv
Introduction *Brooke Richardson and Rachel Langford*	1
1 Reflections on Poststructural Feminisms: Supporting Multiple Performances of Teacher Identities *Kylie Smith*	11
2 Kristevan Early Childhood Teacher: Poststructural Feminist Identities in Australia and New Zealand *Sonja Arndt and Marek Tesar*	27
3 Labouring Relations and the Early Childhood Educator: The Return to Materialism *Jan Newberry*	45
4 Reclaiming Early Childhood Educator(s) *as* Early Childhood Educator(s) through Feminist Ethics of Care *Melinda Bruce and Alana Powell*	61
Commentary 1 *Rachel Langford and Brooke Richardson*	79
5 Waves upon Waves: Highlighting the Invisibility of the Early Childhood Workforce through Conversations with Fourth Wave, Black and Postcolonial Feminisms *Flora Harmon, Erica Ritter and Radhika Viruru*	83
6 Womanist Praxis in Early Childhood Education and Care: Educators' Nourishment of Mind-Body-Spirit Relations *Nnenna Odim, Kia S. Rideaux and Michelle Salazar Pérez*	99
7 Decolonizing Feminisms: Provocations for Early Childhood Educators in Aotearoa/New Zealand *Jenny Ritchie*	115
Commentary 2 *Brooke Richardson and Rachel Langford*	135
8 Queer Bodies in Early Childhood: Gender and Sexuality Disruption(s) and Impure Feminisms to 'Get Us Free' *Janice Kroeger*	139
9 Posthuman Possibilities for the Early Childhood Educator *Meagan Montpetit*	157

10 Early Childhood Pedagogues, Thresholds and the Potentialities of
    Feminisms and New Materialism *Gunilla Dahlberg and
    Ann Merete Otterstad*   175

11 Femme-inist Approaches to Early Childhood Education and Care:
    Cultivating Pedagogies of Care via Femme Theory *Adam W.J. Davies
    and Rhea Ashley Hoskin*   191

    Commentary 3 *Rachel Langford and Brooke Richardson*   209

Concluding Remarks *Rachel Langford and Brooke Richardson*   213

Index   217

Contributors

Sonja Arndt is Senior Lecturer at the Melbourne Graduate School of Education, the University of Melbourne, Australia. Her teaching, leadership and research intersect early childhood education and the philosophy of the subject, with a particular focus on equity and diversity in early childhood settings and the often-unrecognized topic of teacher diversity. She is the coordinator of pre-service teacher placement experiences. Arndt has published widely on related subjects, and actively promotes inclusionary engagements with teacher identity formations in early childhood education. She is currently the Vice President of the Philosophy of Education Society of Australasia.

Melinda Bruce is a Registered Early Childhood Educator and emerging scholar who recently completed her MA in Early Childhood Studies at Toronto Metropolitan University (formerly Ryerson University), Canada. Prior to graduate studies, Bruce was a Professional Practice Analyst with the College of Early Childhood Educators, Ontario, Canada. Her research interests focus on discourses of care, professionalism and early childhood educator identities, and evolving images of the child/childhood within the context of early childhood education and twenty-first-century Canadian society. She co-presented and co-authored *Insights from feminist ethics of care as a contemporary critical theory for contesting binaries and imagining possibilities* (2020) at the Canadian Association for Research in Early Childhood Online Symposium.

Gunilla Dahlberg is Professor Emeritus of Pedagogy at Stockholm University, the Department of Child and Youth Studies, Sweden. Her recent research focuses on experimental work and change in the field of early childhood education. She co-wrote the book *Beyond quality in Early Childhood Education and Care*, with Peter Moss and Alan Pence, and *Ethics and Politics in Early Childhood Education*, with Peter Moss. During the last decades she has carried out research in close cooperation with the preschools in the city of Reggio Emilia, Italy, and is a member of the scientific board of Fondazione Reggio Children, Centro Loris Malaguzzi.

Adam Davies is Assistant Professor at the University of Guelph, Canada in Family Relations & Human Development. Their research interests focus on gender and sexuality in early childhood education, queer masculinities and critical disabilities. They have published on gay masculinities, sexuality education in early childhood education, inclusion and autism, and the regulation of gender in school settings. Davies is an Ontario Certified Teacher and Ontario Registered Early Childhood Educator.

Flora Harmon is a PhD Student specializing in early childhood education in the Texas A&M University School of Teaching, Learning, and Culture, USA. Her research interest focuses on culturally responsive professional development in early childhood education, early childhood workforce advocacy, child welfare, learning philosophies in early childhood education, and Black Feminist Theory in early childhood education. Her most recent work focuses on advocating for equity-based practices for the early childhood workforce.

Rhea Ashley Hoskin is AMTD Waterloo Global Talent Postdoctoral Fellow at the University of Waterloo, Canada, and St. Jerome's University, Canada, where she is cross-appointed to the departments of Sociology & Legal Studies, and Sexuality, Marriage, and Family Studies. Hoskin's research focuses on femininities, femme theory, femme identities, critical femininities and femmephobia. In 2019, she was awarded the Governor General's Academic Gold Medal for her work on Femme Theory. Hoskin's most recent book *Feminizing Theory: Making space for Femme Theory* (2021) is among the first collections to apply femme theory to understand femininity and systems of gender and power broadly.

Janice Kroeger is Professor and Graduate Coordinator of Early Childhood Education at Kent State University, USA. Kroeger's noteworthy publications relate to post-foundational and critical qualitative studies of family-school-community partnerships and to the needs of LGBTQ parents or students, African American communities, and refugee Hmong American families and their children's teachers. Recent works account for the social and political needs of families and students in urban schools as well as an edited book titled *Nurturing Nature and the Environment with Young Children: Children~Elders~Earth* (2019).

Rachel Langford is Professor Emeritus in the School of Early Childhood Studies, Toronto Metropolitan University (formerly Ryerson University), Canada. Her research interests focus on conceptualizations of care in early childhood education, Canadian early childhood policy and the childcare movement. She has published on childcare activism, policy development, the early childhood workforce and visioning care in early childhood education. Her most recent book is *Theorizing Feminist Ethics of Care in Early Childhood: Possibilities and dangers* (2019).

Meagan Montpetit is a PhD candidate at Western University, Ontario, Canada. Thinking with posthuman feminism her research engages with the pedagogical nuances of educator/child/more-than-human assemblages. She has worked as a pedagogist in London, Ontario. She is currently the Pedagogical Coordinator for the British Columbia Early Childhood Pedagogy Network.

Jan Newberry is Professor at the University of Lethbridge, Canada, in the Anthropology Department. Her research interests include social reproduction theory, global early childhood programmes and collaborative ethnographic methods. She has published on the role of working-class Javanese women in delivering community-based social welfare programmes, including early childhood education and care programmes. Her recent collaborations include work with Vina Adriany on neuroscience in early childhood education that has appeared in *Current Sociology* (2021) and work with Amy Mack on multimodal and collaborative ethnographic methods with Indigenous youth and non-profits that has appeared in *Collaborative Anthropologies* (2020).

Nnenna Odim is a PhD candidate at the University of Texas at Austin, USA, at the Department of Curriculum and Instruction, specializing in Early Childhood Education. Her research focuses on how young children reinforce multiple ways of knowing. Sitting in the intersections of Black Geographies, Place-Based Studies and Early Childhood Education, her work forefronts moments where young children offer testimonies of elder and ancestral knowledges. She has published articles about futuristic visions in early childhood, resisting anti-Black violence and inequity in Caribbean childhoods and Black geographies in early childhood studies.

Ann Merte Otterstad is Professor in Early Childhood Pedagogy at Oslo Metropolitan University, Institute of Early Childhood Education, Norway. Her research interests are in the intersection between philosophies in education, new material theories and methodologies. She has published on early childhood policy, decentring and rethinking the child, what is data, different methods and representation. Her recent co-authored book with Lotta Johansson is about posthumanism in early childhood (Hverdagsøyeblikkets dirrende kraft. Posthuman teorier I barnehagen).

Michelle Salazar Pérez is Associate Professor of Early Childhood Education at the University of Texas at Austin, USA. She uses women of colour feminisms to inform her community collaborations, research and pedagogy in early childhood studies. These perspectives not only critically orient her work, but they also foreground the urgency to re-envision the field to support culturally sustaining praxis and programmes for minoritized young children. She is co-editor of the recently published *Sage Handbook of Global Childhoods* and was Host Chair of the 27th international Reconceptualizing Early Childhood Education (RECE) conference in 2019.

Alana Powell is Executive Director of the Association of Early Childhood Educators Ontario (AECEO), Canada. Her research engages in critical exploration of care discourses in early childhood and seeks to reposition care as central in politics, practice and advocacy. At the AECEO, her work also seeks to listen to and centre the experiences and voices of early childhood educators while advocating for decent work and professional pay.

Brooke Richardson is Adjunct Faculty in the Department of Sociology at Brock University, Canada and President of the Association of Early Childhood Educators of Ontario (AECEO). Her research and scholarly work focuses on the privatization of childcare in Canada, political representations of the childcare policy 'problem', reconceptualizing and reasserting care in early childhood education, critically examining mothering within child protection systems and pre-service education for care professionals. She has published and presented international on topics related to Canadian childcare policy. She is currently working on an edited volume titled *Mothering on the Edge: A Critical Examination of Mothering within Child Protection Systems.*

Kia S. Rideaux is an Elementary ESL Language Coach for a school district in north Texas, USA. Over the last seventeen years as an early childhood educator, she has served in the roles of classroom teacher and EC-6 teacher educator. Her research interests centre on marginalized feminist perspectives and utilize critical qualitative methodologies to address issues of equity and diversity in early childhood education. She has published several chapters and journal articles about teacher educators of colour, African American girls, and lensing childhood studies with women of colour theoretical perspectives.

Jenny Ritchie is Associate Professor in Te Puna Akopai, the School of Education, Te Herenga Waka Victoria University of Wellington, Aotearoa New Zealand. Her research, teaching and publications focus on: social, cultural and ecological justice within early childhood education; pedagogies that affirm and support children's cultural, spiritual and emotional well-being and citizenship enactment; and exploring how applying Māori conceptualizations can enhance pedagogies that protect and care for our planet. Her recently completed collaborative research project resulted in the publication, *Young children's community building in action: Embodied, emplaced and relational citizenship* (2019).

Erica Ritter is a third-year PhD student in the Teaching, Learning & Culture Department at Texas A&M University, USA. She is the Director for the Becky Gates Children's Center. Her research interests focus on feminism, workforce and progressivism within the field of early childhood education.

Kylie Smith is Associate Professor at the University of Melbourne, Australia at the Melbourne Graduate School of Education. Her research interests are focused on exploring social justice pedagogies in early childhood classrooms drawing on participatory methods. She has published on gender equality and possibilities for pedagogies for early prevention of gender-based violence, early childhood professional identities, children's rights and citizenship and participatory research methodologies.

Marek Tesar is Associate Professor, Head of School and the Associate Dean International at the Faculty of Education and Social Work, the University of Auckland, New Zealand. His expertise is in early childhood education and childhood studies in Aotearoa New Zealand and international contexts. His focus is on educational policy, philosophy, pedagogy, methodology and curriculum and draws on his background as a qualified teacher. He has published in these fields extensively, and currently he is the President of the Philosophy of Education Society of Australasia (PESA), and chairs the Steering Committee of the Reconceptualising Early Childhood Education society (RECE).

Radhika Viruru is Clinical Professor in the Department of Teaching, Learning and Culture at Texas A&M University, USA. Her research interests include early childhood education and postcolonial childhood studies. She is the author of two books (*Early Childhood Education: Postcolonial Perspectives from India*) published by Sage in 2001 and *Childhood and Postcolonization: Power, Education and Contemporary Practice (co-author)* published by Routledge in 2004 as well as numerous journal articles and edited book chapters. Her current research interests centre around the social construction of the family particularly in the Persian Gulf.

Series Editors' Foreword

The series *Feminist Thought in Childhood Research* considers experimental and creative modes of researching and practising in childhood studies. Recognizing the complex neo-liberal landscape and worrisome spaces of coloniality in the twenty-first century, the *Feminist Thought in Childhood Research* books provide a forum for cross-disciplinary, interdisciplinary and transdisciplinary conversations in childhood studies that engage feminist decolonial, anticolonial, more-than-human, new materialisms, posthumanist and other postfoundational perspectives that seek to reconfigure human experience. The series offers lively examples of feminist research praxis and politics that invite childhood studies scholars, students and educators to engage in collectively imagining childhood otherwise. Until now, childhood studies has been decidedly a human matter, focused on the needs of individual children (Taylor, 2013). In the Anthropocene (Colebrooke, 2012, 2013), however, other approaches to childhood that address the profound, human-induced ecological challenges facing our own and other species are emerging. As Taylor (2013) reminds us, if we are going to grapple with the socioecological challenges we face today, childhood studies needs to pay attention to the more-than-human, to the non-human others that inhabit our worlds and the in human. Towards this end, *Feminist Thought in Childhood Research* series challenges the humanist, linear, and moral narratives (Colebrook, 2013; Haraway, 2013) of much of childhood studies by engaging with feminisms. As a feminist series, the books explore the inheritances of how to live in the Anthropocene and think about it in ways that are in tension with the Anthropocene itself.

This volume in the book series, entitled *The Early Childhood Educator: Critical Conversations in Feminist Theory* and edited by Rachel Langford and Brooke Richardson, is a critical conversation of the feminized figure of the educator. Outlining the possibilities that emerge by rethinking the image of the educator from feminist pedagogical thoughts in various contexts, the authors collectively propose the early childhood educator as a cultural figure. Challenging the neoliberal image of educators as 'useful in their application of technical "skills" in order to produce standardized, objective outcomes in children', the anthology engages with a wide range of feminist theories: standpoint, poststructural feminism, new materialisms, posthumanisms, Black feminist thought, postcolonial feminisms, decolonizing feminisms, femme-inisms, queer theory and womanist praxis. Importantly, these diverse frameworks are meeting points, a commonplace that allows us to understand their complementarity in the challenging task of shifting the masculinist-driven discourse of the developmental early childhood educator.

In the name of child development, we continue to devalue the early childhood educator role to meet neoliberal demands – in this way, some practitioners are valued above educators, educators' voices are made invisible, and some educators (white) are privileged while others (racialized women) are catalogued as second class.

For us, *The Early Childhood Educator: Critical Conversations in Feminist Theory* marks the construction of a transformative early education through the reimagining of alternatives to the hegemonic image of the educator based on a fundamentally economic perspective that leaves aside a socially just, situated and diverse image. Unlike developmental psychology-informed notions of the early childhood educator, this volume starts off from the premise that educators are crucial protagonist in social struggle, the production of knowledge and counter-hegemonic and anti-patriarchal actions. The authors help us not only to rethink the dominant developmental model of the educator (generator of inequalities) but also open paths (from an intersectional axis) to build alternative ways of being, doing, thinking, feeling and living as an educator.

In these comprehensive feminist analyses, we learn that, as a critical protagonist, the educator recognizes that education is never neutral. In fact, the figure of the educator is multiple and constantly emerging and re-emerging in the midst of pedagogical processes and curriculum making in the presence of others. Questioning hegemonic, economic, social and development models, the volume as a whole challenges readers towards the idea that early childhood education demands close exploration of various ways of accessing knowledges, analysing them and thinking with them.

Jayne Osgood and Veronica Pacini-Ketchabaw

Acknowledgements

First and foremost, we acknowledge and thank the Lkwungen People, also known as the Songhees and Esquimalt First Nations communities, and the Haudenosaunee, Anishinaabe, Chippewa and Mississauga of the Credit for allowing us to live, think and write on their land. The two-row wampum belt represents an agreement between the Haudenosaunee and Dutch settlers whereby the two lines (the ship of the settlers and the canoe of the Indigenous peoples) exist both in relation to and separate from one another. The blank spaces between the lines represent peace and friendship, forever. Inspired by being in between, we hope this book has created a space for many different ideas to co-exist and come together through an overarching commitment to sustaining each other in solidarity, peace and friendship. We gratefully acknowledge the steadfast commitment of chapter authors to shining a feminist light on early childhood educators during the tumultuous Covid-19 pandemic. This is their book. We profoundly thank our families for understanding why we spend so much time in a room of our own. We also greatly thank our friends and colleagues for their generous support as we worked through the complex feminist ideas explored in this book. We are deeply grateful to each other for the opportunity to collaboratively embark on and navigate this intellectually and emotionally challenging journey. A great appreciation goes to Jayne Osgood and Veronica Pacini-Ketchabaw, the series editors, who have significantly contributed to keeping feminisms alive in early childhood education. We enthusiastically thank Mark Richardson and Anna Elliss at Bloomsbury Academic for their support in bringing the book to publication. We dedicate this book to early childhood educators around the world for the extraordinary work they do all day, every day.

Introduction

Brooke Richardson and Rachel Langford

Why this Book?

Early childhood education (ECE) is one of the most gendered professions in the majority of countries in the world (Steinberg, 2016). In deeply entrenched neoliberal sociopolitical and economic contexts where provision and delivery of early childhood education are driven by a market model, the work of early childhood educators (ECEs) is systematically undervalued, misunderstood and often rendered invisible. The material conditions of ECEs remain stubbornly inadequate, characterized by long hours, low pay, few opportunities for professional advancement and minimal (if any) benefits. In an effort to prioritize early childhood education as a policy and funding priority, the neoliberally compatible human capital discourse, backed by powerful organizations such as the Organization of Economic Co-operation and Development (OECD) and the World Bank, has come to penetrate early childhood education policy discourse globally. This discourse centres children as vessels of future economic productivity and educators as the mechanisms for tapping this potential. ECEs are understood as useful in their application of technical 'skills' *on* children in order to produce standardized, objective outcomes *in* children. Deeply connected to neuroscientific claims that young children's brains operate on a use-it-or-lose-it principle, the human capital discourse has largely occluded other ways of thinking about early childhood education and ECEs in policy and practice spaces.

At the same time as the human capital discourse has monopolized dominant narratives of early childhood education, there has been a strong push towards the professionalization of ECEs. While increased post-secondary educational requirements are necessary, these requirements have largely been driven by dominant narratives that position ECEs as technicians who maximize children's development rather than as educators who co-navigate the complexities of everyday experiences with children. Also highly problematic is that educators have been expected to take on increased responsibilities often without systematic support (i.e. increased time, financial, human, environmental resources). Inflexible regulatory requirements, the key mechanism through which states attempt to secure the basic health and safety of children in a market model, leave little space for creative pedagogical practice that critically engages with the existing sociopolitical order. What is most troubling to us in all of this is a lack of regard for the day-to-day experiences of ECEs. There is no space in dominant narratives of professionalism for ECEs to express ways of being in relation to children, families, colleagues and policymakers or in their own right. ECEs are increasingly exposed to eternally imposed, strict assessment, and regulation measures with little regard to their values, experiences, knowledges and motivations.

It is this void that this anthology seeks to address. Recognizing that ECEs are overwhelmingly women, this edited volume examines a range of contemporary feminist theories. We begin with the premise articulated by bell hooks (1989) (and referenced by Jenny Ritchie in her chapter) that 'feminism' is a movement 'to end patriarchal domination' (p. 21). At the same, hooks states that 'this feminism, as liberation struggle, must exist apart from and as a part of the larger struggle to eradicate domination in all its forms' (p. 22). In addition, hooks reminds us that while feminism seeks to end patriarchal domination, feminists diverge on how to realize this goal resulting in a proliferation of feminist theories. This sets the context for Susan Hekman's 2014 influential analysis of major contributions to understandings of the feminine subject in feminist theory from the mid-twentieth century to the present. This analysis was the inspiration for this volume. Hekman writes 'our goal should not be to finally get "woman" right, but rather to explore in contemporary terms what we can contribute to our understanding of this central concept, an understanding grounded in previous theories' (p. 3). In this anthology, we wish to apply such thinking through an exploration of a range of feminisms in relation to the early childhood educator subject. In approaching authors to contribute a book chapter, we were transparent that Hekman (2014) had been a key source of inspiration. Thus, Hekman is referred to by several authors while describing their focus on feminism as well as by us throughout our three commentaries and concluding remarks.

We recognize that centring the ECE in discussions of early childhood education is contentious: it has become accepted and expected that discussions of early childhood education focus on the child. In centring educators, we do not suggest that children's experiences are not important – they emphatically are. Further, there seems to be a discomfort about focusing on the ECE because it is assumed that this focus reinforces a hierarchical structure whereby educators are perceived as having power *over* children and families. In this book, we understand that ECEs simultaneously exercise power, hopefully *with* children, and are subjected to it within social relations at the practice and policy levels. Our own experiences and observations suggest that, despite many graduates of post-secondary early childhood education programmes around the world and many textbooks that outline the roles and responsibilities of ECEs, they are not at the centre of practice and policy concerns. If they were at the centre, then ECEs would have good working conditions, decent wages and benefits and be admired by everyone for the extraordinary work they do.

Our starting point is simply that children and family's experiences are inextricably connected to the often, invisible experiences, bodies and understandings of the gendered ECEs who care with them and for them every day (Cumming, 2020). We argue that this invisibility and positioning decentres and marginalizes ECEs in theory and in practice. This anthology, therefore, aims to do something that has not been done: place ECEs at the centre of an extensive discussion that is deeply theoretical, practical, critical and feminist in orientation.

In addition, we have observed siloed theoretical conceptualizations of early childhood educators in the academy. Moss, Dahlberg, Olsson and Vanderbroeck (2016) have called on our field to explore ways to cross paradigmatic divides, particularly between developmentalism and post-foundational ideas. We respond to their call to open boundaries between theoretical positions by exploring a range of feminisms, exposing potential tensions/affinities between them and enriching possibilities for complex understandings of ECE subjectivities. We feel a heightened responsibility to prioritize a conversation about ECEs as we move through the turbulent, post-pandemic waters. Governments, particularly in liberal democracies, are paying attention to early childhood education as a priority policy area. Federal governments in Canada, the United States and Australia have all committed to massive expansion of early childhood programmes largely motivated by a need to address the 'she-cession' brought on by the pandemic. The pandemic revealed the necessity of state-supported social infrastructure to ensure equitable opportunities for men and women in social and economic life through illustrating the highly gendered impact a *lack of* these structures instantiates (Murray, 2020). But this understanding is still quite limited, not necessarily making space for the women who disproportionately do the care work. Early childhood educators are the backbone of any ECE system. We cannot move towards meaningful, sustainable policy change in ECE without critically discussing, exploring and meaningfully incorporating the voices of early childhood educators. This anthology will provide a starting place for these critical conversations.

Who is the Early Childhood Educator?

We adopt the term 'early childhood educator' for several reasons. First, with an understanding that to educate is to care, we view early childhood education as part of an educational continuum (Moss, 2019). We see ECEs in many different locations and contexts. Second, we feel this term allows space for ECEs to be engaged in both theory and practice. Nevertheless, chapter authors may use different terms (e.g. early childhood teacher, pedagogue, practitioner) for different reasons. Central to the spirit and orientation of this book is an understanding of the early childhood educator subject as someone always separate from but in relation with children and families in the early childhood setting. The emphasis on relationality is most evident in chapters by Melinda Bruce and Alana Powell, Sonja Arndt and Marek Tesar and Adam Davies and Rhea Ashley Hoskin.

Tracing postmodernist thinking back to Davies (2000), Pacini-Ketchabaw et al. (2015) describe the formation of subjects or subjectivity as processes of social relations in which one is constituted and reconstituted through participation in various discursive practices. While subjects are subjugated by these practices, they can also resist them and create alternative discourses and subjectivities. Kylie Smith and Janice Kroeger's chapters, among others, explore many forms of resistance while generating new subjective possibilities. This understanding of subject formation is further complicated by feminist new materialists who view the subject as more than just a discursive effect, but as a being constituted and reconstituted through entanglements of 'the human, more-than-human, the material and the discursive' (Hekman, 2014, p. 150). Chapters in this book by Jan Newberry, Megan Monpetit, and Gunilla Dahlberg and Ann Merte Otterstad further our thinking about the ECE subject from this perspective.

It is worth noting how this conceptualization of subjectivity is both distinct from and connected to identity. Identity, a term referred to by many authors, is typically used as means of distinguishing oneself from others or representing to which group(s) one belongs. Identity may be stable over time and across contexts, though neither identity nor subjectivity are ever static or impermeable to change. All ECEs identify as ECEs, yet how they experience being/becoming an ECE – what that feels like and what that means to them – differs substantially. It is the latter that we are particularly interested in here, as well as what possibilities different feminist theoretical understandings may offer ECEs in thinking about their subjective experiences.

The implication of these understandings is that the ECE cannot be regarded as having a fixed universal identity or subjectivity that emerges out of its formation. Rather ECEs as individual and collective subjects actively construct and change their identities (and, therefore, subjective experiences of these identities) drawing on a range of discourses circulating broadly in the field and in particular sociopolitical contexts. Further considering feminist materialist claims that the subject is also a material effect, ECE identities are always being shaped by social practices that include the bodies of ECEs, the more-than-human world, the material and discourse.

This understanding of the ECE as always becoming an educator and/or professional is counter to dominant discourses that seek to position the ECE in a fixed way. At least in North American contexts, a persistent public perception is that ECEs are 'glorified babysitters' who require little knowledge and skills because they are drawn to work by a natural love for children. In the 1970s and 1980s when a childcare system (albeit an incoherent one) began to expand, childcare workers became responsible for ensuring that children were safe and healthy in their care. Unlike half-day nursery programmes in which teachers focused more on early learning, childcare workers or caregivers were regarded as providing custodial care for children whose mothers had to work full-time.

In the 1990s and 2000s, a number of influences from developmentally appropriate practice to OECD prescriptions on how to improve ECE systems converged to position the ECE as a child-development practitioner. However, this practice was not produced by ECEs neither did it belong to them. Rather, ECEs were positioned as handmaidens of developmental psychologists among other experts and expected to rigorously apply child development knowledge others had produced for them. As Moss (2019) has extensively documented, the rise of neoliberalism converged with this understanding of the ECE as the child-development practitioner to produce the image of the ECE as a technician. Moss describes a taken-for-granted and uncontestable technical practice in which 'an education for predetermined outcomes and high returns on investment, and an education based on the marketized delivery of services' is prioritized (2019, p. 48). Drawing on Reggio-Emilia educational philosophy, Moss (2019) proposes a counter image of the ECE as a researcher who he describes as a 'protagonist participating actively in the co-constructive learning process' (p. 77). Such an image of educators is more congruent with conceptualizations of pedagogues embraced in several Nordic countries (Richardson, 2021), as Dahlberg and Otterstad show in their chapter. Importantly, each chapter author in this book also offers alternative visions of who the early childhood educator can be.

In the early childhood education field, there is a tendency to see the ECE as an individualized solitary subject who wrestles internally with educational ideas about who she/they should be. However, some early childhood scholars (e.g. Moss, 2019; Langford, 2020) insist that the ECE is also a political subject or social actor who thinks with others about ideas and material structures in a democratic space that is always (or should be) politically contentious. In this democratic space where individual and collective political choices have to be considered and decisions made, the ECE is also an ethical subject. We reiterate that ECEs are gendered subjects because they are predominantly women affected by gendered discourses and material experiences about who they should be. But this book takes the position that while 'gender matters, it does not always matter in the same way and it is not the only factor that matters' (Altman & Pannell, 2012, p. 292). Acknowledging the theoretical work of Patricia Hill Collins (2019) and Kimberle Crenshaw (1991) among other Black feminist thought scholars, we recognize that thinking about ECEs requires an analysis of an intersectional subjectivity in which the focus is on multiple sources of oppression experienced by ECEs and the ways in which these oppressions produce different kinds of subjects. Chapters by Flora Harmon; Erica Ritter and Radhika Viruru; Nnenna Odim, Kia Rideaux and Michelle Salazar Peréz; and Jenny Ritchie emphasize how intersectionality is taken up in their particular feminism(s).

Since multiple sources of oppression matter, we contend that feminist theories offer critical ways to examine how neoliberal discourses and material realities work to keep ECEs in their place as low-waged female workers who undertake technical work under the direction of developmental experts. Indeed, counter to seeing the work of ECEs as a neutral social issue, we argue that without feminist theory it is impossible to seriously examine the experiences of ECEs. This position is captured in the title of the book – *The Early Childhood Educator: Critical Conversations in Feminist Theory* – which seeks to emphasize that feminist theory can illuminate the problems and possibilities of being an early childhood educator in these contemporary times. At the same time, this anthology recognizes that there is a range of feminisms under the larger tent of feminist theory, all which can push thinking beyond conventional understandings of the early childhood educator in global practice and policy contexts. This anthology, therefore, offers a unique and comprehensive examination of both the subjectivities of the early childhood educators *and* contemporary feminist theories.

Why We Care?

As editors, we have worked extensively over a number of years with a several feminisms: standpoint/materialist feminism, postmodern/poststructural feminism, feminist critical discourse analysis and feminist ethics of care. We have introduced many post-secondary students and practicing ECEs to intersectional, postcolonial and posthumanist feminisms that are profiled in this book. We have both worked as ECEs, experiencing the complexities and frustrations of being and feeling invisible. For over a decade, we have also been active leaders in the Canadian and Ontario childcare movement, advocating for decent work for early childhood educators within broader social structures. Having been immersed in feminisms as scholars, teachers and activists, we are passionate about further exploring the subjective experiences of ECEs through a range of feminisms and how/where this fits in within contemporary ECE scholarship, practice and activism.

Structure of Book

In organizing the structure of the book, we were guided by Hekman's (2014) examination of feminist theories over the last sixty years. Hekman stresses that any chronology of feminisms must be regarded as a 'positive cumulative enterprise' rather than a competitive one in which previous feminist theories must be rejected for a brand new one. This book adopts this stance. It will be evident in reading the chapters that each feminism builds on ones that went before and, importantly, complexifies our understanding of ECE subject. Moreover, at the end of her book, Hekman (2014) reminds us that we should not be 'seduced' into thinking that the most current feminism concludes the development of feminist theory (p. 185).

Chapter authors were invited to contribute to this book because they are passionate about and explicitly work with a particular feminism. While, as editors, we sought authors to represent different geographical and political contexts, we recognize that the book is not truly international. Chapter contributions come from the Global North and postcolonial perspectives represent perspectives from Canada, New Zealand and the United States. We, therefore, enthusiastically welcome other publications that expand the focus of this book. To prepare their chapters, authors worked with several questions that asked how their particular feminism frames understandings of the ECE subject. We asked authors how and/or why their feminism matters for thinking about who ECE subjects are and how they experience these subjectivities. Several chapters include two or three authors who embraced a collaborative, supportive process in their thinking and writing. Many authors powerfully adopt a personal tone when describing the feminism that resonates with them. With this comprehensive focus on feminist thinking, the anthology could only be theoretical in its orientation. At the same time, chapter authors decisively ground their feminist thinking in the lived experiences of and possibilities for ECE subjectivities. Between groups of chapters are three commentaries in which we, as editors, explore solidarities and tensions between the feminisms described by the chapter authors. The aim of the commentaries is to generate critical conversations about how the work and lived experiences of ECEs are constructed and understood in diverse feminisms. We expect readers will generate many more insights into the invigorating ideas explored by chapter authors. In the conclusion, we reflect on all the chapters and offer some ways to envision the subjectivities of early childhood educators going forward in a post-pandemic world.

This anthology fits comfortably into the 'boundary-pushing' book series, *Feminist Thought in Childhood Research* edited by Jayne Osgood and Veronica Pacini-Ketchabaw which focuses on 'feminist research praxis and politics in childhood studies'. As will be seen, feminist theorizing is integral to everything in this anthology. Additionally, several chapter authors rigorously engage with the series' focus on feminist posthumanism and new materialisms. We now invite readers to dive in and join us in thinking differently about early childhood educators, feminisms and the wealth of possibilities for early childhood educator subjectivities.

References

Altman, M. & Pannell, K. (2012). Policy gaps and theory gaps: Women and migrant domestic labor. *Feminist Economics, 18*(2), 291–315. Doi: 10.1080/13545701.2012.704149

Collins, P. H. (2019). *Intersectionality as critical social theory*. Duke University Press.

Crenshaw, K. (1991). Mapping the margins: Intersectionality, identity politics, and violence against women of colour. *Stanford Law Review, 43*(6), 1241–99.

Cumming, T. (2020). A critique of the discursive landscape: Challenging the invisibility of early childhood educators' well-being. *Contemporary Issues in Early Childhood, 21*(2), 96–110. https://doi.org/10.1177/1463949120928430

Davies, B. (2000). *A body of writing 1990–1999*. Altamira.

Hekman, S. (2014). *The feminine subject*. Policy Press.

hooks, b. (1989). *Talking back: Thinking feminist, thinking black*. South End Press.

Langford, R. (2020). Navigating reconceptualist and feminist ethics of care to find a conceptual space for rethinking children's needs in early childhood education. *Journal of Childhood Studies, 45*(4). https://doi.org/10.18357/jcs00019308

Moss, P., Dahlberg, G., Olsson, L. M., & Vandenbroeck, M. (2016). *Why contest early childhood?* Available at: https://www.researchgate.net/publication/305817038_Why_contest_early_childhood#:~:text=https%3A//www.routledge,paign%3D160701429

Moss, P. (2019). *Alternative narratives in early childhood: An introduction for students and practitioners*. Routledge.

Murray, J. (2020). In a time of COVID-19 and beyond, the world needs early childhood educators. *Journal of Early Years Education, 28*(4), 299–302. https://doi.org/10.1080/09669760.2020.1839830

Pacini-Ketchabaw, V., Nxumalo, F., Kocher, L., Elliot, E., & Sanchez, A. (2015). *Journeys: Reconceptualizing early childhood practices through pedagogical narration*. University of Toronto Press.

Richardson, B. (2021). Commodification and care: An exploration of workforces' experiences of care in private and public childcare systems from a feminist political theory of care perspective. *Critical Social Policy*. April 2021. Doi: 10.1177/0261018321998934

Steinberg, S. (2016). Early education as a gendered construction. *Counterpoints: Curriculum: Deconizing the field, 491*, 429–37. Doi: https://www.jstor.org/stable/45157425

1

Reflections on Poststructural Feminisms: Supporting Multiple Performances of Teacher Identities

Kylie Smith

After finishing secondary school, I undertook a two-year associate diploma in early childhood and then began my career as an early childhood teacher working in Australian long day care centres. During my initial training, I learnt about developmental theories and how to use concepts, tools and templates informed by Freud (2014), Piaget (1964), Bronfenbrenner (1989) and Maslow (1987), to see, assess and plan for children's learning and development. As a graduate early childhood teacher, entering the classroom for the first time I struggled to place children into developmental boxes and felt like I had missed something in my training to cause me to question how children were assessed, and how and why routines and programmes were constructed the way they were. I felt like I didn't fit into the model of early childhood teacher that everyone around me performed. I felt like an imposter. I struggled to find language outside of developmental ideologies to express or explain what the issues were and the questions that it raised for me. So, over the course of the next twenty years, I worked full time and studied part time at nights in the pursuit of knowledge in an attempt to 'fit in' and be a 'good' teacher.

I kept going back to study because I thought that if I just undertook the right subject or read the right article or book, I would have the knowledge and skills to connect with and feel comfortable observing and assessing children's development. I wondered if further study might help me be more comfortable using categories and milestones and plan and implement curriculum and routines that privileged white middle-class cultural discourses. In my second year in my diploma training, I met a lecturer, Glenda MacNaughton, who presented a class on anti-bias curriculum which opened up a crack in the early childhood system and allowed a glimmer of light for alternative knowledge to be considered. Twelve years later and I began postgraduate studies with Glenda MacNaughton as my supervisor. She introduced me to a world of different paradigms and invited me to explore feminist poststructuralism in and outside early childhood. I began to read Glenda's work (1996, 1997a, b, 1999, 2000), Bronwyn Davies (1991, 1992, 1993, 2003), Chris Weedon (1987), Valerie Walkerdine (1998), Judith Butler (1988, 1992, 2011) and later work by Kerry Robinson (2013) and Mindy Blaise (2005, 2012). Feminist poststructuralist writing provided me with an introduction to feminism that I had previously limited access to, and introduced me to female academic scholars. Specifically, feminist poststructuralism supported me to question taken-for-granted truths and investigate the operations of power, truth and knowledge, discourses, subjectification and resistance. Concepts and ideas from feminist poststructuralism gave me access to a paradigm that engaged with the multiplicity of identities held by teachers, families and children. This allowed me to explore how, as a teacher, I moved through and within discourses that privileged or silenced the performances of different subject positions of the early childhood teacher. I began to see different possibilities to perform teacher. Gaile Cannella's 1997 book *Deconstructing Early Childhood Education: Social Justice and Revolution* created one of many lightbulb moments for me in my journey to becoming the 'good' teacher. Cannella (1997) wrote:

> The discourses and actions associated with professional institutions and practices have generated disciplinary and regulatory powers over teachers (who are mostly women) and children. Standards have been created through which individuals judge and limit themselves, through which they construct a desire to be 'good', 'normal' or both.
>
> (p. 137)

I began to recognize how I understood myself as the 'good' or 'deficient' early childhood teacher who was tied up in developmental discourses that privileged particular knowledges and understandings of the world and teaching. In this chapter, I explore the background of feminist poststructural thinking and how key concepts of discourse, subjectivity, agency and power help to deconstruct dominant discourses of early childhood teacher identity to consider alternative discourses.

Feminist Engagement with Poststructuralism

Feminist thinkers began to engage with poststructuralism in a struggle to question the universal, singular category of women. In the post-1980s, feminists from diverse racial, cultural, class, religious and sexuality backgrounds began to problematize and challenge a unified, homogenic feminist narrative of women's experiences and inequities within society. Feminist engagement with poststructuralist ideas made available ways to explore the multiplicity of the feminine subject and illuminate differences between women. It's important to note that poststructuralism rather than a singular theory is a 'collection of theoretical positions' (Gavey, 1989, p. 460), with influences from linguistics, Marxism, psychoanalysis, feminisms and the work of Derrida and Foucault. Poststructuralism emerged in the late twentieth century within philosophy and literary theory as a critique or reaction to structuralism, questioning and challenging the systems of knowledge and truth-seeking meaning making that knowledge was based on (Gutting, 1998). Within structuralist ideologies meaning is not understood through the experiences of individuals; rather truth-seeking meaning is established 'by elucidating the impersonal systems of relationships that bind the world together. In other words, the individual doesn't explain the system of relationships – the system "explains" the individual' (Hughes, 2010, pp. 45–6). Poststructuralist thought disrupted singular knowledge truths and explored the relationships between knowledge, power and identity. It challenges the concept that the individual or subject can be understood as unitary, coherent, integrated, rational and fixed, instead viewing the world as socially constructed, incoherent and discontinuous (Dahlberg, Moss & Pence, 1999; Hughes, 2010; Weedon, 1987).

Feminist engagement with poststructuralism was contentious creating turmoil, tension and dissensus across feminist writers. During the post-1980s, there were debate and challenges between some feminists questioning the engagement with poststructural theories. Theory was seen particularly by radical feminist writers such as Mary Daly (1984), as a patriarchal tool that oppressed women and framed women as inferior subjects separated from knowledge and theory (Weedon, 1987). Women were seen and (not) heard as carers, mothers and nurturers with white men as thinkers, theorists and gatekeepers of knowledge and power where women's experiences were (and still often) silenced. Engaging with theory, in this case poststructural theories, was seen by some feminists as taking up patriarchal masculine discourses and working against the feminist struggle for recognition and equality (Weedon, 1987). However, Weedon (1987) argues that experience is not enough and to create change requires engagement with theories that disrupt power relationships within dominant discourses. She (1987) wrote that we need to engage with theory as a way of becoming empowered:

> Rather than turning our backs on theory and taking refuge in experience alone, we should think in terms of transforming both the social relations of knowledge

production and the type of knowledge is produced and by whom, and of what counts as knowledge. It also requires a transformation of the structures which determine how knowledge is disseminated.

(p. 7)

The need to transform the *structures which determine how knowledge is disseminated* particularly resonates with me as I often hear academics and policymakers argue that early childhood educators will not understand theories and so we need to keep teaching and training practical so that knowledge is accessible. This attitude or belief continues to remove early childhood teachers from accessing theories that challenge dominant discourses and disempowers their capacity to speak back using alternative ways to understand or frame the world. Access to poststructural knowledge allowed me to recognize that during my early childhood training the knowledge that counted was developmental psychology and behaviourism and the producers of this knowledge were predominantly white middle-/upper-class men. Today neuroscience and developmental theories continue to dominate early childhood education across systems through policy, training and curriculum. How do higher education institutions and researchers stand accountable for presenting and explaining multiple theoretical perspectives in accessible ways?

Judith Butler was a significant scholar who brought feminist thinking into poststructuralist theories. Feminist poststructuralism attempts to examine and decentre discourse, language and the cultural formation of gender roles and power, highlighting how patriarchal society continues to position women in the margins (Aston, 2016; Lather, 1991; Weedon, 1987). Butler (1992) explored the concept of identity as performance. She describes performativity as the way that a person internalizes or performs in a particular way through their understanding of language or discourse (Butler, 1992). Considering performativity as a way to explore teacher identity allows opportunities to understand identity as fluid, partial and shifting or in motion. Identity becomes multiple and performances can become strategic and political depending on the moment and the relationship with the people you are performing teacher to. Butler (1988) argues that it is important to investigate what performances are authorized, by who and under what conditions. She wrote:

> When Simone de Beauvoir claims 'one is not born, but, rather, becomes a woman,' she is appropriating and reinterpreting this doctrine of constituting acts from the phenomenological tradition. In this sense, gender is in no way a

stable identity or locus of agency from which various acts proceed; rather, it is an identity tenuously constituted in time – an identity instituted through a stylized repetition of acts.

(p. 519)

A person performs across and within multiple discourses often through a desire to fit in or have approval within the context of the community or group of people. For the early childhood teacher, identity politics are embedded in discourses of professionalism with continual battles to be recognized within educational systems as important and valuable to society. How do we perform teacher identit(ies) differently for different children and families, for other teachers, for regulatory bodies and assessors of quality and accreditation systems?

Discourses

Feminist poststructuralism calls for me to explore discourses that are available to early childhood teachers and how they shape, privilege and silence different subject positions. There are many different definitions of discourse. Within a poststructural paradigm discourse is about what can be said and thought, and who can speak, when, and with what authority. Foucault (1972) wrote that discourses are 'practices that systematically form the objects of which they speak… Discourses are not about objects; they do not identify objects, they constitute them and in the practice of doing so conceal their own invention' (p. 49).

Meaning and definition are inscribed in discourse within the social, historical and political positions held by those who use them. Ball (1990) argues that meanings emerge through power relations within institutional practices rather than from merely language. Within early childhood classrooms, institutional practices of routines, observation, documentation and accreditation create meanings about what knowledge is privileged and how people perform professional identities. Discourses contain multiple ideas and thoughts and position a person in a discourse as a subject that is rational, conscious, non-agentic, fixed and coherent (Weedon, 1987).

> A discourse gains a position of power over others in the way it is supported and 'activated' by individuals in society, such as governments, religious bodies, and the legal and education systems, take up a discourse, its power is reinforced and its ability to persuade individuals that it is the most appropriate view

of the world is increased. Those position themselves in the discourse will share in the privilege, advantage and power that are culturally sanctioned through the dominant culture's support for this 'truth'. Those who locate outside this dominant discourse will frequently experience inequities, diminish power and little or no support from this dominant culture for their perspective.

(Robinson & Jones Diaz, 2006, p. 35)

As I reflect of Robinson and Jones Diaz's (2006) words, I ask: how do early childhood systems *support* and *'activate'* teacher discourses through teacher training, teacher certification, curriculum frameworks and assessments, and accreditation? Further, how are discourses taken up that *persuade individuals that the most appropriate view of the world* is the well-trained expert (in developmental ideologies) professional, who is objective, and has managerial skills to maintain records of assessment and learning to report on?

Identifying discourses makes possible opportunities to undertake discourse analysis which provides a way to investigate the historical, economic and political context of how the social world influences our subjectivity. Subjectivity is 'the conscious and unconscious thoughts and emotions of the individual, her sense of herself and her ways of understanding her relation to the world' (Weedon, 1987, p. 26). This raises questions about the gender politics within discourses and how language constructs gendered positions and creates or limits identity performances for early childhood teachers. Feminist poststructuralism helps to investigate the gender politics in dominant discourses of teacher identity in operation within early childhood. Early childhood is a highly feminized space with women as the vast majority of teachers in the profession. Historically, early childhood services and particularly kindergarten and long day care services in Australia were established in the late 1800s and early 1900s as a philanthropic endeavour by women to help the poor (Brennan, 1998). The care of young children was and continues to be threaded through dominant discourses as women's work, that is natural. With this discourse, women are understood universally as having innate skills and dispositions to care and mother due to the biology of being women (Osgood, 2012). The continuing effects of these discourses are poor salaries and conditions, particularly for people working in long day care compared to teachers in other educational systems (primary and secondary teachers). The discourse of caring teacher or teacher as carer has often been rejected in recent times by early childhood teachers as an inferior subject position in education, positioning the discourse as the binary opposite of the discourse of the teacher as professional and educator (Osgood, 2012). This has created hierarchies and binaries both outside of early childhood and within. Binaries such as education/care, teacher/caregiver and professional/parent circulate within our field, which places one identity against another. Ailwood (2008 cited in Osgood, 2012, p. 87) notes that:

> ECEC teachers continue to have their skills and knowledge regularly and enduringly attributed to a natural mothering instinct. These links between nature, maternalism and the work of the ECEC teacher are difficult and contradictory. It needs to be acknowledged that many women in ECEC take others attempts to refuse this discourse, pointing out their years of university education and the need for early childhood teachers to be recognised as professionals. For those women, the naturalisation of their work undermines their struggle for professional status.

Interrogating Neoliberalism and Professional Identities

The professionalization of early childhood has been taken up in an endeavour to increase the status of being seen as teachers with expert knowledge and skills (Dahlberg, Moss & Pence, 2007; Osgood, 2012). At a government policy level, discourses of professionalism have become entangled with neoliberal and human capital discourses of quality assurance and workforce strategies (Martin, Nuttall, Henderson & Wood, 2020). This played out in the *Early Childhood Education and Care Workforce Strategy for Australia* (2012–16) (Standing Council on School Education and Early Childhood, 2012) which stated:

> A skilled workforce is essential to delivering high-quality ECEC services and to achieving the best outcomes for children and their families. There is increasing recognition that the work of caring for and educating young children is complex and requires enhanced qualifications and ongoing professional development. Programs delivered by qualified educators are particularly effective in improving outcomes for vulnerable children.
>
> (p. 4)

This document was significant in Australia, as it placed the importance of early childhood education and educators at a national level for the first time.

Neoliberal ideologies work to support discourses of the early childhood teacher as technician (Moss, 2014). The operation of power/knowledge within these discourses shape performances of technician where managerial and accountability performances are acted out through movement, languages and utterances (Butler, 2011) of assessment of children's learning outcomes, quality assurance monitoring and reporting, 'evidence based' planning, objective, intentional teaching and evaluation. The teacher as technician creates a promise that teacher quality and effectiveness can be seen, monitored and assessed to ensure good outcomes for children which equals future productive citizens of the future (Moss, 2014; Roberts-Holmes & Moss, 2021). Care discourses within neoliberal policy contexts is a commodification as part of economic trade. Care is often seen as messy, emotional, subjective and non-scientific. Care is a commodification as part of economic trade. Osgood (2006) wrote that within 'neo-liberal discourses there is little room for emotionality or such feminine characteristics that are seemingly unquantifiable or auditable' (p. 8). Since the 2009, early childhood policy reform care discourses in Australia have been silenced through the removal of care in the naming of early childhood teachers. Previously, people working in long day care or family day care (also known as home-based care) were named as carers. With the introduction of the EYLF (Department of Education, Employment and Workplace Relations, 2009), all people working in early childhood services are referred to as educators to universalize the role to those who educate children.

Poststructural theories provide the tools to examine how neoliberal ideologies privilege discourses of individualism. This means that to be a 'good' teacher sits at the site of the individual teacher. It is the responsibility of the teacher to continue to engage in training and/or upgrade qualifications to ensure current expertise. Teacher success is demonstrated by the teacher through honing their skills to ensure children's learning is assessed and reported on; and curriculum is developed, documented and evaluated to produce high-quality standards is maintained. Where there are gaps or this is not maintained, then the teacher needs to work harder with the notion that everyone can be successful if they work/try hard enough – irrespective of gender, sexuality, class, race, culture or religion. The result is a good neoliberal teacher/citizen who is contributing to society and the future economic success of the nation through setting the foundations of the next generation.

The Early Childhood Teacher/Subject

It is important to consider how the early childhood teacher navigates or takes up discourses and meanings. Within poststructuralist discourses, language and the social construction of meaning is explored to investigate how these meanings are acted on through discursive practices (Davies, 2000; Weedon, 1987). Weedon (1987) explained that 'language is the place where actual and possible forms of social organization and their likely social and political consequences are defined and contested' (p. 21). Discursive practice is a term Davies (2000) describes as '… all the ways in which people actively produce social and psychological realities' (p. 88). One of the challenges for early childhood teachers is access to alternative realities outside of developmental ideologies. While I have had access to the work of Bronwyn Davies, Glenda MacNaughton, Kerry Robinson and Mindy Blaise, much of this literature does not filter down into professional development books and materials. Feminist poststructuralist (or any kind of feminism) informed professional development is extremely rare or non-existent within Australia. This is despite the fact that the EYLF (Department of Education, Employment and Workplace Relations, 2009) acknowledges that there are many different theoretical perspectives to understand children's learning and development and invites teachers (educators) to draw on these in practice. Weedon (1987) wrote:

> The problems of the relationship between experience and theory, access to knowledge and the patriarchal structure and content of knowledge are of central importance to feminism. To dismiss all theory as an elitist attempt to tell women what their experience really means is not helpful, but it does serve as a reminder of the importance of making theory accessible and of the political importance of transforming the material conditions of knowledge production and women's access to knowledge. It is arguable that a feminist transformation of both knowledge and access to knowledge would enable all feminists to see the relevance and inescapability of theory.
>
> (p. 7)

In Australia, and in early childhood teaching access to and authorization of feminist theories is limited. Developmental, socio-cultural, critical and post-structuralist theories are named in the EYLF list with no feminist theories in sight. Further, while these different theories are listed, developmental ideologies are embedded throughout the EYLF. Feminist theories are not identified, and the only discussion related to poststructuralist theories is that they 'offer insights into issues of power, equity and social justice in early childhood settings' (p. 12). There is no further discussion about poststructuralism throughout the document resulting in no exploration of the construction of the concept of power, knowledge, identity or discourse. One of the learning outcomes is for children to have a *strong sense of identity* where the grammatical tense of the word identity marks it as singular which runs counter to feminist poststructural thinking.

The concept of power is understood within differently across different paradigms. Early childhood understandings of power are often informed through a developmental lens where children can be powerful if they learn social and emotional skills and language skills to enable them to negotiate play and resources with other children. Alternatively, teachers can draw on critical theory and a Freirean lens where power is redistributed through education of the oppressor supporting them to understand how they are silencing others' ideas, knowledge and cultures and educating the oppressed to challenge the oppressor (Freire, 1996). Within these modern paradigms, power is seen as a product, object or gift that can be given, taken, received, shared or equalized. Power is seen as being possessed by someone or a person holding or having power over another. Poststructural scholars conceptualize power very differently than scholars within critical theory such as Freire (1996) and Habermas (1984). Power is seen as always in circulation and in motion within and through discourses and at the site of the body. Foucault (1980) wrote:

> Power is not to be taken to be a phenomenon of one individual's consolidated and homogenous domination over others, or that of one group or class over others. What, by contrast, should always be kept in mind is that power, if we do not take too distant a view of it, is not that which makes the difference between those who exclusively possess and retain it, and those who do not have it and submit to it. Power must be analysed as something which circulates, or rather as something which only functions in the form of a chain. It is never appropriated as a commodity or piece of wealth. Power is employed and exercised through a net-like organization. And not only do individuals circulate between its threads; they are always in the position of simultaneously undergoing and excising this power. They are not only its inert or consenting target; they are always the elements of its articulation. In other words, individuals are the vehicles of power, not its points of application.
>
> (p. 98)

Feminist poststructuralist scholars' focus is on the operation of power and gender. When we explore the operation of power, gender, discourses and subjectification we can gain insight into the ways early childhood teachers take up, perform and navigate identity politics in and outside early childhood classrooms. Davies (2003) explains that

> People are not *socialised* into the social world, but that they go through a process of *subjectification*. In socialisation theory, the focus is on the process of shaping

the individual that is undertaken by others. In poststructuralist theory the focus is on the way each person actively takes up the discourses through which they and others speak/write the world into existence *as if they were their own*.

(p. 14)

How do we perform feminist teacher identities where we create gender pedagogy that promotes the multiple discourses so that children, families, community and teachers can perform multiple gendered identities? How can moving through discourses open up diverse gendered subject positions for multiple understandings of femininity, masculinity, non-conforming gendered positions? What might that mean for teachers' sense of belonging?

Gaps

While feminist poststructuralisms support alternative exploration of gender and teacher identities, it is partial and other theories are needed to open up ways to examine the intersections of oppression. Feminist postcolonial theories (Srinivasan, 2019, 2014), Black feminist theories (Pérez, 2017) and Indigenous knowledges (Moreton-Robinson, 2000) open up ways to explore the intersections of gender and race. This is particularly important for early childhood teachers to explore with many women of colour working in the early childhood field. There are many questions to be asked. Who gets to be an educational leader? Who is the director of the service? Who is trained and who is untrained? How do dominant white Western ideologies silence diverse ways of knowing and learning? How are dominant white teacher discourses performed and take centre stage? Queer theories are also often silenced in the early childhood space which means gendered identities are recognized as binary rather than fluid and multiple. How might queer theories support performances of non-conforming or non-binary identities by teachers, children, families and the community? Exploring diverse feminisms creates opportunities for educators to see, respect and engage with different professional identities in order to feel a sense of belonging to the early childhood service or community. Ortlipp, Arthur and Woodrow (2011) argue that:

> Understanding professional identity as provisional and discursively produced allows the prospect of reshaping professional discourses in the context of changing social and historical conditions, contributing to expanded possibilities for new forms of professional identity.
>
> (p. 57)

How might different theoretical knowledge and paradigms support new discourses of professionalism so that early childhood educators can consider alternative ways to recognize themselves and teacher? This may create different opportunities to develop a sense of belonging in and out of the early childhood classroom.

Reflection

I learnt early into my journey of exploration into feminist poststructuralism that this feminism would not provide a single answer to my questions. Key within feminist poststructuralism is the epistemological understanding that there are multiple truths about the world and therefore multiple understandings about who, what and how early childhood teachers are, can be and the identities they perform. How we discursively take up different subject positions will shift; change; and be contingent, strategic and political.

> All subjects – including the transformed (or more correctly, the transforming) poststructuralist subject, who is capable of critically analysing the constitutive force of discourse – are always inside language. To change discourse is also, at least in part, at least for the moment, to change oneself. But while critique of discourse may work to make it, as Foucault says, *unthinkable*, the deconstructive process is always partial, messy and incomplete. The transforming poststructuralist subject is not the rational, unified subject, newly liberated from liberal humanism. The newly transforming subject is aware of its own messiness.
>
> (Davies et al., 2006, p. 90)

This messiness is difficult at times when dominant neoliberal discourses and dominant conversations about ways to be a professional early childhood educator demand answers, certainty and universal truths that can be compared, contrasted and benchmarked across the nation and globally. Feminist poststructuralism gave me language, to create cracks in the developmental foundations of early childhood ideologies to find a light or space to feel connected or excited about and have an understanding of why I felt or feel disconnected – and possibilities to be comfortable, exhilarated, energized and inspired in the disconnect and discomfort. Feminist poststructuralism has given me alternative discourses to resist, rebel, revolt and be in solidarity with others. Resistance is multiple and changing within the context of a world that is complex, shifting, contingent and pluralistic (Foucault, 1978). Foucault (1978) wrote:

These points of resistance are present everywhere in the power network. Hence there is no single locus of great Refusal, no soul of revolt, source of all rebellions, or pure law of the revolutionary. Instead there is a plurality of resistances, each of them a special case: that are spontaneous, savage, solitary, concerted, rampant, or violent; still others that are quick to compromise, interested, or sacrificial; by definition, they can only exist in the strategic field of power relations.

(pp. 95–6)

As an early childhood teacher, feminism invited me to engage with 'the politics of the personal' where my 'subjectivities and experiences of everyday life become the site of the redefinition of patriarchal meanings and values and of resistance to them, [and] feminism generates new theoretical perspectives from which the dominant can be criticized and new possibilities envisaged' (Weedon, 1987, p. 6). As I think back and reflect on my early performances of teacher identity, I can now understand the scripts I took up to perform within dominant discourses through my engagement with feminist poststructural theories. I move through a repertoire of teacher identities in and out of the classroom. My performances are at times conscious, strategic and political contingent on the desired outcome – accreditation, certification, funding, increased wages, advocacy for the recognition for care as an ethical encounter (Dahlberg, 2003), action for gender equity and safe spaces for women in and outside the workplace. At other times I am unconsciously drawn into discourses through unrecognized desires of acceptance or approval. Conscious or unconscious, every day I navigate and perform teacher discourses of professionalism, good neoliberal citizen, feminist, activist, carer and nurturer, technician, researcher and critically reflective practitioner. The difference for me now is I can name the discourses, recognize what knowledges are privileges and by who, and the language and the way meanings are attached. This knowledge allows me to speak and perform differently/politically and be 'comfortable' and embrace this (well most times)!

References

Aston, M. (2016). Teaching feminist poststructuralism: Founding scholars still relevant today. *Creative Education, 7*(15), 2251.

Ball, S. (1990). Introducing Monsieur Foucault. In S. J. Ball (Ed.), *Foucault and education, discipline and knowledge* (pp. 1–8). Routledge.

Blaise, M. (2005). A feminist poststructuralist study of children 'doing' gender in an urban kindergarten classroom. *Early childhood research quarterly, 20*(1), 85–108.

Blaise, M. (2012). *Playing it straight: Uncovering gender discourse in the early childhood classroom*. Routledge.

Brennan, D. (1998). *The politics of Australian child care: Philanthropy to feminism and beyond*. Cambridge University Press.

Bronfenbrenner, U. (1989). Ecological systems theory. *Annals of Child Development*, 6(1), 187–249.

Butler, J. (2011). *Gender trouble: Feminism and the subversion of identity*. Routledge.

Butler, J. (1992). Contingent foundations: Feminism and the question of 'postmodernism'. In J. Butler, & J. Scott (Eds.), *Feminists theorize the political* (p. 3). Routledge, Chapman and Hall, Inc.

Butler, J. (1988). Performative acts and gender constitution: An essay in phenomenology and feminist theory. *Theatre Journal*, 40(4), 519–31.

Cannella, G. (1997). *Deconstructing early childhood education: Social justice and revolution*. Peter Lang.

Cheek, J. (2000). *Postmodern and poststructural approaches to nursing research*. Sage Publications.

Dahlberg, G. (2003). Pedagogy as a loci of an ethics of an encounter. In M. N. Bloch, K. Holmlund, I. Moqvist, & T. S. Popkewitz (Eds.), *Governing children, families, and education* (pp. 261–86). Palgrave Macmillan.

Dahlberg, G., Moss, P., & Pence, A. R. (1999). *Beyond quality in early childhood education and care: Postmodern perspectives*. Falmer Press.

Dahlberg, G., Moss, P. & Pence, A. (2006). *Beyond quality in early childhood education and care*. London, UK: Taylor and Francis. https://doi.org/10.4324/9780203966150

Daly, M. (1984). *Pure lust: Elemental feminist philosophy*. The Women's Press.

Davies, B., Browne, J., Gannon, S., Hopkins, L., McCann, H., & Wihlborg, M. (2006). Constituting the feminist subject in poststructuralist discourse. *Feminism & Psychology*, 16(1), 87–103.

Davies, B. (2000). *A body of writing, 1990–1999*. Rowman & Littlefield.

Davies, B. (2006) Subjectification: The relevance of Butler's analysis for education. *British Journal of Sociology of Education*, 27(4), 425–38.

Davies, B. (1993). *Shards of glass: Children reading and writing beyond gendered identities*. Hampton Press.

Davies, B. (2003). *Frogs and snails and feminist tales: Preschool children and gender*. Hampton Press.

Davies, B., & Gannon, S. (2011). Feminism/post-structuralism. In B. Somekh & C. Lewin (Eds.), *Theory and methods in social research* (pp. 312–19). Sage.

Davies, B. (1991). The concept of agency: A feminist poststructuralist analysis. *Social Analysis: The International Journal of Social and Cultural Practice* (30), 42–53.

Davies, B. (1992). A feminist poststructuralist analysis of discursive practices in the classroom and playground. *The Australian Journal of Education Studies*, 13(1), 49–66.

Department of Education, Employment and Workplace Relations (DEEWR). (2009). *Belonging, being and becoming: The early years learning framework for Australia*. Canberra, Australia.

Foucault, M. (1972). *The archaeology of knowledge and the discourse on language.* New York: Pantheon.

Foucault, M. (1978). *The History of Sexuality: Volume 1 Introduction.* Edited and Translated by R. Hurley, Random House.

Foucault, M. (1980). *Power/Knowledge: Selected Interviews and Other Writings 1972-1977.* Edited by C. Gordon. Pantheon Books.

Freire, P. (1996). *Pedagogy of the oppressed (revised).* Continuum.

Freud, S. (2014). *Inhibitions, symptoms and anxiety.* Read Books Ltd.

Gavey, N. (1989). Feminist poststructuralism and discourse analysis: Contributions to feminist psychology. *Psychology of Women Quarterly, 13*(4), 459-75.

Gore, J. (1993). *The struggles for pedagogies: Critical and feminist discourses as regimes of truth.* Routledge.

Gutting, G. (1998). Post-structuralism. In Edward Craig, (Ed.), *The Routledge Encyclopedia of Philosophy.* Taylor and Francis. 5 July 2021. https://www.rep.routledge.com/articles/thematic/post-structuralism/v-1. doi:10.4324/9780415249126-N045-1

Habermas, J. (1984). *The theory of communicative action: Reason and the rationalization of society* (Vol. 1). Beacon Press.

Hughes, P. (2010). Paradigms, methods and knowledge. In G. MacNaughton, S. A. Rolfe, & I. Siraj-Blatchford (Eds.), *Doing early childhood research* (pp. 35–61). Allen & Unwin.

Lather, P. (1991). *Getting smart: Feminist research and pedagogy within/in the postmodern.* Routledge.

MacNaughton, G. (2000). *Rethinking gender in early childhood education.* Allen & Unwin.

MacNaughton, G. (1999). Promoting gender equity for young children in the South and South East Asian Region. *International Journal of Early Years Education, 7*(1), 77-84.

MacNaughton, G. (1997a). Feminist praxis and the gaze in the early childhood curriculum. *Gender and Education, 9*(3), 317-26.

MacNaughton, G. (1997b). Who's got the power? Rethinking gender equity strategies in early childhood. *International Journal of Early Years Education, 5*(1), 57-66.

MacNaughton, G. (1996). Is Barbie to blame?: Reconsidering how children learn gender. *Australasian Journal of Early Childhood, 21*(4), 18-24.

Martin, J., Nuttall, J., Henderson, L., & Wood, E. (2020). Educational leaders and the project of professionalisation in early childhood education in Australia. *International Journal of Educational Research, 101,* https://doi.org/10.1016/j.ijer.2020.101559.

Maslow, A. H. (1987). *Motivation and personality* (3rd ed.). Pearson Education.

Moreton-Robinson, A. (2000). *Talkin'up to the white woman: Aboriginal women and feminism.* University of Queensland Press.

Moss, P. (2014). *Transformative change and real utopias in early childhood education: A story of democracy, experimentation and potentiality.* Routledge.

Moss, P. (2006). Structures, understandings and discourses: Possibilities for re-envisioning the early childhood worker. *Contemporary issues in early childhood, 7*(1), 30-41.

Ortlipp, M., Arthur, L., & Woodrow, C. (2011). Discourses of the early years learning framework: Constructing the early childhood professional. *Contemporary Issues in Early Childhood, 12*(1), 56–70.

Osgood, J. (2012). *Narratives from the nursery: Negotiating professional identities in early childhood*. Routledge.

Osgood, J. (2006). Deconstructing professionalism in early childhood education: Resisting the regulatory gaze. *Contemporary Issues in Early Childhood, 7*(1), 5–14.

Pérez, M. S. (2017). Black feminist thought in early childhood studies: (Re)centering marginalized feminist perspectives. In K. Smith, K. Alexander, & S. Campbell (Eds.), *Feminism(s) in early childhood* (pp. 49–62). Springer.

Piaget, J. (1964). Part I: Cognitive development in children: Piaget development and learning. *Journal of research in science teaching, 2*(3), 176–86.

Roberts-Holmes, G., & Moss, P. (2021). *Neoliberalism and early childhood education: Markets, imaginaries and governance*. Routledge.

Robinson, K. H. (2013). *Innocence, knowledge and the construction of childhood: The contradictory nature of sexuality and censorship in children's contemporary lives*. Routledge.

Robinson, K. H., & Jones Diaz, C. (2006). *Diversity and difference in early childhood education: Issues for theory and practice*. Open University Press.

Standing Council on School Education and Early Childhood (SCSEEC). (2012). *Early Years Workforce Strategy: The Early Childhood Education and Care Workforce Strategy for Australia 2012-2016*. Education Services Australia.

Srinivasan, P. (2019). Pookey, poory, power: An agentic performance. *Contemporary Issues in Early Childhood, 20*(2), 121–32.

Srinivasan, P. (2014). *Early childhood in postcolonial Australia: Children's contested identities*. Palgrave Macmillan.

Walkerdine, V. (1998). *Daddy's girl: Young girls and popular culture*. Harvard University Press.

Weedon, C. (1987). *Feminist practice and poststructuralist theory*. Basil Blackwell Ltd.

2

Kristevan Early Childhood Teacher: Poststructural Feminist Identities in Australia and New Zealand

Sonja Arndt and Marek Tesar

Introduction: On possibilities

This chapter discusses early childhood teachers' identities in Australia and Aotearoa New Zealand. It uses Julia Kristeva's French poststructural feminist lens to help us to reconceptualize the complexities of theories and practices that affect them. Central to this chapter is Kristeva's work on the formation of the subject, and her notion of the 'foreigner'. The chapter argues that this perspective is important in the two countries in which we are situated as teacher educators and scholars, that is, Australia and Aotearoa New Zealand, and further, that it also opens up imaginaries for global ramifications and new possibilities.

Being and becoming an early childhood teacher is influenced by teachers' relations with, and within, a local place. In Aotearoa New Zealand, for example, *Te Whāriki* is a curriculum framework that early childhood teachers are asked to implement that brings together neo-colonial and neoliberal discourses (Tesar, 2015), while at the same time it offers solace through the mantra of 'people, places and things' (Ministry of Education [MoE], 2017, p. 12) and the potential for opening up to other theoretical frameworks which may further shape early childhood teacher identities (Tesar & Arndt, 2020). These identities are, thus, linked to the local people, places and things, where Kristeva's poststructural feminism serves as a springboard to different thinking, being and doing in the familiar, the human and the more-than-human world (Malone, Tesar & Arndt, 2020).

The early childhood landscape in our two countries is a place where the key elements in Kristeva's thinking come alive. Kristeva's poststructural framing brings the focus on early childhood teachers and on the ethics of identity constructions, as it emphasizes the disruption of homogenizing, simplistic and universal expectations (see also Arndt & Tesar, 2019). In this sense, Kristeva's work offers an opening of critical and uncomfortable spaces that not only recognize, but facilitate a shift towards a gaze of multiplicities through which early childhood teachers can be seen as weaving Indigenous and non-Indigenous subject formations. With this chapter, we argue that Kristeva's feminism is helpful to examine and enhance understandings of the multiplicities and potential discomforts embodied in early childhood teacher identities in Australia and Aotearoa New Zealand and to inspire ways of thinking that could be adapted to other places also.

Becoming Julia Kristeva

First, however, we ask: who is Julia Kristeva, and why does her work matter in early childhood education? Kristeva is a French philosopher, psychoanalyst and linguist. As an immigrant from her native Bulgaria, Kristeva's theories reflect the notion of foreignness that she has experienced in her own life. As a foreigner, she arrived in Paris in 1965, as a young student, immersing herself in the male-dominated philosophical, psychoanalytical and linguistic milieu. She was 'pushed' as she says 'to the limits of [her] abilities … of society, language, and culture' (France Culture Broadcast, 1988/1996, p. 4). Her experiences led to her referring to herself as 'a mosaic' (Midttun, 2006, p. 169), of different cultures, nationalities and identities. Strongly influenced by her relational and academic connections, Kristeva's work elevates notions of difference not focused on labels or binaries, whether sexual, cultural or others (Oliver, 1993, 2002). Kristeva's positioning towards feminism is an ethical one. In an examination of Kristeva's feminist revolutions, Oliver (1993) outlines:

> Kristeva is concerned to formulate an ethics that allows all individuals to avoid sheer conformity to the Law, on the one hand, and complete ostracism from the social, on the other. She wants an ethics in which women are neither mere conformists nor absolute outlaws. She wants an ethics that unravels the doublebind of identity.
>
> (p. 110)

Despite being seen by critics in various ways as feminist and representing feminist thought, others oppose this idea and see her as un-feminist. Kristeva herself rejects the label of feminism, simultaneously contributing to disruptions of singular conceptions of women, the body, identity and foreignness, and to her contributions to feminist thought overall (Oliver, 1993). In particular, Oliver says, Kristeva 'criticizes feminist movements which maintain some fixed notion of a feminine essence or "woman" because they cover over differences between individual women' (p. 98). Despite Kristeva's lack of personal alignment with feminism and feminist practices, her work significantly affects the application of a feminist lens to the identity of the early childhood teacher. According to Moi (1986), Kristeva 'used to belong to the movement' (p. 9) but is 'now more radical' (Midttun, 2006, p. 174), as Kristeva herself claims in an interview. Aggressive feminism is 'archaic' (p. 174), Kristeva says, and contrary to her aim of speaking 'of each and every woman's freedom and creativity' (p. 174). Kristeva's concerns have been labelled as a 'third generation postmodern feminism' (McCance, 1996, p. 155). In other words, Kristeva's stance is labelled, like many feminisms (Smith, Campbell & Alexander, 2017), as a feminism that is conscious of, and argues against, the prevailing social contract and ideological contexts. Whilst for Kristeva the resistance to a particular label may be more of a resistance to any perceived permanence that labelling may cause, a different lack of alignment with such a feminism wrestles in the early childhood milieu in Australia and Aotearoa New Zealand. Embedded within an increasingly inescapable neoliberal, business-focused model of early childhood education, teachers who remain ideologically committed in their daily practice, narratives and discourses to feminist orientations are placed in direct tension with shareholders, business managers and the transformation of their profession into an industry (Duhn, 2010). A Kristevan feminist disruption of early childhood teacher identities becomes increasingly important, then, in a sector that is held up as an 'attractive investment opportunity' where the aim is to sell 'a commodity to parent consumers as they [the teachers] participate in the workforce' (Mitchell, 2014).

Kristeva's thinking sees the subject as ongoing in formation, in relation to and by all that is and that occurs in and around the subject. Her 'more radical' approach that elevates the intricacies of all women's lives spurs an investigation of identity that recognizes the specificities of individual and collective realities. Early childhood teachers in Australia and Aotearoa New Zealand – all of us – are always 'infinitely in construction, deconstructible, open and evolving' (Kristeva, 2008, p. 2), meaning that there is also always an element of foreignness involved. Explicating her notion of the foreigner, Kristeva notes that we are not only always – at least to a certain extent – foreigners not only to each other, but also to ourselves. In other words, as identities are constantly in construction, there remains always some part or parts of an individual that is unknown (Kristeva, 1991).

Thinking with early childhood teachers in Australia and Aotearoa New Zealand, recognizing the foreignness within each of us, or as Kristeva (1991) says, living not only 'with others' but also '*as* others' (p. 2), unsettles normalized and universalized conceptions of early childhood teachers. It pushes an 'ability to accept new modalities of otherness' (p. 2) which may or may not be knowable, comfortable or practical. Despite critics having argued against Kristeva's feminism (Oliver, 1993), its ethics of engagements, of confronting strangeness in 'the other and [of] oneself, toward an ethics of respect for the irreconcilable' (Kristeva, 1991, p. 182) is critical for understanding Kristeva's contribution to examinations of early childhood teacher identities. It impacts in important ways on Kristevan notions of feminism that recognize the inability of establishing once and for all, any one way of being, of truth, accuracy or direction of their formation and realities.

Kristeva's Poststructural Feminism Matters

The challenge of constructing early childhood teacher identities in Australia and Aotearoa New Zealand through a poststructural feminist lens is grounded in postmodern theory. Postmodernism calls for an ontological and epistemological breaking down of universal truths and metanarratives. It is a radical departure from the structuralism of modernity. Postmodernism offers a useful foundation for an investigation of teacher identity and subject formation (Tesar, Gibbons, Arndt & Hood, 2021), and fundamentally frames the discussion in an orientation towards multiple meanings and truths, multiple places, spaces, localities and diverse ways of thinking, being and doing early childhood education. It shows a possibility of how poststructural feminism shapes early childhood teacher subjectivities, how the histories and subjectivities, and their intersections with philosophy and education, matter (Tesar, 2021).

Poststructuralism thus arises from postmodern theory. Deconstructing fixed notions of early childhood teacher identity through a postmodern school of thought and through Kristeva's poststructural feminism is a productive exercise that neither offers nor seeks a singular lens, approach, method or outcome. What it does is it offers a way of feminist poststructural rethinking of meaning and dominant understandings of teachers' subject positions. A poststructural central focus on the subject and subjectivity marks, as Weedon says (1997), 'a crucial break with humanist conceptions of the individual' (p. 32), especially those which insist on a limited, narrow or static conception of the individual subject as unchanging, already formed. In contrast to 'this irreducible humanist essence of subjectivity, poststructuralism proposes a subjectivity which is precarious, contradictory and in process, constantly being reconstituted in discourse each time we think or speak' (Weedon, 1997, p. 32). Viewing early childhood teacher identities through a Kristevan feminist poststructuralist lens, then, acknowledges the precarity and tensions within which these teachers work and within which their identities are formed not only in Australia and Aotearoa New Zealand, but also globally (Yelland et al., 2021).

The importance and uniqueness of Kristeva's poststructural feminist lens is its mosaic nature. In relation to early childhood teachers, a Kristevan stance and its poststructural feminist standpoint are concerned with shifting 'the boundaries, the limits, of the subject's enclosure' (McCance, 1996, p. 155) as formed through encounters with the self, other beings, other things and the structural, political and policy environment. In its deconstruction of the dominant narratives on teacher identities and of the self, this stance thus gives hope to teachers' complex subject formations and their implications for the teacher workforce and early childhood education and care. Kristeva's notion of subjects as always in process embodies this poststructural feminist stance. The ongoing construction of the subject – and the early childhood teacher – is always only alive if we recognize that it is constantly changing, and constantly affected by its environment (Kristeva, 2002).

The notion of the foreigner further confronts the ongoing formation of early childhood teacher identities. Elevating the discomfort of such a confrontation, Kristeva's concern is with '[t]he challenge of confronting the foreigner', which lies in 'the challenge of confronting alterity' (Purcell, 2010, p. 575), or that which is different. The importance of a Kristevan lens is therefore that it does not allow us to rest in any comfortable space of superficiality or normality. As her mentor Roland Barthes says, Kristeva's work changes 'the order of things' (Barthes, n.d., cited in Moi, 1986, p. 1): it *intends* to disrupt, by challenging and questioning. Importantly, then, a Kristevan lens works to unsettle early childhood teacher subjectivities by taking thought and questioning seriously. Suggesting that there is a lack, in today's society, of dissent or disruption of the dominant narrative, or of rethinking norms to question realities, understandings and meanings, true dissidence, according to Kristeva (1977/1986), 'is perhaps simply what it always has been: thought' (p. 299). A Kristevan poststructural feminist lens thus not only *gives us permission* to create openings to disrupt and question teacher realities and identities, it *implores* us to do so.

Early Childhood Teacher Identities in Process

Applying Kristeva's poststructural feminist lens in early childhood education in Australia and Aotearoa New Zealand recognizes the intersectionalities that permeate the early childhood sector, and how teachers' identities are produced. Reference to the term 'intersectionalities' acknowledges the Kristevan (1991) notion of our inner unknowability and multiple realities, as it 'refutes the idea of a primary category' (Evans & Lépinard, 2019, p. 2). Instead, as with the evolving construction of identities on the basis of all with which we are surrounded, 'categories are co-constructed, and therefore cannot be artificially separated' (p. 2). Early childhood teacher identities are challenged within this recognition and consequent de-elevation of dominant exceptionalism, through exposing inequities that arise within the sector and between the sector and society. As in other parts of the world, contemporary constructions of early childhood teachers in our two countries are impacted by the highly feminized nature of the early childhood profession, and thus by conceptions of women within society in general. Smith, Campbell and Alexander (2017) argue that 'feminism(s) are more than oppositional discourses' (p. 3), but rather they are transformational. The importance of bringing a Kristevan lens to bear through the notion of intersectionalities is thus that it aims not only to achieve transformation within the sector and within society, but also to do so from the beginnings of inner transformations. Immersed in past, present and future tensions on the basis of gender, understandings of power arise for instance in recognizing historical gendered marginalizations in our countries and feminist goals of social justice and activisms to reduce women's subjugations, especially for women of colour (Smith et al., 2017).

Political histories illustrate some of the transformations that have occurred for women in both Australia and Aotearoa New Zealand (although there remains a dominant and recently overt sexism within politics and society). In Australia, women were given the right to vote in 1902, but this only included Indigenous women in two states. Indigenous people across the country were only granted the same voting rights as non-Indigenous in 1983 (Coady, 2017). Aotearoa New Zealand on the other hand preceded this by almost a century, being the first country to grant all women the right to vote with the passing of the Electoral Act 1893 (Ministry for Culture and Heritage [MCH], 2018). A Kristevan poststructural feminist encounter of the foreigner within creates an opening to rethink our own relations and enactments of power within these historical and contemporary contexts. Although the story of teacher identity for us is closely tied to our own localities in the Australian and Aotearoa New Zealand contexts, the stories and philosophies of subject formation that arise can be related to other teachers and other places. Concerns such as Ladson-Billings (2021) highlights, of racial discrimination and ongoing marginalization are, like a pandemic, raging within Western societies. On the other hand, perceptions of early childhood teachers as in some way less valued than teachers in other educational sectors remain concerning and in need of transformation, beyond being merely governed, structured, predetermined and normalized behaviour managers or workers on a factory floor (Arndt, Gibbons & Fitzsimons, 2015; Arndt et al., 2018, 2020; Gibbons, 2018).

It is interesting to note some similar tendencies between Australia and Aotearoa New Zealand. Both remain deeply affected by a consciousness of colonization in education, the early childhood sector and teacher identities (Lopez-Atkinson, 2017; Ritchie & Skerrett, 2014). We suggest that perhaps it is not too bold a move to suggest that Kristeva's poststructural feminism permits us to question any hesitancy to rethink attitudes towards a feminism that recognizes Indigeneities in new ways. As Aboriginal women reclaim and reimagine their place in education and society (Lopez-Atkinson, 2017), for example, a critical engagement with the notion of the foreigner within shifts the process of recognizing each of us as foreign and unknowable, to a cautious space taking care not to revert to a feminism that amounts to nothing more than a 'middle class and Anglo Centric... form of colonisation in itself' (Lopez-Atkinson, 2017, p. 26). De-elevating ourselves begins, according to Kristeva (1991), when citizens (including all groups of society, policymakers, politicians) cease to 'consider [themselves] as unitary and glorious' (p. 2), unexceptional, equally unknowable foreigners to those who are openly othered and marginalized.

A Kristevan poststructural feminist lens pushes towards a de-escalation of whitestream (Ritchie & Skerrett, 2014) models of education by challenging institutional and structural regimes of racism and ongoing colonization, including early childhood teachers and their pedagogies. Recognizing the foreigner within, Kristeva (1991) says, leads to a discovery of the 'incoherences and abysses' or 'strangenesses' (p. 2) within each of us, and, by extension we argue here, within our institutions, communities and societies. A Kristevan poststructural feminist examination in itself is an inadequate tool for clearing all unresolved and contested personal, land and legal concerns facing Indigenous people in our countries. Challenging 'the boundaries, the limits, of the subject's enclosure' as McCance (1996, p. 155) suggests, however, gives us a starting point for challenging, rearticulating and redefining the hegemony and dominance of non-Indigenous teachers and teacher educators (including ourselves), to elevate Aboriginal, Torres Strait Islander and Māori teachers and their pedagogies. It opens us up to our own raw and intricate Otherness, represented in Kristeva's (1991) call to live 'as' (p. 2) the other, meaning to confront and experience the discomfort of our own difference.

Beyond the intersecting gender relations, both Australia and Aotearoa New Zealand are impacted by immigration policies, and the prevalence of immigrant early childhood teachers employed within early childhood settings. In both countries, this is a useful measure to fill shortages of teachers in early childhood settings (Immigration New Zealand, 2011). Early childhood teachers with whom we work tell stories of their own lived, felt realities, of how they migrate to our countries often from Asian countries and some from European countries. Many teachers have given up everything in their home countries to take up their position in what was to be a new life, a new job, in a new country. We hear how they leave their home countries as qualified teachers and arrive to our countries where their qualifications are not recognized, where they have to apply to work with young children (Victorian Government, 2021), and upgrade their qualifications to the levels required for teacher registration (New Zealand Teachers Council, 2014).

A Kristevan lens that recognizes early childhood teachers as constantly in construction usefully acknowledges such dynamic assemblages of times, histories and realities. That is, it recognizes that historical, present and future possibilities and realities are always in relation, weaving (Barthes, 1977) the stories of teacher selves. As we hear their stories, we perceive a real excitement in these teachers about working 'down under', as our two countries are sometimes referred to, where the growing enrolments of ever younger children in early childhood education have led to the rapid demand for early childhood education and childcare services. Tensions in the sector are exacerbated more recently as a global pandemic causes increasing problems with teacher retention due to a lack of acknowledgement of the profession and the work of qualified professional teachers (Arndt et al., 2020; Jackson, 2021). Through teachers' stories it also becomes clear that, like ours, early childhood teachers' experiences cannot be labelled in universalized or consistent, static ways. They are physical, emotional, personal and professional, raw, intimate, intricate and difficult to share or articulate. And, like ours, they appear to be rising and falling, a roller coaster, at times elated and then sorrowful, grappling with new emotional, cultural and material early childhood, cultural and societal environments. Kristeva (1991) points to such highs and lows as ways of being that are 'brought up, relieved, disseminated' (p. 3) in our foreignness. Grappling with such a foreignness within – the profession, society and ourselves – is the goal and work of a Kristevan poststructural feminist lens.

Possibilities for a New Wave of Down under Feminism

As already indicated, the importance of Kristeva's philosophy for re-visioning early childhood teacher identities lies not only in its contestation of homogenizing truths. Her notion of the foreigner offers a subversion of the dominant societal and to a large extent the profession-specific discourses in diverse contexts (Arndt et al., 2020). In suggesting that not only do we all not know each other, but that there is also always an element of the unknown in ourselves, the recognition of the stranger within opens up to new understandings through a notion of revolt. Revolt is central to Kristeva's (1998) theory of subject formation. Its purpose is to provoke continually questioning attitudes and approaches, towards individuals (ourselves), diverse team members, social groups, and Others. Following Kristeva, it is the basis of an ethical and moral obligation for revolt. Revolt, in relation to who the early childhood teacher is, is an attitude, towards community, towards teaching teams, towards political states, and most crucially of all, this attitude, like dissident thought, according to Kristeva, is sorely lacking in contemporary politics and society (Kristeva, 2000). As early childhood teachers and teacher educators, Kristeva's notion of subject formation resonates with the intricate rawness of all of our identity constructions. Diverse attitudes and orientations within teaching teams, approaches and practices, and personal and professional experiences underlie those emerging in the professional discourses.

A Kristevan notion of revolt calls for a permanent state of questioning. It is a 're'-volt', that involves an evolution through the past and the present (Kristeva, 1996/2000). The disruption and ongoing questioning that is necessary according to Kristeva is an intimate, inner process of interrogation that is necessary and unceasing (Oliver, 2002). New understandings of the early childhood teacher subject arise through this intimate process of revolt. It is not intended that it (re)introduces or focuses on already existing occurrences, understandings or situations, but rather that it elevates, shifts into and exposes new ways of thinking and thus uncertainties. Such an intimate process has the potential to open up to new articulations of power, to new understandings and operations of intersectionalities, to new ways of governing the teacher self and to how she perceives herself and is perceived by others. Kristeva suggests that a culture of revolt must be cultivated. It acts as a critical conscience, she claims, and indeed, without it, we would neither come to 'realise ourselves as autonomous and free' (Kristeva, cited in Oliver, 2002, p. 420), nor confront dominant and often oppressive normalizations in society.

Cultivating a culture of revolt unsettles normalizations that perpetuate conceptions of the early childhood teacher as inferior and worthy of lower esteem, status and pay than teachers in other sectors (Arndt et al., 2018; Mitchell et al., 2019), of unquestioningly remaining at the disposal of society as essential frontline workers in times of a pandemic (Arndt et al., 2020), or the narratives of governing agencies during the pandemics (Gibbons & Tesar, 2021). Such normalizing conceptions of the early childhood teacher – as unworthy, or as mere *minders* of young children – therefore call for attitudes of revolt to unsettle, dethrone and simultaneously elevate how we call, see and treat them.

Down under, in Australia and Aotearoa New Zealand, whether deeply seeped in the local place, newly migrated from another, or somewhere in between, early childhood teachers are constantly confronted by the influences of local and global societal orientations: towards children, childhoods, teaching, learning and practice. All of these affect others and their own orientations towards themselves and who they are as early childhood teachers. Taking Kristeva's urging of considering the stories of all women (extended to all teachers of all genders) means taking the importance of each teacher's historicized and felt values and beliefs and how they inform their lives and teaching, what they choose to celebrate, how they choose to speak, who they choose to relate to and how. If, for instance, it is 'culture day' and their culture is deemed to be somehow a way to illustrate 'richness' or 'diversity', taking up Kristeva's calls for revolt means not only reflecting in sufficiently critical ways on the associated practices, but also transforming them. What are teachers asked to do, on culture day and why? It means asking not only what is the purpose of this day as a pedagogical activity, but in what ways is it an elevation of identity – of the children, families, community – and of the teachers enacting it? For whose benefit are such practices integrated into the curriculum, and what benefits or hurt might they be causing?

The increased focus on revolt as an inner questioning is a key consequence of aligning with a Kristevan feminist poststructuralist approach to teacher identity. What in a Kristevan sense is seen as 'true' dissidence, that is, critical thought and a permanent state of questioning, provokes an attitude of increased attention, of truly noticing. It urges inner confrontations of ways in which teachers become valued, sidelined, marginalized, in their early childhood settings and in society. Any objectification in their teams, such as being merely, celebratorily, 'put on show' on culture day, may be just a tip of the iceberg indication of deeper orientations towards teachers in general and teachers who are in any way Other. When teachers internalize their sensitivities and/or hide their hurt or isolation, they are able to be neither really true, nor completely false, in their situatedness in the dominant early childhood setting and community or societal milieu, this is a cause for concern. While programming and planning questions may have been asked within the team, and 'on paper' connections can be drawn to justify certain practices, a Kristevan inner revolt and questioning of teacher identity may raise and for the first time confront such concerns as what even constitutes 'richness', for instance, in light of the dangers of a superficial 'tourist' approach (Papastephanou, 2015) to identity. Such questioning may raise doubt as to whether it is possible even to know and value 'richness', or questions of ethics (Buchanan et al., 2021), when we are all foreigners not only to each other, but also to ourselves.

Coupled with a political neoliberal elevation of economic freedom, early childhood teachers have become situated in a context of overwhelmingly narrow definitions, competition and expectations of neoliberal constructs of achievement, outputs and success (Duhn, 2010; Kelsey, 2015; Springer, 2016). Increasingly, it seems that what and who they should and could be or become has already been predetermined: a tidy fit into a productive, non-disruptive teacher mould. Particularly in the past three decades, there have been strengthened efforts; activism and research; espousing reconceptualist, feminist and poststructuralist ideals, and arguing against the marginalization of minority or subjugated groups within early childhood education and in the role of the early childhood teacher (Arndt, Gibbons & Fitzsimons, 2015; Arndt & Tesar, 2016; Bloch, Swadener & Cannella, 2014; MacNaughton, 2005; Taylor, 2005; Tesar & Arndt, 2016). Even so, the risk of becoming enveloped by the individualist, competitive neoliberal drive remains, and penetrates common ideals and pedagogies. Rather than enhancing fairness or rights, such a focus then can resemble the superficial practices and assumptions that Papastephanou

(2015) highlights as exoticizing, in a superficial disconnectedness from the realities of individuals, teams in localized settings and their communities.

An inner revolt may expose questions of programming, policy and pedagogical practices as more akin to exploitation, rather than valuing. To return to the previous example, when interest in a teachers' culture is expressed only on 'culture day', but not at any other time, what focus does this bring on the quality of the teaching and learning, on teachers' strengths, diverse and intricate knowledges and multiple ways of being? These are the considerations that arise when we return to Kristeva's calls for a 'more radical' feminism, that creates space for *all* realities, expectations and experiences. There is a certain permission that this feminist poststructural stance gives us, to retrieve from the margins teachers considered to be 'a nobody', tamed into a dominant teacher mould. With this permission early childhood teachers in contemporary times, and those of us who advocate for them, might come closer to accentuating the intimacy and delicacy of their – and all of our – Otherness, as a permanent feature in our identities, constantly in construction, and always evolving (Kristeva, 2008).

Kristeva's feminist poststructural approach to Otherness offers an opportunity to rethink identity. If identity is constantly in construction, then what teachers can be, should be or are, becomes inevitably also always evolving. Who the early childhood teacher is and can be then moves beyond seemingly flippant and surface level acts that affect teachers in ways that are far deeper than they show or make evident. A Kristevan permanent state of questioning through an inner attitude of revolt opens spaces for new understandings of teacher identity. It allows inner attitudes to shift towards the dominant moral universalisms that shape and perpetuate liberal attitudes to individual freedom in Australian and New Zealand early childhood education and society. In the Australasian down under context the early childhood education sector's liberal, rights and equity focused societal and educational policies mirror this orientation (Loveridge et al., 2012). A Kristevan feminist poststructuralist lens helps to explicate and elevate expectations of respectful relations, tolerance and pluralism, and what might be associated conceptions of universally cosmopolitan citizens (Peters, 2013) widens, rather than reduces, the gap, depending on their interpretations. It complicates early childhood teacher identity to problematize what risk being narrow or simple interpretations, leading to marginalizing, tokenistic or (unwittingly) harmful practices. A revoltful inner questioning thus strengthens inner relationships with societal and wider global liberal interests in issues of race, gender, culture, freedom, rights and equity.

Concluding Comments

Just as a culture of revolt is necessary for the life of society, this chapter has argued that it is necessary for rethinking early childhood teachers' identities. A Kristevan poststructural feminist lens urges a critical intimate engagement with identities and implores us to reconceptualize the down under early childhood teacher as forever in process. That is, in a process where their – and all of our – identities are constantly in construction, where we are all strangers not only to each other, but also to ourselves (Arndt, 2018; Kristeva, 1991). Conceptualizing constructions of early childhood teacher identities therefore needs to remain alive and in process, to avoid stagnation, fixed presumptions and the risk of becoming (or perhaps already being) irrelevant, misinformed or misplaced. A Kristevan poststructural feminism offers re-volt-ful provocations as valuable openings for igniting and indeed elevating the nuances, rawness and intricacies of early childhood teachers' identities. It creates conceptual spaces in which to elevate locally relevant, constantly shifting and entangled meanings and multiple ways of being. Most crucially, a Kristevan poststructural feminist lens depends at its core on a shift away from fixed notions of who the early childhood teacher is. It urges us to confront the shifts and uncertainties within each of us.

References

Arndt, S. (2018). Early childhood teacher cultural otherness and belonging. *Contemporary Issues in Early Childhood Special Issue: Interrogating Belonging in Diverse Early Years Settings, 19*(4), 392–403. Doi: 10.1177/1463949118783382

Arndt, S., Gibbons, A., & Fitzsimons, P. (2015). Thriving and surviving, and the incredible problem of constructions of normality and otherness in early childhood settings. *Global Studies of Childhood Special Issue: Regulating Childhoods: Disrupting Discourses of Control*, 1–12. Doi:10.1177/2043610615597144

Arndt, S., & Tesar, M. (2016). A more-than-social movement: The post-human condition of quality in the early years. *Contemporary Issues in Early Childhood, 17*(1), 16–25. Doi:10.1177/1463949115627896

Arndt, S., Urban, M., Murray, C., Smith, K., Swadener, B., & Ellegaard, T. (2018). Contesting early childhood professional identities: A cross-national discussion. Special issue: The lived and sometimes clandestine professional experiences of early childhood educators. *Contemporary Issues in Early Childhood, 19*(2), 97–116. Doi:10.1177/1463949118768356

Arndt, S., & Tesar, M. (2019). Re-configuring an ethics of care in culturally diverse early childhood settings: Towards an ethics of unknowing. In R. Langford (Ed.), *Theorizing feminist ethics of care in early childhood practice* (37–58). Bloomsbury Academic Press.

Arndt, S., Smith, K., Urban, M., Ellegard, T., Swadener, B.B., & Murray, C. (2020). Reconceptualising and (re)forming early childhood professional identities: Ongoing transnational policy discussions. *Policy Futures in Education*. Doi: 10.1177/1478210320976015

Barthes, R. (1977). *Image – Music – Text* (S. Heath, Trans.). Fontana.

Bloch, M., Swadener, B., & Cannella, G. S. (2014). Introduction: Exploring reconceptualist histories and possibilities. In M. Bloch, B. Swadener, & G. S. Cannella (Eds.), *Reconceptualising early childhood care & education: A reader. Critical questions, new imaginaries & social activism* (pp. 1–18). Peter Lang Publishers.

Buchanan, R., Forster, D., Doughlas, S., Nakar, S., Boon, H., Heath, T., Heyward, P., D'Olimpio, L., Ailwood, J., Eacott, S., Smith, S., Peters, M, & Tesar, M. (2021). Philosophy of education in a new key: Exploring new ways of teaching and doing ethics in education in the 21st century. *Educational Philosophy and Theory*. https://doi.org/10.1080/00131857.2021.1880387

Coady, M. M. (2017). Feminism and the development of early childhood education in Australia. In K. Smith, S. Campbell, & K. Alexander (Eds.), *Feminism(s) in early childhood: Using feminist theories in research and practice* (pp. 11–24). Springer.

Duhn, I. (2010). 'The centre is my business': Neo-liberal politics, privatisation and discourses of professionalism in New Zealand. *Contemporary Issues in Early Childhood*, *11*(1), 49–60. Doi:10.2304/ciec.2010.11.1.49

Evans, E., & Lépinard, É. (2019). Confronting privileges in feminist and queer movements. In E. Evans & É. Lépinard (Eds.), *Intersectionality in feminist and queer movements: Confronting privileges* (1st ed., pp. 1–26). Routledge.

France Culture broadcast. (1988/1996). Julia Kristeva in person (R. M. Guberman, Trans.). In R. M. Guberman (Ed.), *Julia Kristeva Interviews* (pp. 3–11). Columbia University Press.

Gibbons, A. (2018). Not the bottom, but the beginning: The failure of the teaching profession to value early childhood education. *New Zealand Journal of Teachers' Work*, *15*(1), 5–9. Auckland University of Technology.

Gibbons, A., & Tesar, M. (2021). The 'new normal' and new normalisations in Early Childhood Education policy in Aotearoa New Zealand: A post-COVID 19 perspective? *New Zealand Annual Review of Education* (25). https://doi.org/10.26686/nzaroe.v25.6911

Immigration New Zealand. (2011). *Essential skills in demand lists review*. http://www.immigration.govt.nz/migrant/general/generalinformation/news/esidreview.htm

Jackson, J. (2021). Early childhood educators are leaving in droves. Here are 3 ways to keep them, and attract more. *The Conversation* (15 January). https://theconversation.

com/early-childhood-educators-are-leaving-in-droves-here-are-3-ways-to-keep-them-and-attract-more-153187

Kelsey, J. (2015). *The FIRE economy: New Zealand's reckoning*. Bridget Williams Books.

Kristeva, J. (1977/1986). A new type of intellectual: The dissident. In T. Moi (Ed.), *The Kristeva reader* (pp. 292–300). Blackwell Publishers Ltd.

Kristeva, J. (1991). *Strangers to ourselves*. Columbia University Press.

Kristeva, J. (1996/2000). *The sense and non-sense of revolt* (J. Herman, Trans.). Columbia University Press.

Kristeva, J. (1998). The subject in process. In P. Ffrench (Ed.), *The Tel Quel reader* (pp. 133–78). Routledge.

Kristeva, J. (2000). *Crisis of the European subject* (S. Fairfield, Trans.). Other Press.

Kristeva, J. (2002). My memory's hyperbole (1984), from New York Literary Forum. In K. Oliver (Ed.), *The portable Kristeva* (pp. 3–21). Columbia University Press.

Kristeva, J. (2008). '*Does European culture exist?*'. Paper presented at the Dagmar and Václav Havel Foundation VIZE 97 prize, Prague Crossroads. http://www.vize.cz/wp-content/uploads/2016/05/laureat-julia-kristeva-en-speech.pdf

Ladson-Billings, G. (2021). I'm here for the hard re-set: Post pandemic pedagogy to preserve our culture. *Equity & Excellence in Education, 54*(1), 68–78. Doi: 10.1080/10665684.2020.1863883

Lopez-Atkinson, S. (2017). The didgeridoo, an instrument of oppression or decolonisation? In K. Smith, K. Alexander, & S. Campbell (Eds.), *Feminism(s) in early childhood: Using feminist theories in research and practice* (pp. 25–34). Springer.

Loveridge, J., Rosewarne, S. M. J, Shuker, M. J., Barker, A., & Nager, J. (2012). Responding to diversity: Statements and practices in two early childhood education contexts. *European Early Childhood Education Research Journal, 20*(1), 99–113. Doi:10.1080/1350293X.2011.634998

McCance, D. (1996). L'écriture limite: Kristeva's postmodern feminist ethics. *Hypatia, 11*(2), 141–60. http://www.jstor.org/stable/3810268

MacNaughton, G. (2005). *Doing Foucault in early childhood studies: Applying poststructural ideas*. Routledge.

Malone, K., Tesar, M., & Arndt, S. (2020). *Theorising posthuman childhood studies*. Springer.

Midttun, B. H. (2006). Crossing the borders: An interview with Julia Kristeva. *Hypatia, 21*(4), 164–77. http://content.ebscohost.com.ezproxy.auckland.ac.nz/pdf18_21/pdf/2006/HYP/01Sep06/22856093.pdf?T=P&P=AN&K=22856093&S=R&D=a2h&EbscoContent=dGJyMNHX8kSep7M40dvuOLCmr0qeprRSr6m4TLKWxWXS&ContentCustomer=dGJyMPGotkiwq7JRuePfgeyx44Dt6flA

Ministry for Culture and Heritage. (2018). *Suffrage 125 Whakatū Wāhine*. 6 August 2021 https://mch.govt.nz/suffrage-125

Ministry of Education. (2017). *Te Whāriki he whāriki mātauranga mō ngā mokopuna o Aotearoa Early Childhood Curriculum*. Wellington: New Zealand Government.

Mitchell, L. (2014, 2 December). Linda Mitchell: Put children's education before shareholders. *The New Zealand Herald*. http://www.nzherald.co.nz/nz/news/article.cfm?c_id=1&objectid=11367139

Mitchell, L., Clarkin-Phillips, J., Archard, S., Arndt, S., & Taylor, M. (2019). What do they do all day? Exploring the complexity of early childhood teachers' work. *EC Folio, 23*(1), Doi: 10.18296/ecf.0062

Moi, T. (1986). Introduction. In T. Moi (Ed.), *The Kristeva Reader* (pp. 1–22). Blackwell Publishing Ltd.

New Zealand Teachers Council. (2014). Overseas teachers. http://www.teacherscouncil.govt.nz/content/overseas-teachers

Oliver, K. (1993). Julia Kristeva's feminist revolutions. *Hypatia, 8*, 94–114. http://www.jstor.org/stable/3810407.

Oliver, K. (2002). Kristeva's revolutions. In K. Oliver (Ed.), *The portable Kristeva* (pp. xi–xxix). Columbia University Press.

Papastephanou, M. (2015). On ugliness in words, in politics, in tour-ism. *Educational Philosophy and Theory, 47*(13–14), 1493–515. Doi:10.1080/00131857.2014.963493

Peters, M. A. (2013). *Citizenship, human rights and identity: Prospects of a liberal cosmopolitan order*. Addleton Academic Publishers.

Purcell, E. (2010). Torn flesh: Julia Kristeva and the givenness of the stranger. *Religion and the Arts, 14*, 572–88. Doi:10.1163/156852910X529340

Ritchie, J., & Skerrett, M. (2014). *Early childhood education in Aotearoa New Zealand: History, pedagogy and liberation*. Palgrave Macmillan.

Smith, K., Campbell, S., & Alexander. (2017). Introduction. In K. Smith, K. Alexander, & S. Campbell (Eds.), *Feminism(s) in early childhood: Using feminist theories in research and practice*. (pp. 1–7). Springer.

Springer, S. (2016). *The discourse of neoliberalism: An anatomy of a powerful idea*. Rowman & Littlefield International.

Taylor, A. (2005). *Towards a transformative pedagogy of self/other*. Paper presented at the AARE Conference, Parramatta, NSW, Australia.

Tesar, M. (2015). *Te Whāriki* in Aotearoa New Zealand: Witnessing and resisting neoliberal and neo-colonial discourses in early childhood education. In V. Pacini-Ketchabaw & A. Taylor (Eds.), *Unsettling the colonial places and spaces of early childhood education* (pp. 145–70). Routledge.

Tesar, M., & Arndt, S. (2020). Re-reading and Re-activating Te Whāriki through a posthuman childhood studies lens. In A. Gunn and J. Nuttall (Eds.), *Weaving Te Whāriki: Aotearoa New Zealand's Early Childhood Curriculum Document in Theory and Practice* (pp. 181–94). NZCER Press.

Tesar, M. (2021). Philosophy as a method: Tracing the histories of intersections of 'philosophy', 'methodology' and 'education'. *Qualitative Inquiry, 27*(5), 544–53. https://doi.org/10.1177/1077800420934144

Tesar, M., Gibbons, A., Arndt, S., & Hood, N. (2021). Postmodernism in education. In *Oxford research encyclopedia of education*. Oxford University Press. Doi: https://doi.org/10.1093/acrefore/9780190264093.013.1269

Victorian Government. (2021). *Working with children check*. 10 August. https://www.workingwithchildren.vic.gov.au/

Weedon, C. (1997). *Feminist practice and poststructuralist theory*. Blackwell Publishing.

Yelland, N. J., Peters, L., Fairchild, N., Tesar, M., & Pérez, M. S. (Eds.) (2021). *The SAGE handbook of global childhoods*. SAGE Publications Ltd.

3

Labouring Relations and the Early Childhood Educator: The Return to Materialism

Jan Newberry

My brother gave me a set of feminist books when I was in high school. Apparently, he found my horizons too narrow. Reading *The Second Sex* by Simone de Beauvoir (2010) marked the beginning of my identification as a feminist, a thread woven through my life since. Although it manifested as a passionate defence of the Equal Rights Amendment during my high school years (an amendment still not made to the US constitution), it later shaped the research questions and methods I used as an ethnographer on Java, the central island in Indonesia.

My early theoretical, political and analytical enthusiasms centred on women's voice and women's work, reflecting the materialist feminism of the 1970s and 1980s. Later, my focus on the shaping of domestic labour by global political economy seemed misaligned with the move towards poststructuralism in feminism and anthropology. When research in the early 2000s led me to the neoliberal globalization of early childhood education and care, my work shifted towards a poststructural analysis of governmentality that draws from Foucault's analysis of power as distributed through the active participation of subjects in their regulation rather than as imposed by sovereign power. I confess I made this shift reluctantly, although ultimately my work demonstrated strong threads of connection between the two approaches. This later phase of research also marked a move to child and youth studies, particularly early childhood education and care.

One gift of a long career is to watch the times and tides of theoretical change, and so it is gratifying to witness the return of materialism, now understood as 'new', here at the end of my career. Fittingly, my own work has returned to social reproduction theory where I began as a researcher. In the following, I trace the path from my early enthusiasms to their return in new forms to follow the thread of materialist feminism that connects them and to consider its relevance for understanding feminist constructions of the early childhood educator.

Finding Women's Work

My graduate training in the late 1980s overlapped with a florescence of feminist materialist theorizing (for recent overviews, see Ferguson, 2014; Hekman, 2014; Luxton, 2014). At this time, the 'add-women-and-stir' approach to the anthropology of women in the 1970s was being replaced with an anthropology of gender that emphasized how categories of difference are made and experienced in relation to one another. This was again replaced in the 1990s by a feminist anthropology in line with poststructuralism's focus on sexuality, performance, discourse and subjectivity (Moore, 1988, 1994).

My initial research project was an ethnographic one in Yogyakarta, a court city in central Java. I had gone to the field to study the agriculture in relation to global political economy. Informed by Marxian approaches to the historical role of capitalism in producing an international division of labour that marginalized small-scale producers through primitive accumulation and the commodification of their labour, the transformation of peasant agriculture was taken as a site for understanding the power of capital to rewrite social relations (Polanyi, 1944). My specific interest was the role of women in agricultural change in the Global South. The literature on women in development (WID) in international development circles was, like the trajectory outlined above, shifting to gender and development (GAD) (Razavi, 2007), and so mirroring scholarly calls to consider the erasure of women in historical and ethnographic work.

As often happens in ethnographic research, my topic changed in the field. My work came to focus on a national organization of all adult (read: married) women as *ibu rumah tangga* or housewives. The government dictated the structure of this quasi-public organization of all women across the archipelago as housewives and helpmeets. This relegation of women to a domestic sphere mimicked the historical process of producing separate spheres in Europe. Materialist feminism of the 1970s and 1980s emphasized both the power of capital and the role of the state in securing the long-term interests of the capitalist class. One focus was the historical process through which both male political rule and women's economic subordination were realized. Carole Pateman's *The Sexual Contract* (1988) was a critical text linking European forms of rule to women's prior subordination through relegation to heteronormative marriage and domestic work in the private home. This separation was predicated on the presence of marginalized women working as domestics in the homes of other women while denied the same privilege in their own (Scott & Tilly, 1975). The domestic angel and the home as a haven in a heartless world represented an ideology built on the foundational imbrication of capitalism, patriarchy, nation and empire as systems of domination and expansion (Fraser, 2017). The extension of this model of the family and women's proper role to colonies, like the Dutch East Indies, manifested the power of capital to reorganize the world (Stoler, 1989).

As newly independent Indonesia enthusiastically pursued modernization post-1945, national campaigns encouraged women to take up the role of housewife and attend to women's duties (*dharma wanita*) to address mass unemployment produced by mechanization in the countryside. The national organization of housewives encouraged women who had worked for wages in agriculture and elsewhere to stay home and care for their homes, their husbands and their families. During my research, I saw women actively take up the term *ibu rumah tangga* to explain their felt sense of unemployment, an indication of the newness of this category as women were interpellated into a new global form of subjectivity as housewives (Mies, 1986).

To understand the differential effects of colonialism and their elaboration under nationalist modernizing in Indonesia, I looked to social reproduction theory (SRT). The 1970s and 1980s were not only a time of florescence in materialist approaches to political economy, but in feminist engagements with these theories. Lise Vogel's (1983) *Marxism and the Oppression of Women: Toward a Unitary Theory* is particularly noteworthy. The essence of social reproduction theory is that capitalism depends on the unwaged and often invisible labour of social reproduction, including the work to reproduce humans and the social formations that support them. Fraser (2017) provides a contemporary elaboration of social reproduction:

> The work of birthing and socializing the young is central to this process, as is caring for the old, maintaining households and family members, building communities, and sustaining the shared meanings, affective dispositions and horizons of value that underpin social cooperation.
>
> (p. 23)

In older Marxian terms, this is the socially necessary labour that subsidizes the reproduction of workers. That is, the unwaged and invisible work that takes place in the domestic sphere underwrites low wages in the capitalist economy.

In my fieldwork in a lower-class neighbourhood, I saw women not only working inside and outside the home for cash and wages, but also working in their communities in support of government programmes designed to provide low-cost social welfare. At monthly meetings, women received government directives to organize cooperatively to support the family planning programme, improve child nutrition and health and support the harmonious functioning of the neighbourhood *as* a community. For this 'volunteered' labour, they received the gratitude of the nation, but little else. They were also meant to be the first educators of their children. Kindergarten programmes had started during the Independence era in the early twentieth century, but otherwise there was no early childhood education other than that provided by these mothers of the nation, a conflation of mother and educator with long-standing threads (Ailwood, 2008). This state version of the feminine subject was wife and mother with a naturalized role as caregiver whose unpaid work supported the social reproduction of a flexible, very low-waged labour force needed by an Indonesian economy based on surplus labour.

In 2017, Lise Vogel wrote that 'the fundamental insight of SRT is, simply put, that human labour is at the heart of creating or reproducing society as a whole' (p. 2). Vogel's words appear in the foreword to Bhattacharya's (2017) recent collection, *Social Reproduction Theory: Remapping Class, Recentering Oppression*, which marks a return to this kind of theorizing after a long period of stagnation. Picking up the thread on the historical contingency of the separate spheres – understood as a contrast between production and reproduction – Bhattacharya (2017) argues that these two spheres must be 'theorized integratively' (p. 9). The boundary problem here is at the centre of Fraser's (2017) recent attention to the care crisis under finance capitalism with its reliance on debt (Newberry & Rosen, 2020). Fraser identifies again how capitalism 'free-rides on' the activities of provisioning and caregiving that produce and maintain social bonds. 'Variously called *care, affective labor,* or *subjectivation,* this activity forms capitalism's human subjects, sustaining them as embodied natural beings while also constituting them as social beings' (Fraser, 2017, p. 23).

Bhattacharya (2017) and Fraser (2017) usefully update central concepts in SRT to incorporate care labour (see Rosen, 2019) and its relationship to subjectivity, elements missing in my own first analysis. My early work had been devoted to locating the source of women's domination through a focus on their labour and lives as they were shaped by colonialism, capitalism and nationalism. The feminine subject in this work was a *woman* located in a structure of domination that muted her voice and erased her history even as it exploited her social reproductive labour. The work of early materialist feminists, like second-wave feminism generally, was inattentive to forms of intersectional difference (Ferguson, 2014). I too took the category of woman perhaps too uncritically. The form of difference that dominated my analysis then was the subjection of poor women of the Global South through the structuring power of capitalism.

Early Childhood Education and Care: Reproducing the Feminine Subject through Neoliberal Democratization

Returning to fieldwork in the early 2000s, much had changed, not only in Indonesia but also in theory, feminist and otherwise. Hekman (2014, p. 147) notes that work on materialist approaches has receded, in part due to the power of postmodern approaches that emphasize linguistic constructionism. Simultaneously it seemed, Indonesia had undergone a democratic transition sparked by the Asian financial crisis of the 1990s, amplified through a series of natural disasters, including the 2004 Indian Ocean tsunami. These disasters, financial and seismic, had softened the ground for the rapid influx of early childhood education and care (ECEC) programmes. My focus shifted with the landscape to the rise of these globalized programmes and the burgeoning field of child and youth studies.

Work with activists, educators and government officials at this time of tremendous change identified the World Bank's push to improve the lives of the very young through improved education, development and care. This work was extended through the explosion of private, corporate early child programmes appearing in Indonesia. Education was the focus of democratization efforts by young activists, but it was equally seen as an entrepreneurial opportunity. Programmes and curricula ranged from small-scale programmes with an emphasis on local culture to larger for-profit programmes with an internationalized approach drawing upon curricular materials from the Global North. The emergence of ECEC exemplified a critical set of issues in neoliberal democratization: an emphasis on privatization and marketization in education, the role of inter-governmental organizations like the World Bank and the OECD (Organization for Economic Co-operation and Development) in providing expert knowledge and standardized measures of development, and an emphasis on the development of human capital and parental 'choice'.

To make sense of this, I turned my own analytical lens to governmentality (Foucault, 1991). The material effects of the ECEC programmes were not ignored in this poststructuralist analysis. Rather, the emphasis on power was distributed across the spectrum of programmes, policies and standards produced to guide ECEC in Indonesia as elements of global neoliberalism (Newberry, 2017). The state and capital dropped from their central position. Instead, the multiple discursive, biopolitical and pedagogical effects of the local/global, private/public push for programmes aimed at early childhood were foregrounded (Dahlberg, Moss & Pence, 1999).

The dramatic explosion in ECEC programmes in Indonesia was marked. The spirit of reform, opportunity and democratic transformation was everywhere (Newberry, 2017). Young women entrepreneurs were opening programmes to offer services from day care to preschool as were democratization activists who saw education as central to reform in Indonesia generally. The role of women in this work was striking. Some programmes were explicitly aimed at linking women's welfare with childcare and child development, including a lab school project begun by feminists (Marpinjun et al., 2018).

The subjectivation of early childhood educators, mostly women, was inflected with the entrepreneurial and self-help energy enshrined in the global neoliberal policies endorsed by the World Bank and other inter-governmental organizations. The push for human capital development (Adriany & Saefullah, 2015) and democratic reform were intertwined with the growth in middle-class consumption. Yet, as I documented (Newberry, 2014), some of these new programmes – billed as helping build better brains in young children along with pathways for academic achievement – did little to support the working lives of the women. Even so, the accompanying growth in training opportunities for early childhood educators at local universities and through professional organizations meant that ECEC offered opportunities for young, educated and middle-class women.

But in the shadow of this work, another group of women was stepping back into a familiar role: the unpaid community worker now charged with offering neighbourhood ECEC programmes. The 'housewives' organization I had described more than a decade before was being tasked with the delivery of early childhood programmes, again with little or no financial support, and as an extension of their position as mothers and wives with a responsibility for the welfare of not just their own families but their communities.

It was striking to see the mechanisms of the previous authoritarian modernizing government re-engaged as a part of neoliberal democratization. So much had changed, including the proliferation of early childhood programming, but here again was the reproduction of the feminine subject as helpmeet and community worker, whose skills and inclinations as mother and wife required her to expand ECEC in lower-class communities across Indonesia. Drawing on the poststructuralist concept of global assemblage (Ong, 2005), I described the durability of this assemblage of 'volunteered' labour by women, one rooted in years of organizing the self-help of communities through a separate spheres model begun during colonialism and carried through the thirty-two years of Suharto's rule (Newberry, 2017). Their unpaid social reproductive work was in some contrast to the entrepreneurial approach of others. Yet both referenced the naturalized role of woman as carer and first educator. To see its uptake through newly globalized neoliberalism was to be reminded forcefully of the connective tissue between democratic neoliberalism of the late twentieth and early twenty-first centuries and Indonesia's long history shaped by global capitalism.

The Problem of Womenandchildren

This work also led me beyond the boundaries of the feminine subject to that of the child. Rapid growth in the transdisciplinary studies of children and youth since the 1990s has added new dimensions to the question of intersectionality, although not without critique (Konstantoni & Emejulu, 2017). In asking how we understand what a child is, this work has taken up many of the questions at the heart of feminist scholarship (Rosen & Twamley, 2018). At the same time, growing activist and scholarly work on global care chains was identifying how the work of social reproduction connects the material circumstances of women with that of children (Parrenas, 2012). The disparate fortunes of the children cared for versus the children who become carers themselves are connected through the mother/caregiver who travels across a global topography of racialized inequality (Katz, 2001; Kofman, 2014).

The term 'womenandchildren' has been used to identify the unitary subject position constituted through the shared vulnerability of women and children through patriarchal state power founded on the need to protect (Enloe, 2014). This mutual subjectivation conflates the infantilization of women with the vulnerability of the child even as it feminizes the young as helpless under the cover of the humanitarian protection of human rights (Hudson, 2017). Burman (2008) uses the tension between womenandchildren and women vs. children to argue both for the power of feminist analysis but also for the agency of women and children elided in the conflation of their subject positions. As Burman notes, both formulations are problematic but also productive. Here, I retool the 'indivisibility' asserted in womenandchildren in early childhood education from the perspective of social reproduction.

Razavi (2007) writing on the political and social economy of care describes how 'a feminist vision of childcare as a cornerstone for women's full citizenship, economic autonomy and well-being that was dominant in the 1960s and 1970s has given way to a redefinition of childcare as an issue that is about children' (p. 31). And, Dobrowolsky and Jenson (2004) describe the decentring of women as global welfare regimes shifted to social investment in the 1990s: 'Those advocating in the name of women find themselves increasingly excluded or find themselves compelled to use the language of children's needs' (p. 155). While there are no inherent or irreconcilable conflicts of interest between women and children, tensions arise 'when policies and programmes designed to benefit children assume and take for granted the work women undertake in ensuring their children's needs as something that mothers "do"' (Razavi, 2007, p. 31). When this happens, 'the social relations of reproduction remain unproblematized, and the work performed easily naturalized' (Molyneux, 2006, p. 439).

In Indonesia, the assumption that women's work is what mothers do was extended – yet again – as the boom in ECEC led to government-mandated programmes for the poor offered in neighbourhoods and villages. Such early childhood education programming brings together two aspects of social reproduction that produce linked but differentiated forms of subjectivity: the work of female or feminized caregiver and the work of the child being educated. Some have attended to the emotional labour of the teacher-educator (Colley, 2006) while others have identified the work that the young must undertake in the classroom as workers of the future (Ferguson, 2017). Qvrotrup (1995) describes the unidentified economic contributions of children in schools as a form of labour. Others point to the close relationship between investment in human capital and an emphasis on educating children (Campell-Barr & Nygard, 2014).

Child labour has been central to the global problematization of child rights since at least the UN Convention on the Rights of the Child in 1989. Aligned with the humanitarian goal to protect the young, the drive to outlaw child labour has often neglected the historical relationship between factory labour and the development of formal schooling as a means both to protect and control children. Nieuwenhuys (2005) both identifies this neglect and demonstrates how the lens of protection has misconstrued and overlooked the work of children – both in the Global North and South. Given the entangled nature of work and schooling begun during industrialization in Europe and subsequently extended through colonization, it should be no surprise that changes in capital that reframe labour will change how we understand education.

It was in this context that Rachel Rosen and I (2018) advocated a reconceptualization of social reproduction that keeps 'women and children in the frame' (p. 131). This work was marked not only by an explicitly feminist approach to the politics of childhood, but also by a focus on what SRT offers to understanding some of the dilemmas in early childhood education. To do so, we looked back to the groundbreaking work of Lise Vogel (1983, 2000). Our analysis highlighted that while the interests of women and children are often aligned, they also can be differentiated and 'made antagonistic' as each seeks to satisfy needs not legitimated under neoliberal capitalism, yet still met through someone's labour. We considered how women and children are differentiated not only by their needs but also in how and when those needs are met. That is, some women are required to provide low-cost non-familial early childcare for others, while others purchase it. Some children provide social reproductive labour in their families. Some are sent (or send themselves) to long-term schooling as a labour of investment. To attend to this stratification in social reproduction, we argued for a rethinking of the concept of appropriation, conventionally understood in Marxist analysis as the exploitation of taking value produced by labour without compensating for it through wages, and its temporal differentiation across time and space in the uneven and situated productivity of capital (Newberry & Rosen, 2020).

Returning to Womenandchildren with New Materials

We were not alone in returning to social reproduction theory and the power of materialist feminism to make sense of the twenty-first century. There were not only Bhattacharya's edited volume (2017), but also Federici's (2020) essays reflecting on SRT's early dynamism and the unresolved dilemmas of social reproduction (and see Bezanson & Luxton, 2006). Yet this is not a 'new' materialism so much as a return to long-standing issues in materialist feminist thought.

Hekman (2014) distinguishes new materialism as arising not only from feminism but also from 'philosophy of science, cultural studies, animal studies, and what has come to be called the posthuman' (p. 148). This trajectory appears different from that which led to SRT with its attention to the historical role of capital and the state in oppressing women and framing the feminine subject as helpmeet, mother, and caregiver. Yet the new materialism resurfaces my initial enthusiasms for understanding the centrality of labour in producing possibilities for women – and children – and the early childhood educator.

In our return to SRT and socially necessary labour, Rosen and I referred to an old squib of an idea from Marx: species-being. 'The central point that Marx makes is that it is through productive activity that human beings actualize themselves as human beings' (Wartenberg, 1982, p. 79). That is, we are made as humans – realize our species-being – through our labour. The larger philosophical implications of this argument are beyond my scope here. Yet, although not recognized as such by Marx, the socially necessary labour of reproduction is the heart of species-being. That is, the labour social reproduction described above by Fraser, with its reference to sustaining embodied natural beings, which includes care, affect and subjectivation, is species-being. This use of the species-being is consonant with theoretical moves to centre the body and practical activity (Grosz, 2004; Mol, 2008) as a means to unsettle the modernist dualism that haunts theory, feminist and otherwise. We were careful to note that while species-being connects female bodies with child bodies, it does not limit care to the female-bodied beyond the act of parturition (McDowell, 1986). Rather, the labour of species-being directs us to the bodily engagement of humans through practical activity with others, humans and the more-than-human.

Here, I go farther to make a claim that extends Grosz's assertion that 'sexual difference is the ontological condition of human bodies' (Hekman, 2014, p. 154). The labour of social reproduction is the ontological condition of species-being. This assertion is more than a reminder that Marxian-inflected theory remains a powerful way to understand the making of the human under the conditions of capital. Species-being also suggests how this making can precede and exceed its logic and offer the grounds for recognizing and privileging other relationships and other ways to relate. In making this claim, I draw upon feminist science studies (Haraway, 2010; Mol, 2008) and work in anthropology that recognizes the entangled natures that are the basis for relationships that exceed the human body (Tsing, Matthews & Bubandt, 2019).

Species-being brings us again to Fraser's boundary problems, even as it allows for a return to the 'off-limits subject' of biology. '[I]t is Grosz's contention that we must bring biology back into feminist theory if we are to develop the political critiques that feminism needs to further its cause' (Hekman, 2014, p. 157). As Rosen and I (2020) noted, Marx's species-being describes human nature as neither fixed nor given but rather as made through practical activity and relations of labour that are historically specific and contingent. It is 'the medium through which we recognize both others and ourselves' (Held, 2009, p. 146). Centring the labour of species-being as an ontology – that is, the making of the real – identifies the relation of womenandchildren as more than a source of oppression and also as the basis for human freedom, creativity and love.

By thinking of the labour of species-being as part of the biological that prefigures and makes possible 'the various permutations of life that constitute natural, social and cultural existence' (Grosz, 2004, p. 1, cited in Hekman, 2014, p. 157), we can begin to meld the insights of the old materialism with the new. We can return to the biological in way that focuses not on the standpoint of women but from the standpoint of the relations made through species-being. These relations are not limited to the female-bodied or the heteronormative. Relationality is another term that has new life (Strathern, 2014), this time in the context of multi-species relationships long acknowledged in Indigenous ways of knowing (Simpson, 2014) and now used to reimagine education (Keddie, 2014).

Species-being directs us to an intersectionality that troubles the limits of bodies, needs and subject positions. It directs attention again to the centrality of social reproductive labour to human life and the forms differentiation produced through its exploitation. Yet it also allows us to see the materialist making of subjects both before and after being rewritten under capitalism and the possibility that the labour shared in species-being offers a path through the impasse of womenandchildren and the contradictions in the materiality of reproduction as a biological and embodied practice towards other possible ways to be *in it* together.

Materializing the Early Childhood Educator: A Source for Change and Imagined Possibilities?

The flowering of materialist feminism beginning in the 1970s and 1980s was marked by Marxist approaches to social reproduction theory, with an emphasis on the historical emergence of the domestic sphere in tandem with industrial capitalism in Europe and a concern with the role of state power in shaping women's appropriate roles. The household understood as the site of women's oppression was extended to non-European women through its use in the colonies. This powerful critique of Western capitalism and its relationship to rule and imperial expansion was extremely productive. Yet, its force waned as capitalism and globalization shapeshifted and social theory likewise moved towards postmodern and poststructuralist approaches to power.

Understanding the early childhood educator as a subject has likewise shifted to its discursive production and away from the structural subordination of women's labour. As global development regimes came to emphasize human capital and social investment, the goal of education – including early childhood education – has moved from the production of working-class bodies to the shaping of the entrepreneurial spirit through better brains and improved executive function (Hasan, Hyson & Chang, 2013). The neoliberal self so imagined was promulgated through the expansion of a global early childhood assemblage that draws upon the confluence of developmentalism, global health mandates and neuroscience.

Yet, in my own work, the newly empowered young child was to be guided by an early childhood educator whose subject position was that of a housewife cum community manager, the very position I had analysed through the lens of Marxist feminism in my early work. For this reason, I have welcomed the chance to return to social reproduction theory, this time moving beyond its gaps and its reliance on modernist dualism in feminist thinking to embrace the relations between those figured as women and those understood as children. Here is intersectionality refigured along new dimensions.

Revivifying species-being offers a way to approach the problematic of womenandchildren central to the localizing of global ECEC programmes in Indonesia. My Indonesian collaborators have identified the feminist dilemma in the conflation of mothering with teaching (Adriany, 2016): the low pay, the community pressure to serve and the gendered expectations of delivering care. Many of these collaborators are working directly to resolve these contradictions through their work in communities, early childhood programmes and university early childhood departments. This is work that I respect and support, and it mirrors the struggles of feminists in the Global North. Because of them, I start with the relationship that brings educator and young person together, without assuming the subjectivities engaged and produced.

I end by asking: can a resurgent materialism refigure the possibilities of subjectivation by acknowledging the shared labour of species-being? Can considering the early childhood educator from the standpoint of the mutual relations of social reproduction open the possibility of other futures? Can this amalgam of old and new materialism retain the power of SRT's critique of capitalism, its shapeshifting and its exploitative stratification of difference? Is it possible for the early childhood educator positioned in a necessary relationship to the young in their care shape social worlds in which this shared labour is central rather than marginalized and exploited?

References

Adriany, V. (2016). Gender in pre-school and child-centred ideologies. In J. Warin, I. Wernersson, & S. Brownhill (Eds.), *Men, masculinities and teaching in early childhood education* (pp. 70–82). Routledge.

Adriany, V. & Saefullah, K. (2015). Deconstructing human capital discourse in early childhood education in Indonesia. In T. Lightfoot-Rueda, R. L. Peach, & N. Leask (Eds.), *Global perspectives on human capital in early childhood education: Reconceptualizing theory, policy, and practice* (pp. 159–79). Palgrave Macmillan US.

Ailwood, J. (2007). Mothers, teachers, maternalism and early childhood education and care: Some historical connections. *Contemporary Issues in Early Childhood, 8*(2), 157–65. http://dx.doi.org/10.2304/ciec.2007.8.2.157

Bezanson, K. & J. Luxton, M. (2006). *Social reproduction: Feminist political economy challenges neo-liberalism*. McGill-Queen's Press-MQUP.

Bhattacharya, T. (2017). *Social reproduction theory: Remapping class, recentering oppression*. Pluto Press.

Burman, E. (2008). Beyond 'women vs. children' or 'womenandchildren': Engendering childhood and reformulating motherhood. *The International Journal of Children's Rights, 16*(2), 177–94. http://dx.doi.org/10.1163/157181808X301773

Campbell-Barr, V., & Nygård, M. (2014). Losing sight of the child? Human capital theory and its role for early childhood education and care policies in Finland and England since the mid-1990s. *Contemporary Issues in Early Childhood, 15*(4), 346–59. http://dx.doi.org/10.2304/ciec.2014.15.4.346

Colley, H. (2006). Learning to labor with feeling: Class, gender and emotion in childcare education and training. *Contemporary Issues in Early Childhood, 7*(1), 15–29. http://dx.doi.org/10.2304/ciec.2006.7.1.15

Dahlberg, G., Moss, P., & Pence, A. R. Pence (1999). *Beyond quality in early childhood education and care: Postmodern perspectives*. Falmer Press.

De Beauvoir, S. (2010). *The second sex*. Knopf.

Dobrowolsky, A. & Jenson, J. (2004). Shifting representation of citizenship: Canadian politics of 'women' and 'children'. *Social Politics, 11*(2), 154–80. http://dx.doi.org/10.1093/sp/jxh031

Enloe, C. (2014). *Bananas, beaches and bases*. University of California Press.

Federici, S. (2020). *Revolution at point zero: Housework, reproduction, and feminist struggle*. PM Press.

Ferguson, S. (2014). A response to Meg Luxton's 'Marxist feminism and anticapitalism'. *Studies in Political Economy, 94*(1), 161–8. http://dx.doi.org/10.1080/19187033.2014.11674958

Ferguson, S. (2017). Children, childhood and capitalism: A social reproduction perspective. In T. Bhattacharya (Ed.), *Social reproduction theory: Remapping class, recentering oppression* (pp. 112–30). Pluto Press.

Foucault, M. (1991). Governmentality, ideology and consciousness. In G. Burchell, C. Gordon, & Miller, P. (Eds.), *The Foucault effect: Studies of governmentality* (pp. 87–104). The University of Chicago Press.

Fraser, N. (2017). Crisis of care? On the social-reproductive contradictions of contemporary capitalism. In Bhattacharya, T. (Ed.), *Social reproduction theory: Remapping class, recentering oppression* (pp. 21–36). Pluto Press.

Grosz, E. (2004). *The nick of time*. Duke University Press.

Haraway, D. (2010). When species meet: Staying with the trouble. *Environment and Planning D: Society and Space, 28*(1), 53–5. http://dx.doi.org/10.1068/d2706wsh

Hasan, A., Hyson, M., & Chang, Chang (2013). *Early childhood education and development in poor villages of Indonesia: Strong foundations, later success.* International Bank for Reconstruction and Development/The World Bank.

Hekman, S. J. (2014). *The feminine subject*. Polity Press.

Held, J. M. (2009). Marx via Feuerbach: Species-being revisited. *Idealistic Studies, 39*(1/3), 137–48. http://dx.doi.org/10.5840/idstudies2009391/319

Hudson H. (2017). The power of mixed messages: Women, peace, and security language in national action plans from Africa. *Africa Spectrum, 52*(3), 3–29. http://dx.doi.org/10.1177/000203971705200301

Hultqvuist, K. & Dahlberg, G. (Ed.) (2001). *Governing the child in the new millennium.* RoutledgeFalmer.

Katz, C. (2001). Vagabond capitalism and the necessity of social reproduction. *Antipode, 33*(4), 709–28. http://dx.doi.org/10.1111/1467-8330.00207

Keddie, A. (2014). Indigenous representation and alternative schooling: Prioritising an epistemology of relationality. *International Journal of Inclusive Education, 18*(1), 55–71. http://dx.doi.org/10.1080/13603116.2012.756949

Kofman, E. (2014). Gendered migrations, social reproduction and the household in Europe. *Dialectical Anthropology, 38*(1), 79–94. http://dx.doi.org/10.1007/s10624-014-9330-9

Konstantoni, K. & Emejulu, A. (2017). When intersectionality met childhood studies: The dilemmas of a travelling concept. *Children's Geographies, 15*(1), 6–22. http://dx.doi.org/10.1080/14733285.2016.1249824

Luxton, M. (2014). Marxist feminism and anticapitalism: Reclaiming our history, reanimating our politics. *Studies in Political Economy, 94*(1), 137–60. http://dx.doi.org/10.1080/19187033.2014.11674957

Marpinjun, S., Rengganis, N., Riyanto, Y. A. Riyanto & Dhamayanti, F. Y. (2018). Feminists' strategic role in early childhood education. In R. Rosen & Twamley, K. (Eds.), *Feminism and the politics of childhood: Friends or foes* (pp. 218–24). UCL Press.

McDowell, L. (1986). Beyond patriarchy: A class-based explanation of women's subordination. *Antipode, 18*(3), 311–21. http://dx.doi.org/10.1111/j.1467-8330.1986.tb00370.x

Mies (1986) *Patriarchy & accumulation on a world scale: Women in the international division of labour.* Zed Books.

Mol, A. (2008). I eat an apple. On theorizing subjectivities. *Subjectivity*, 22, 28–37. http://dx.doi.org/10.1057/sub.2008.2

Molyneux, M. (2006). Mothers at the service of the new poverty agenda: Progresa/Oportunidades, Mexico's conditional transfer programme. *Social Policy & Administration*, 40(4), 425–49. http://dx.doi.org/10.1111/j.1467-9515.2006.00497.x

Moore, H. L. (1994). *A passion for difference: Essays in anthropology and gender*. Indiana University Press.

Moore, H. L. (1988). *Feminism and anthropology*. University of Minnesota Press.

Newberry, J. (2017). 'Anything can be used to stimulate child development': Early childhood education and development in Indonesia as a durable assemblage. *Journal of Asian Studies*, 76(1), 25–45. http://dx.doi.org/10.1017/S0021911816001650

Newberry, J. (2014). Women against children: Early childhood education and the domestic community in post-Suharto Indonesia. *TRaNS: Trans – Regional and – National Studies of Southeast Asia*, 2, 271–91. http://dx.doi.org/10.1017/trn.2014.7

Newberry, J. & Rosen, R. (2020). Women and children together and apart: Finding the time for social reproduction theory. *Focaal*, 86(112–20). http://dx.doi.org/10.3167/fcl.2020.860109

Nieuwenhuys, O. (2005). *Children's lifeworlds: Gender, welfare and labor in the developing world*. Routledge.

Ong, A. (2005). Ecologies of expertise: Assembling flows, managing citizenship. In Ong, A. & Collier, S. J. (Eds.), *Global assemblages: Technology, politics and ethics as methodological problems* (pp. 337–53). Blackwell.

Parrenas, R. S. (2012). The reproductive labor of migrant workers. *Global Networks*, 12(2), 269–75. http://dx.doi.org/10.1111/j.1471-0374.2012.00351.x

Pateman, C. (1988). *The sexual contract*. University of California Press.

Polanyi, K. (1944). *The great transformation: Economic and political origins of our time*. Beacon.

Qvortrup, J. (1995). From useful to useful: The historical continuity of children's constructive participation. In Mandell. N. & Amber, A. (Eds.), *Sociological Studies of Children* (pp. 49–76). JAI Press.

Razavi, S. (2007). *The political and social economy of care in a development context: Conceptual issues, research questions and policy options*, Gender and Development Programme Paper Number 3. United Nations Research Institute for Social Development.

Rosen, R. (2019). Care as ethic, care as labor. In Langford, R. (Ed.), *Theorizing feminist ethics of care in early childhood practice: Possibilities and dangers* (pp. 79–96). Bloomsbury Academic.

Rosen, R. & Newberry, J. (2018). Love, labor and temporality: Reconceptualising social reproduction with women and children in the frame. In Rosen, R. & Twamley, K. (Eds.), *Feminism and the politics of childhood: Friends or foes* (pp. 117–33). UCL Press.

Rosen, R. and Twamley, K. (Eds). (2018). *Feminism and the politics of childhood: Friends or foes*, UCL Press.

Simpson, L. B. (2014). Land as pedagogy: Nishnaabeg intelligence and rebellious transformation. *Decolonization: Indigeneity, Education & Society, 3*(3), 1–25.

Scott, J. & Tilly, L. (1975). Women's work and the family in the nineteenth-century Europe. In Rosenberg, C. (Ed.), *The family in history* (pp. 145–78). University of Pennsylvania Press.

Stoler, A. L. (1989). Rethinking colonial categories: European communities and the boundaries of rule. *Comparative Studies in Society and History, 31*(1), 134–61. http://dx.doi.org/10.1017/S0010417500015693

Strathern, M. (2014). Reading relations backwards. *The Journal of the Royal Anthropological Institute, 20*(1), 3–19. http://dx.doi.org/10.1111/1467-9655.12076

Tsing, A. L., Matthews, A. S., & Bubandt, N. (2019). Patchy anthropocene: Landscape structure, multispecies history, and the retooling of anthropology: An introduction to supplement 20. *Current Anthropology, 60*(S20), S186–S197. http://dx.doi.org/10.1086/703391

Vogel, L. (1983). *Marxism and the oppression of women: Toward a unitary theory*. Rutgers University Press.

Vogel, L. (2000). Domestic labor revisited. *Science & Society, 64*(2), 151–70.

Vogel, L. (2017). Foreward. In Bhattacharya, T. (Ed.), *Social reproduction theory: Remapping class, recentering oppression* (pp. x–xii). Pluto Press.

Wartenberg, T. E. (1982). 'Species-being' and 'human nature' in Marx. *Human Studies, 5*(1), 77–95. http://dx.doi.org/10.1007/BF02127669

4

Reclaiming Early Childhood Educator(s) *as* Early Childhood Educator(s) through Feminist Ethics of Care

Melinda Bruce and Alana Powell

Recent early childhood education scholarship has attended to the early childhood educator (ECE) subject calling for a reimagining of individual and collective ECE identities expressing a vision of multiplicity, uncertainty, and de-centred and relational interpretations of subjectivity (Arndt & Tesar, 2019; Arndt et al., 2018; Canella, 2018; Cumming, Sumison & Wong, 2013; Moss, 2006; 2010; Osgood, 2006, 2010; Skattebol, Adamson & Woodrow, 2016; Urban, 2008; Woodrow, 2008). In light of the ethical and political urgency to respond to the violently uncaring patriarchal, neoliberal and colonial conditions of the twenty-first century, this is important work for early childhood education. However, this move to complexify and reimagine the ECE has not adequately acknowledged the multiplicity of existing ECE subjectivities or the deeply complex and situated relationality of the ethical care in which they are engaged. Too often ECEs are called upon to be more, to resist and to break rules. At the same time, they have been omitted from the very discussion in which they are intimately apart and, to whom the gendered, precarious, devalued care and pedagogical work falls.

As women, feminists, ECEs, scholars and activists in Ontario, Canada, we argue for, in the words of feminist ethics of care scholar Carol Gilligan (2011), 'a discovery of a voice I knew but had forgotten' (p. 178). If we are to ask ourselves and all ECEs to be more, to be different in order to enact a response(ability) to children, families, colleagues and more-than human-worlds on the edge of environmental collapse and mired in neoliberal, colonial and white supremist logics, let us first return, reclaim and centre the complex relationality and plurality of existing ECE subjectivities.

In this chapter, we reclaim and remember by reading the ECE subject through feminist ethics of care. Feminist ethics of care exposes an in-between space, an ethical and political coming home that, on the one hand, resists singular identity constructions, oppressive uncaring conditions, and, on the other hand, affirms a relational subjectivity that is constituted by situated, entangled, embodied and provisional ways of being and doing. We argue that reclaiming the forgotten voice, the obscured multiplicity of ECE subjectivities, requires abandoning (for now) new constructions, re-writes and articulations of the ECE. Early childhood educator(s) *as* early childhood educator(s) sufficiently responds to twenty-first-century response(abilities) of early childhood education despite uncaring conditions and systems.

We begin by discussing feminist ethics of care as a 'critical, political theory' (Robinson, 2020, p. 11) and 'relational ontology' (Robinson, 2011, p. 4). We then trace the ECE subject through maternal, technical and professional identity constructions all of which silo and constrain ECE's within uncaring contexts. Next, we offer a mode of resistance to these conditions and singularities by embracing care and orienting the ECE towards the relational through Joan Tronto's (1993, 2013) phases of care. In this, the ECE is not only construed as multiple (ECEs *as* ECEs) and complex but, always (and already) situated and embodied as both caregiver(s) and care receiver(s).

Feminist Ethics of Care and Subjectivity

Feminist ethics of care developed at the end of the twentieth century in response to and resistance of traditional liberal moral theories that equate moral thinking, value and worth with rational, patriarchal notions of individuality that argue for universal principles for moral guidance. Instead, early care ethicists Held (2006) and Gilligan (1993, 2011) centred the voices and experiences of women to suggest another way of thinking and doing ethically. As described by Held (2006), feminist ethics of care 'takes the experience of women in caring activities such as mothering as central, interprets and emphasizes the values inherent in caring practices … and then considers generalizing the insights of caring to other questions of morality' (p. 26). Where traditional moral theories rely on individual actors to draw upon universal principles, feminist ethics of care understands 'people as relational and interdependent, morally and epistemologically' (Held, 2006, p. 13). Further, feminist ethics of care scholar, Fiona Robinson (2020) writes that ethics of care 'emphasises the *relationality* of moral agents, as well as the importance of *contextual* and *revisable* moral judgement ... and understands all people as embodied, vulnerable and mutually interdependent' (p. 3).

Although feminist ethics of care emerged from women's experiences, care is conceived as a universal experience necessary for human (and more-than-human) survival and flourishing. Fisher and Tronto (1990) famously define care as

> *a species activity that includes everything that we do to maintain, continue, and repair our "world" so that we can live in it as well as possible.* That world includes our bodies, our selves, and our environment, all of which we seek to interweave in a complex, life-sustaining web.
>
> (p. 40)

According to Tronto (1993, 2013), this definition opens to a broad use of care ethics and different understandings of what constitutes good, ethical care in varying contexts. Tronto (1993) notes that care understood as value and practice does not restrict caring activities to the interactions and relations occurring between two individuals. Rather it creates space to consider how care works in and between institutions and broader systems. Tronto (1993, 2013) also articulates interrelated moral values and phases of care that include: attentiveness – caring about; responsibility – caring for; competence – caregiving; responsiveness – care receiving; solidarity – caring with.

As a critical, political theory, feminist ethics of care also responds to and resists neoliberal, colonial, patriarchal ways of knowing and being by foregrounding relationality and interdependence, and honouring vulnerability and need. The hierarchies, binaries and dichotomies created by oppressive and disciplinary systems work to divide the self from the other, the mind from the body, while ethics of care resists and confronts these systems in 'its repudiation of the modern, disembodied moral subject ... [and] opens the door to the relational subject – connected, situated, heterogeneous, plural' (Robinson, 2020, p. 4).

Negotiating Identities: Situating the Early Childhood Educator in Uncaring Conditions

This door to the relational subject is also the door that opens towards a more complex understanding of the ECE than has otherwise been offered. Through feminist ethics of care, the ECE subject is constituted within and through situated and ongoing relations and evolving contexts. Langford's (2020) work, writing on care ethics and intersubjectivity, aptly applies to the ECE whereby 'there is no separate self outside of being relational; relationality then, constructs the self' (p. 27). Without question, early childhood education is an ethical and political practice that primarily engages educators, children and families in care and pedagogical work that is embodied and relational. Though ECE practice it is not exclusively a humanist engagement, our discussion, through feminist ethics of care, examines the ECE subject through human relations. Further, as feminist ethics of care is understood as both value and practice (Held, 2006; Tronto, 1993, 2013), the relational, plural subject of the ECE is constructed within the overlapping and nested spheres of knowing, being and doing and always within contexts.

However, identity discourses and the material conditions and practice realities for ECEs in primarily Euro-Western contexts continue to reduce, constrain and silo the complexities and pluralities of ECE subjectivities. ECEs must not only negotiate between limited and incomplete (and often imposed) identity constructions but also navigate complex social and political systems, institutional rules and regulations and unequal circulating power relations. We agree with Langford and Richardson (2020) who assert that 'educators cannot separate themselves from the embodied and subjective experiences of their social locations and the inequities in their political and policy contexts in which their care is practised' (p. 37). To that end, the negotiations between identity constructions always occur in time and space and through power relations, and for ECEs, this is largely framed by the devaluation of early childhood education and care labour, and the uncaring conditions of early learning spaces created by patriarchal, neoliberal and colonial systems.

While ECE identity discourses are numerous, as are detailed accounts of specific practice realities and conditions, we focus here on three dominant identity constructions: substitute mother, technician and professional. These identities continue to reinforce commonly held beliefs and gendered stereotypes of ECEs drawing them away from complex, embodied ethical care, their relationality and plurality. Ultimately, these singular identities cause harm.

Substitute Mother

The ECE as 'substitute mother' (Moss, 2006, p. 34) is perhaps the most contentious and controversial image of the ECE. Broadly, this identity construction asserts that the ECE is a mere extension of the maternal – a gendered image that 'assumes that little or no education is necessary to undertake the work, which is understood as requiring qualities and competencies that are either innate to women... or else are acquired through women's practice of domestic labour' (Moss, 2006, p. 34). This identity continues to uphold an unfortunate and inaccurate divide between care labour and early childhood education, relegating care work to an 'inferior positioning' (Langford & Richardson, 2020, p. 33) within the private, maternal realm. The substitute mother, also, asserts a view of care as easy, natural and well-suited to the subordinate moral subject of the woman echoing much of the traditional, liberal and patriarchal moral theories to which feminist ethics of care scholars like Gilligan (1993, 2011) and Held (2006) contest. Further, Moss (2006) and Pacini-Ketchabaw et al. (2015) note that the substitute mother identity is borne out of child development theories that focus on 'attachment pedagogy' (Moss, 2006, p. 34) and the importance of fostering secure relationships all of which demand the ECE embody a 'mother's love' (Pacini-Ketchabaw et al., 2015, p. 62).

Considerations of maternalism, love and care have had a strong place in feminist ethics of care theorizing (Noddings, 2010; Ruddick, 1995), and have extended to early childhood scholarship in conceptualizing complex moral thinking and action as 'care-full pedagogy' (Luff & Kanyal, 2015, p. 1748) or 'professional love' (Page, 2018, p. 126). Langford (2019) writes: 'in the context of ECEC, maternalism is typically understood as natural care and love that enhances the dyadic attachment between a practitioner and child' (p. 5). Though such maternalism discussions open to complexifying educator practice and subjectivity by centring emotions, intimacy, attachment and even reciprocity, they offer only a partial view and do not sufficiently enrich or resist the narrow and negative, gendered construction of the ECE as substitute mother. The ECE as substitute mother is harmful – construing the work of ECEs as natural and constructing a subject who is devoid of complex moral thinking. It also contributes to the unspoken rationale for the devaluation of early childhood education and care labour that leads to poor working conditions and low wages for ECEs.

Technician

The ECE as 'technician' (Moss, 2006, p. 35) has long been established as a dominant identity discourse (Johnston, 2019; Moss, 2006; Moss, 2010; Moss, Dahlberg, Olsson Mariett & Vandenbroeck, 2016; Pacini-Ketchabaw et al., 2015). Crudely, the technician is a direct product of the political economy of neoliberalism of which governs and regulates early childhood systems and institutions. The ECE as technician 'appl[ies] prescribed human technologies of effectiveness ("what works") to produce predetermined outcomes' (Moss, 2010, p. 12), with a focus on 'best practices' that guide children towards linear developmental milestones. While neoliberalism, as a political and economic paradigm, is focused on the free market, productivity and the exchange of goods and services, it is also concerned with the individual as *'homo economicus'* (Moss, 2014, p. 3; Smith & Campbell, 2018, p. 341). The alignments between homo economicus and the construction of the ECE as technician are clear. Canella (2018) writes: 'Human beings are no longer partners in market exchange, but are now individuals who must invest in themselves… Neoliberal forms of governmentality consume freedom… this form of governmentality silences multiplicity' (p. 341). For this reason, the technician identity is, of course, flawed and wildly out of touch with the complex, relational and ethical care work of early childhood education and the plurality of ECE subjectivities.

In some ways, ECE as technician serves as an initial response or resistance to the ECE as substitute mother identity with its commitment to autonomous, rational, objective knowledge about children and learning outcomes. And as Langford and Richardson (2020) explain, 'the primary path to professionalization in the field has been to focus on technocratic, standardized teaching and "learning" discourses distancing the profession from care' (p. 33). This move, or false resistance, has gone too far. The ECE as technician, in its narrow conception of being and doing, works to distance the ECE subject from themselves, their relationality and results in a disembodiment from ethical caring practice and subjectivity.

Professional

The ECE as professional, largely informed by technician discourses and the neoliberal, autonomous self, places a larger emphasis on expertise, ethical decision-making, curriculum and pedagogy, and building relationships. Complex ethical care and care relations do not feature strongly in the ECE as professional and often sit on the periphery of ethical decision-making and pedagogical work, rendering care and relationality as instrumental and in support of child development. As professionals, ECEs are required to align their identities (individually and collectively) with traditionally patriarchal regulated professions such as teachers, doctors or lawyers. In this conceptualization of a professional, ethical codes of conduct, professional standards, and regulations and legislation are required to guide, inform and adjudicate practice decisions and behaviours and, importantly, to regulate caring/uncaring acts. ECE as professionals are highly surveilled with professional boundaries placed on their subjectivity constraining their enactments of care and yet, they are routinely reminded of their capacity to exercise their autonomy and make complex ethical decisions (College of Early Childhood Educators, 2017; 2018). This disconnect also points to what Powell et al. (2020) refer to as the 'professionalization gap' (p. 155) whereby ECEs are required to adhere to ever increasing regulatory expectations and obligations without improvements to wages and working conditions, ultimately remaining uncared for by these institutions and systems.

Importantly, some researchers have moved away from the autonomous, expert model of professionalism and towards a collaborative, relationship-based approach of what it means to be an ECE (Miller, 2008; Peeters, 2008; Skattebol et al., 2016), while others have reconceptualized the ECE professional identity through a poststructuralist lens, calling for resistance to regulation addressing the importance of provisional, contextual knowledge and multiple professional identities (Arndt et al., 2018; Fenech, Sumsion & Goodfellow, 2008; Osgood, 2006, 2010; Woodrow, 2008). However, the ECE as professional in these newer, albeit provisional, multiple and relational renderings, have not infiltrated regulatory powers and mechanisms enough to shift expectations, and ethical care too, remains on the sidelines. The ECE as professional, even in these nuanced and complex articulations is asked to do more, to be more but still with less.

Broadly, the identities of the ECE as substitute mother, technician and professional are narrow, disembodied and fixed subjectivities. These conceptualizations of the ECE sever ties to complex ethical care and push the image of the ECE as multiple and fundamentally relational to the margins. No one identity construction works. ECEs resist and reformulate, and yet, continue to negotiate these identities and expectations within oppressive conditions, institutions and systems. Situated within uncaring conditions, ECEs continue to be constrained and silenced, making engaging in ethical care challenging (Langford & Richardson, 2020; Langford & White, 2019). While some scholarship (Moss, 2006; Pacini-Ketchabaw et al., 2015) gestures towards the relational subject of feminist ethics of care by pointing to multiplicity and provisional identities that are always 'in-process' (p. 64) through relationships, ethical care and reciprocity is largely ignored. Constructions of the ECE as 'researcher' (Moss, 2006, p. 36), 'educator in relationship' (Pacini-Ketchabaw et al., 2015, p. 65) or even as pedagogue, do not go far enough. They do not capture the ECE situated as both caregiver and care receiver who embodies complex, ethical care relations. Furthermore, like others, these constructions continue to place additional demands on the ECE subject without acknowledging what is already present.

Resisting Singularities, Embracing Care: Turning towards the Relational Early Childhood Educator

In this discussion, we consider what becomes possible when instead of looking away from the ECE to understand, define, attempt to know who the ECE is, we turn *towards* the early childhood educator. We seek to reclaim and remember a relational and plural understanding of the ECE. Notably, ethics of care scholarship within early childhood education has made considerable space for the multiplicity, complexity and relationality of the ECE subject but has done so largely within the scope of pedagogical encounters, ethical interactions and cultivated dispositions required to meet the needs of children (Hodgins, Yazbeck & Wapenaar, 2019; Langford & White, 2019; Langford & Richardson, 2020; Taggart, 2019). Here, we consider how feminist ethics of care also places ethical, political and complex care relations at the centre of the ECE subject. In doing so, feminist ethics of care challenges and resists singular identity constructions (i.e. substitute mother, technician, professional) and uncaring conditions that constrain and harm ECE subjectivities.

We also offer an in-between space in which the ECE's relational caring and multiple subjectivities are centred. We do this with caution of the danger Langford and White (2019) describe where ECEs become 'essentialized as simply a carer rather than as a subject in her own right' (p. 70). We agree with care theorists (Langford & White, 2019; Tronto, 2013) who argue that care is a suppressed moral value and requires uncovering, attuning and turning towards. We do not introduce a new conceptualization of the ECE but seek to show what is already there. We suggest feminist ethics of care that offers ways of thinking/being/doing that embraces the ECE relational subject as a highly ethical and political actor who is not only immersed in care acts, but who also values, enacts and requires ethical care.

We resist the singular ECE subject by thinking with Tronto's (2013) interconnected phases and moral qualities of care to provide a coming home for the ECE – where she/they is, in her/their ethical, political, complex care relations, enough. We offer a reading of the ECE in conversation with Tronto's (1993, 2013) four phases of care. We call upon Tronto's (2013) later added fifth phase *caring with*, not in addition to the four phases, but woven throughout to see the ECE beyond the caregiver/receiver dyad and acknowledge multiplicity, plurality, power and the political, ethical and relational ECE.

Caring with

We start with Tronto's (2013) fifth phase of care, *caring with*, to acknowledge and centre the incompleteness of the dyad relationship, the four phases of care, and their related moral qualities in understanding the relational ECE subject. As Tronto (2013) suggests, 'care rarely happens between two people, only. And to create opportunities to "triangulate" care also creates opportunities to break up a relentless hierarchy of power' (p. 153). She continues, writing that 'in order fully to appreciate care, any concept of it needs to be placed within a political theory, a complete "way of seeing" a society' (Tronto, 2013, p. 155). Similarly, we suggest that we need a more complex way of seeing the ECE, one that constructs them not singularly. Rather, we need to acknowledge the ECE as having nested, intersecting identities and lived experiences entangled within broader political, social and discursive contexts in early childhood settings (Langford & White, 2019; Tronto, 2013).

Acknowledging Crenshaw's (1991) theory of intersectionality, which emerged from the lived experiences of Black women, feminist ethics of care opens to an understanding of the 'self' through intersections of oppression. Drawing from feminist scholar Susan Hekman, Robinson (2020) argues that 'the assumption of difference *inheres in the very core of the relational subject of care ethics*. The relational self has no separate, essential core; rather, it becomes a "self" through relations with others' (p. 4). In this way, we suggest the relational ECE must also be understood through an intersectional (Crenshaw, 1991) lens, where the multiplicity of their identities, marginalization, oppression, power relations and possibilities are central to how we think about and know the ECE. Langford and White (2019) describe 'early childhood institutions as sites of minor politics in which care as ethical interactions is fraught with power relationships implicating gender, race, class, sexuality, and disability among other social factors' (p. 69) to gesture to the intertwined care needs and power relations in an ethical caring interaction. In looking only towards singular identities, we risk that the ECE as caregiver/receiver with needs becomes silenced in the name of what they produce, create or give to others. Through solidarity – caring with – we disrupt this silencing, resist singularity and embrace care to open to the relational ECE and their complexity in embodied caring relations.

Caring about

Caring about is the first phase of care where an unmet care need is noticed. Caring about 'calls for the moral quality of attentiveness, of a suspension of one's self-interest, and a capacity genuinely to look from the perspective of the one in need' (Tronto, 2013, p. 34). In articulating the ECE subject, caring about calls for attentiveness, noticing and actually caring about the ECE themselves. This noticing begins the unravelling of the autonomous self, and opens towards the relational and provisional self.

In resisting the singularity of the ECE subject we think with Tronto's (2013) claim 'we are care receivers, all' (p. 120) alongside Casalini (2019) who writes:

> While care ethics emphasizes care for others over care of the self, it is nevertheless also true that the moral qualities… that Joan Tronto (1993) regards as essential to care may be considered as implicitly linked to practices and exercises in relation to the self.
>
> (p. 7)

In noticing a need for care, the relational ECE is simultaneously becoming, being and doing, not merely fulfilling an instrumental or technical function. The ECE is attentive—valuing and honouring the needs and interdependencies of others. However, in our uncaring systems, the relational ECE subject is often materially and discursively restricted with their own subjectivities going unnoticed. ECEs are not just a vehicle to care about others. We agree with Tronto (2013) that the function of the caregiver/care receiver dyad requires deep, critical thought, and we must consider what it creates and obscures for the ECE – how their needs, voices and complexities are lost in the service to children and outcomes. Recovering this loss requires attuning to the ECE, listening and paying attention to them as caregiver *and* care receiver and attending to the relational self that is provisionally and contextually constituted – this requires *caring with*.

Caring for

Caring for is the second phase of care. Tronto (2013) describes that 'once needs are identified, someone or some group has to take on the burden of meeting those needs. This is responsibility' (p. 34). The significance of this responsibility cannot be understated. As Langford and White (2019) articulate, ECEs are negotiating competing discourses of who and what they should be and do, all while being embedded in punitive and restrictive regulatory, political and social structures that make their work near impossible and reduce the relational ECE into a fixed, singular self. Despite this, and with great moral courage, the ECE resists these discourses and structures, takes responsibility for another and attempts to care ethically (Langford & White, 2019). However, the caring encounter and caring responsibility do not end with the ECE subject. We must turn our attention to who is, or who is not, taking responsibility for the ECE subject.

Care and care work have been and continue to be marginalized, devalued, sidelined as the patriarchal, neoliberal and colonial structures and systems uphold the autonomous, rational and disembodied self as desirable. As Tronto (2013) describes, 'Autonomous actors, who think of themselves primarily as caregivers rather than as care receivers, are thus apt to misunderstand the nature of their own situation. The result is to misconstrue both care and its place in society' (p. 150). We see this misunderstanding woven into the subjective experiences of ECEs, who are both caregiver and care receiver, yet function in systems/structures that devalue need and dependencies and promote them as autonomous actors, caregivers. Misconstruing care for the ECE subject results in an absconding of their own care needs, a resistance to valuing their care work, and obscuring the great moral saliency of taking responsibility for others.

This requires a democratic rethinking of care responsibilities (Tronto, 2013), a *caring for* and also *caring with* the ECE to create openings for the coming home of the relational ECE. This requires others (e.g. government, institutions) to take responsibility for caring for the ECE subject by creating conditions that honour and uphold messy, hard, contextual, ethical and political care.

Caregiving

Caregiving is the third phase of care and involves doing the work of caring. It is where the caring act occurs. Tronto (2013) describes, 'to be competent to care, given one's caring responsibilities, is not simply a technical issue, but a moral one' (p. 35). The ECE is often described as a caregiver, with identities that attempt to define who a good ECE is (and what good care is); however, we must think critically beyond their technical competencies in caregiving and consider what ethical caregiving makes possible for her/their subjectivity. The notion of the ECE as caregiver is complex, and in our context is devalued and underappreciated. However, we argue it is central in turning towards the relational ECE. This requires a centring and valuing of care both in early childhood practice, and in broader systemic *caring acts* to support of the relational ECE.

We think with Dingler (2015) who asserts that 'caring practice shows that the subjectivities of both [caregiver and care receiver] are constituted and altered in an open and unpredictable way' (p. 214). In their caring practice, ECEs embrace provisional and incomplete ways of knowing, being and doing, where subject formation happens discursively and embodied in these relations. They do this in unspoken, unrecognized and unsupported ways – it is the making do of their work. Yet through an ethics of care we understand this work as valuable, critical, ethical and rich.

Caring acts occur across the relations of early childhood spaces, a constant becoming and undoing with children, colleagues, families, materials and the more-than-human. As Langford and White (2019) describe, care holds reiterative potential, where caring acts can generate more (or better) care. We similarly suggest that this reiterative potential is possible for ECE subjects, whose caring acts, when appropriately recognized and valued, would generate possibilities of care for themselves as care receiver and iterations of care for past, present and future ECE subjects. To create spaces that value care and turn towards the relational ECE, we must centre care in our institutions and recognize that 'care is multidimensional, and so any democratic caring practice must make provision for this complexity' (Tronto, 2013, p. 147).

Care-receiving

Care-receiving is the fourth phase of care, where the caregiver and receiver evaluate, judge and determine if care has been received (Tronto, 2013, p. 35). We think with Tronto (2013) who writes that 'no judgment about whether care is good can be accomplished from a singular perspective, not that of caregivers or care receivers' (p. 140). Care, as multiplicity, is negotiated alongside power relations, intersecting oppressions (Crenshaw, 1991), and is interdependent with often conflicting needs. Any judgement or claim of care as good or bad, successful or not, must centre this complexity.

The ECE subject through giving and receiving care, resists the singular telling of who they are. Instead, they are being/doing/becoming in the complexities of our interdependencies with children, families, communities and the more-than-human. Yet they are being/doing in constant tension with narratives that abstract, disembody, constrain and are incomplete in acknowledging this complexity. The ECE subject, in this way, can only provisionally value and understand their self, and they continue to look elsewhere for value, judgement and definition. This is untenable and must be rejected.

While the ECE subject, in being/doing, is resisting singularities and abstractions, they continue to be constrained by the systems that tell them otherwise. This entangled tension must be unravelled. This requires we no longer look to conceptual abstractions and singularities or look away from the ECE subject to understand their identities. It requires a responsive, intentional *caring with* the relational ECE as provisional, as caregiver and receiver, and, as enough.

Reclaiming the Forgotten: Early Childhood Educator(s) *as* Early Childhood Educator(s)

In a recent collaborative report, *Forgotten on the Frontlines: A Survey Report on Ontario's Early Years and Child Care Workforce* (Powell, Ferns & Burrell, 2021), ECEs in Ontario described their experiences while working in the midst of Covid-19: 'We are important too. I feel we are the forgotten frontline staff. Nobody is taking care of our concerns and rights' (p. 7). While this is not a new charge levelled at early childhood institutions and systems, nor is it new that Canadian provincial or federal governments fall short in their caring responsibilities for ECEs (see Langford & Richardson, 2020 and Powell et al., 2020), the global pandemic has further exposed, like many other forms of intersecting oppressions and racial inequities, this failure.

As ECEs, we reclaim what is forgotten through feminist ethics of care by choosing to *care with* and stand in solidarity with early childhood educator(s) understood *as* early childhood educator(s). Crucially, this construction does not intend to smooth over differences and conflicting tensions in care and pedagogical work; rather, it is an invitation for multiplicity, and acknowledges complex power relations, lived experiences and intersecting identities and oppressions. ECE(s) *as* ECE(s) is both a mode of resistance to the narrow and singular identity constructs (i.e. substitute mother, technician, professional) within uncaring conditions, and an affirmation of what is already known. We call for a pause on the external re-articulation, re-naming and reconceptualization of ECE subjectivity(ies). ECEs are none and all of these things – the singular past, present or future construct will always be incomplete. Without this pause, the ECE will continue to be alienated from their complex ethical, caring relationality and asked to ignore the harmful, uncaring conditions and practice realities they experience or, asked to be more in spite of it. ECEs are enough. Instead, let us collectively require existing early childhood institutions and systems to care *better*, care *more* and care *with* early childhood educators.

References

Arndt, S., Urban, M., Murray, C., Smith, K., Swadener, B., & Ellegaard, T. (2018). Contesting early childhood professional identities: A cross-national discussion. *Contemporary Issues in Early Childhood, 19*(2), 97–116. https://doi.org/10.1177/1463949118768356

Arndt, S. & Tesar, M. (2019). An ethics of care in culturally diverse early childhood settings: Toward an ethics of unknowing. In R. Langford (Ed.), *Theorizing feminist ethics of care in early childhood practice: Possibilities and dangers* (pp. 37–55). Bloomsbury.

Canella, G. (2018). Critical qualitative research and rethinking academic activism in childhood studies. In M. Bloch, B. Swadener, & G. Cannella (Eds.), *Reconceptualizing early childhood education and care – A reader: Critical questions, new imaginaries & social activism* (2nd ed. pp. 337–49). Peter Lang.

Casalini, B. (2019). Care of the self and subjectivity in precarious neoliberal societies. https://ethicsofcare.org/wp-content/uploads/2019/04/BC-IA.pdf

College of Early Childhood Educators. (2017). *Code of ethics and standards of practice*. College of Early Childhood Educators.

College of Early Childhood Educators. (2018). *Practice guideline: Professionalism*. https://www.college-ece.ca/en/Documents/Practice_Guideline_Professionalism.pdf

Crenshaw, K. (1991). Mapping the margins: Intersectionality, identity politics, and violence against women of color. *Stanford Law Review, 43*(6), 1241–99. https://doi.org/10.2307/1229039

Cumming, T., Sumsion, J., & Wong, S. (2013). Reading between the lines: An interpretative meta-analysis of ways early childhood educators negotiate discourses and subjectivities informing practice. *Contemporary Issues in Early Childhood, 14*(3), 223–40. https://doi.org/10.2304/ciec.2013.14.3.223

Dingler, C. (2015). Disenchanted subjects? On the experience of subjectivity in care relations. *Ethics and Social Welfare, 9*(2), 209–15. https://doi.org/10.1080/17496535.2015.1023059

Fisher, B. & Tronto, J. (1990). Toward a feminist theory of caring. In E. K. Abel & M. K. Nelson (Eds.), *Circles of care: Work and identity in women's lives* (pp. 35–62). State University of New York.

Fenech, M., Sumsion, J., & Goodfellow, J. (2008). Regulation and risk: Early childhood education and care services as sites where the 'laugh of Foucault' resounds. *Journal of Education Policy, 23*(1), 35–48. https://doi.org/10.1080/02680930701754039

Gilligan, C. (1993). *In a different voice: Psychological theory and women's development*. Harvard University Press.

Gilligan, C. (2011). *Joining the resistance*. Polity.

Held, V. (2006). *The ethics of care: Personal, political, and global*. Oxford University Press.

Hodgins, B. D., Yazbeck, S., & Wapenaar, K. (2019). Exacting twenty-first-century early childhood education: Curriculum as caring. In R. Langford (Ed.), *Theorizing feminist ethics of care in early childhood practice: Possibilities and dangers* (pp. 203–25). Bloomsbury.

Johnson, L. (2019). The (not) good educator: Reconceptualizing the image of the educator. *eceLINK, 3*(2), 40–54. Toronto: Association of Early Childhood Educators of Ontario. https://d3n8a8pro7vhmx.cloudfront.net/aeceo/mailings/1631/attachments/original/eceLINK_Fall2019_Finalweb.pdf?1570820616

Langford, R. (2019). Introduction. In R. Langford (Ed.), *Theorizing feminist ethics of care in early childhood practice: Possibilities and dangers* (pp. 1–15). Bloomsbury.

Langford, R. (2020). Navigating reconceptualist and feminist ethics of care to find a conceptual space for rethinking children's needs. *Journal of Childhood Studies, 45*(4). https://doi.org/10.18357/jcs00019308

Langford, R. & Richardson, B. (2020). Ethics of care in practice: An observational study of interactions and power relations between children and educators in urban Ontario early childhood settings. *Journal of Childhood Studies*, 33–47. https://doi.org/10.18357/jcs00019398

Langford, R. & White, J. (2019). Conceptualizing care as being and doing in ethical interactions and sustained care relationships in the early childhood institution. In R. Langford (Ed.), *Theorizing feminist ethics of care in early childhood practice: Possibilities and dangers.* (pp. 59–77). Bloomsbury.

Luff, P. & Kanyal, M. (2015). Maternal thinking and beyond: Towards a care-full pedagogy for early childhood. *Early Child Development and Care, 185*(11–12), 1748–61. https://doi.org/10.1080/03004430.2015.1028389

Miller, L. (2008). Developing professionalism within a regulatory framework in England: Challenges and possibilities. *European Early Childhood Education Research Journal, 16*(2), 255–68. https://doi.org/10.1080/13502930802141667

Moss, P. (2006). Structures, understandings and discourses: Possibilities for re-envisioning the early childhood worker. *Contemporary Issues in Early Childhood, 7*(1), 30–41. https://doi.org/10.2304/ciec.2006.7.1.30

Moss, P. (2010). We cannot continue as we are: The educator in an education for survival. *Contemporary Issues in Early Childhood, 11*(1), 8–19. https://doi.org/10.2304/ciec.2010.11.1.8

Moss, P. (2014). The story of neoliberalism: A grand narrative of our time. In *Transformative change and real utopias in early childhood education: A story of democracy, experimentation and potentiality* (pp. 60–74). Routledge.

Moss, P., Dahlberg, G., Olsson Mariett, L., & Vandenbroeck, M. (August 2016). Why contest early childhood? Working Paper. https://www.routledge.com/education/posts/10150?utm_source=shared_link&utm_medium=post&utm_cam

Noddings, N. (2010). *The maternal factor: Two paths to morality.* University of California Press.

Osgood, J. (2006). Deconstructing professionalism in early childhood education: Resisting the regulatory gaze. *Contemporary Issues in Early Childhood, 7*(1), 5–14. https://doi.org/10.2304/ciec.2006.7.1.5

Osgood, J. (2010). Reconstructing professionalism in ECEC: The case for the 'critically reflective emotional professional'. *Early Years*, *30*(2), 119–33. https://doi.org/10.1080/09575146.2010.490905

Pacini-Ketchabaw, V., Nxumalo, F., Kocher, L., Elliott, E., & Sanchez, A. (2015). *Journeys: Reconceptualizing early childhood practices through pedagogical narration*. University of Toronto Press.

Page, J. (2018). Characterising the principles of professional love in early childhood care and education. *International Journal of Early Years Education*, *26*(2),125–41. https://doi.org/10.1080/09669760.2018.1459508

Peeters, J. (2008). *The construction of a new profession: A European perspective on professionalism in early childhood education and care*. SWP Publishers.

Powell, A., Ferns, C., & Burrell, S. (2021). *Forgotten on the frontlines: A survey report on Ontario's early years and child care workforce*. Association of Early Childhood Educators Ontario and Ontario Coalition for Better Child Care. https://d3n8a8pro7vhmx.cloudfront.net/aeceo/pages/2614/attachments/original/1621392971/Forgotten_on_the_frontline.pdf?1621392971

Powell, A., Langford, R., Albanese, P., Prentice, S., & Bezanson, K. (2020). Who cares for carers? How discursive constructions of care work marginalized early childhood educators in Ontario's 2018 provincial election. *Contemporary Issues in Early Childhood*, *21*(2), 153–64. https://doi.org/10.1177/1463949120928433

Robinson, F. (2011). *The ethics of care: A feminist approach to human security*. Temple University Press.

Robinson, F. (2020). Resisting hierarchies through relationality in the ethics of care. *International Journal of Care and Caring*, *4*(1), 11–23. https://doi.org/10.1332/239788219X15659215344772

Ruddick, S. (1995). *Maternal thinking: Toward a politics of peace*; with a new preface. Beacon Press.

Skattebol, J., Adamson, E., & Woodrow, C. (2016). Revisioning professionalism from the periphery. *Early Years*, *36*(2), 116–31. https://doi.org/10.1080/09575146.2015.1121975

Smith, K. & Campbell, S. (2018). Social activism: The risky business of early childhood educators in neoliberal Australian classrooms. In M. Bloch, B. Swadener, & G. Cannella (Eds.), *Reconceptualizing early childhood education and care – A reader: Critical questions, new imaginaries & social activism* (2nd ed., pp. 313–23). Peter Lang.

Taggart, G. (2019). Cultivating ethical dispositions in early childhood practice for an ethic of care: A contemplative approach. In R. Langford (Ed.), *Theorizing feminist ethics of care in early childhood practice: Possibilities and dangers* (pp. 97–123). Bloomsbury.

Tronto, J. (1993). *Moral boundaries: A political argument for an ethic of care*. Routledge.

Tronto, J. (2013). *Caring democracy: Markets, equality, and justice*. New York University Press.

Urban, M. (2008). Dealing with uncertainty: Challenges and possibilities for the early childhood profession. *European Early Childhood Education Research Journal, 16*(2), 135–52. http://doi.org/10.1080/13502930802141584

Woodrow, C. (2008). Discourses of professional identity in early childhood: Movements in Australia. *European Early Childhood Education Research Journal, 16*(2), 269–80. http://doi.org/10.1080/13502930802141675

Commentary 1

Rachel Langford and Brooke Richardson

The purpose of this commentary is to draw out some key themes evident in the first four chapters that describe feminisms that emerged in the 1980s and 1990s. Although we organized the book based on the temporal emergence of each feminism, we do not consider any of the feminisms included in this book as 'old'. Chapter authors have made a convincing case that the central ideas of these feminisms evolved over time and are as relevant as ever. It is also important to note that the theoretical perspectives explored in this volume can be articulated without a feminist orientation. Therefore, authors carefully explain why their choice of theoretical perspective is feminist. The first four chapters reflected on here provide insights into the subject constructions of early childhood educators (ECEs) in contemporary, diverse geographical contexts through poststructural feminism (two chapters), feminist materialism and feminist ethics of care.

Like Hekman (2014), we use postmodernism and poststructuralism interchangeably in that they both 'attack the fundamental roots of western thought', particularly the normative subject of 'man' (p. 114). Chapters 1 and 2 further describe these intellectual movements. Despite concerns that influential poststructural theorists did not prioritize feminist concerns in their writings, feminist scholars found this framework helpful in problematizing the patriarchal roots of Western thought. We have included two chapters on poststructuralism as its focus on the discursive construction of subjectivity produces multiple, non-linear ways of being has been particularly influential in feminist studies. Hekman (2014) explains this influence succinctly: 'to say that postmodernism overwhelmed the feminist community is an understatement' (p. 114). Bringing poststructuralism to life, Kylie Smith draws on poststructural themes of discourse, subjectivity, identity and resistance integrating them into her own narrative of being/becoming an early childhood educator (ECE) in Australia. Sonja Arndt and Marek Tesar argue that a Kristevian poststructural approach provides unique theoretical tools to explore the subjective possibilities for ECEs. For Arndt and Tesar, Kristeva's idea that one is a foreigner to others and oneself and always in a process of becoming is key to considering these possibilities.

Interestingly, even chapters that do not extensively focus on feminist poststructuralism – such as Jan Newberry's chapter rooted in Marxism and feminist materialism and Melinda Bruce and Alana Powell's chapter focused on the ethics of care – still carry important traces of poststructural thinking. For example, Newberry uses the Foucauldian concept of governmentality to examine the effects of neoliberal globalization of early childhood education and care (ECEC) in Indonesia and Bruce and Powell emphasize ECE subjectivity as multiple, fluid, ever-changing, unknowing and never fully knowable through a feminist ethics of care analysis. As will be seen, there are also traces of poststructuralism or a complex layering of other feminisms onto poststructuralism in later chapters.

As we read through the chapters (many times over) we asked ourselves how a feminism opens up or shuts down possibilities for ECEs struggling to be in a world that often misunderstands who ECEs are and what ECEs do. We asked in particular how these feminisms interact with and/or challenge dominant, neoliberal, developmental and technical approaches to constructing the ECE subject and what the implications of the feminism might be for ECEs interested and/or having the opportunity to be another way.

Smith's narrative, particularly early in her career, positions her as an outsider whereby she felt uncomfortable and distant from the technical discourses her profession expected her to take up. Smith describes the relief she felt when learning about poststructural feminisms in her undergraduate and graduate studies. Finally, she was permitted to not know, remain curious and feel and think multiple, sometimes contradictory, emotions and thoughts without threatening her 'professional' identity. Particularly poignant in Smith's chapter is how her subjective experience of being an ECE positively changed when she was able to name and problematize ways of being that did not feel authentic to her as an ECE. Still, she describes the constant tensions she feels between the structural, material realities of being an ECE in contemporary Australia and more authentic possibilities she continues to explore.

Similar to Smith, Arndt and Tesar draw on key poststructural themes of becoming, multiplicity and resisting dominant discourses that narrowly define who the educator is supposed to be. Arndt and Tesar introduce us to Julie Kristeva whom Hekman (2014) states began 'with the premise that the western tradition offers women no place to be subjects' (p. 37). Similar to Smith's feelings of being an 'outsider', Arndt and Tesar lean on a Kristevian concept of being a foreigner both to others and to oneself to describe the ever-changing nature of learning about, discovering and becoming a subject. Through their Kristevian theoretical approach, this idea of subject multiplicity is even more pronounced than in Smith's chapter. As the authors explain, Kristeva herself was resistant to the idea that feminism could be considered a unified theoretical concept and, therefore, resisted being labelled a feminist. Their chapter makes clear that we are never one, stable 'thing', but always multiple becomings with no clear beginning or end point.

Another important theme in Arndt and Tesar's chapter is revolt, the idea that a key element of being an ECE is engaging in resistance to dominant, oppressive social, economic and political structures. Revolt in the early childhood setting, they say, is to 'provoke continually questioning attitudes and approaches, towards individuals (ourselves), diverse team members, social groups, and Others' (p. 35). This chapter as well as Smith's chapter push us to consider that creating space to critically question ourselves, and to recognize our foreignness in relation to ourselves and with others may be the grounding to fully exploring our own creativity, curiosity, interests and drive. It may also be at the heart of having the courage to *be* and *do* in ways that challenge the oppressive status quo. In engaging in revolt of this kind, we move closer to recognizing, learning from and being with the foreigner within. At the same time, Bruce and Powell in their chapter wonder if this is asking more of ECEs in a context where they are already overworked, underpaid and systematically unsupported materially, socially and emotionally to do this difficult intellectual, emotional and physical work.

Embracing a feminist Marxist/materialist perspective in the Indonesian early childhood education and care context, Newberry's chapter seeks to tie ECE subjectivity to embodied labour. Hekman (2014) describes the core of Marxism and its feminist problem: it is 'is a theory of labour; labour makes man [*sic*] what he is and defines the parameters of human society. The problem for women is that women's connection to labour under capitalism is different than that of men' (p. 97). Reflecting on her 30-plus-year career, Newberry makes clear connections between how changing social conditions in Indonesia – particularly from an agricultural to an industrial economy – have differently positioned women as labourers over time yet continues to reproduce a feminine subject necessary for capitalism to flourish. Unique to this chapter is how she has had the opportunity to observe the emergence of two groups of women who care for children outside of the home: mothers who take up voluntary care/education work in community programme and entrepreneurs, who establish and run private ECEC programmes. She points out that both groups are vulnerable to being lumped into 'womanandchildren' or 'a unitary subject position' (p. 53). If/when this occurs both early childhood educators and children are infantilized, positioned as helpless and understood as needing patriarchal protection. Newberry returns to the Marxist concept of 'species-being' and social reproduction theory while taking up new materialism's focus on the body and practical activity as a possible way out of the 'womenandchildren' conundrum. She envisions a way 'to be in it together' whereby the shared labour of ECEs and children 'is central rather than marginalized and exploited' and the relationality of ECEs and children is 'the basis for human freedom, creativity and love' (p. 55). This is the 'labouring relations' in Newberry's chapter title and the imagined possibilities of child and ECE subjectivities.

Similar to Newberry, the chapter by Bruce and Powell focuses on ECEs' care work and its inherent relationality, analysed through feminist ethics of care. Hekman (2014) locates the emergence of feminist ethics of care in Carol Gilligan 1982 book, *In a different voice* which 'challenges the hegemony of the masculine subject' and defines an alternative relational subject (p. 58). Coming from this theoretical orientation, Bruce and Powell make a radical assertion: ECEs, as they are, multiple, embodied, situated and relational subjects, 'are enough' (p. 73). They suggest that through a feminist ethics of care approach and a turning towards the ECE, we can find beneath the imposed singular subject constructions, an *already* multiple and relational ECE subjectivity. Through this reclaiming and remembering ECEs as they are, they call for a 'pause' on reconceptualizing the ECE subject until the important, complex care they are already doing is recognized, valued and supported. They further argue that instead of putting the onus of resistance and revolt on individual ECEs, we need to 'stand in solidarity' and 'collectively require existing early childhood institutions and systems to care *better*, care *more* and *care with* early childhood educators' (p. 73).

References

Gilligan, C. (1982). *In a different voice: Psychological theory and women's development.* Harvard University Press.

Hekman, S. J. (2014). *The feminine subject.* Polity Press.

5

Waves upon Waves: Highlighting the Invisibility of the Early Childhood Workforce through Conversations with Fourth Wave, Black and Postcolonial Feminisms

Flora Harmon, Erica Ritter and Radhika Viruru

It has been long recognized that investing in early childhood education (ECE) has long-term benefits for both children and society (Garcia, Heckman, Leaf & Prados, 2017; Heckman, 2008, 2011; Tebes, 2019). However, the early childhood workforce continues to be an 'amorphous and complex' body spread across a variety of settings other than schools and funded institutions (Tebes, 2019, p. 472). Additionally, many early childhood educators are women of colour with limited economic resources and social mobility (Kagan, Kauerz & Tarrant, 2008; Saluja, Early & Clifford, 2002). Although the ECE field has known systemic issues such as low compensation and high rates of turnover (Bassok et al., 2013), few studies have explored what guides educators to commit to the ECE field in spite of these realities. Recent studies, however, do suggest a contributing factor could lie within feminist structures and pedagogies (Lash, 2018). Whereas, historically, pre-school educators' career trajectories have aligned with the expectations of a traditionally feminized profession (Arndt et al., 2018), contemporary ECE literature indicates a high degree of vigour, activism and resilience within the field (Nislin et al., 2016). Thus, feminist theories have an important contribution to make in developing a more complete understanding of the nature of the ECE workforce. In this chapter, we draw from postcolonial, Black and fourth-wave feminist schools of thought to develop that understanding. Through personal narratives, counter storytelling and interconnected conversations, the foundations and theoretical positions of each feminism are revealed, grounded and connected to the trajectories of the early childhood workforce. We argue that each feminism is a necessary and critical tool for moving forward progressive practices in early childhood education.

Fourth-Wave Feminism (Erica)

It was 1997, I was a college dropout, living in a stark, thrift store furniture filled apartment. I didn't have a car nor a driver's license but needed a job to pay the bills. I quit my first job at a shoe store because of transportation issues and therefore had to find a job I could walk to. I was young with a limited skill set and only one year of college. There was a children's learning centre across the street. I did not think I was qualified for the job, but I walked in and applied. I was offered an interview and was hired quickly as a part-time teaching assistant. with a starting salary of $4.75/hr. I was making $570 gross pay monthly without benefits. My apartment was $475/month, and I was responsible for half, not including utilities. I didn't have health benefits and then became pregnant. I didn't know what to do and was scared to tell my family. I took pride in being an independent person and did not want to move back home. I went to the Social Security Administration building and applied for and got Medicaid and the Special Supplemental Nutrition Program for Women (WIC). My boyfriend and I got married since our son 'could not' be born out of wedlock. Since I had to work to live, I enrolled my child at the centre I worked at. Childcare was expensive and was going to take my entire pay cheque. I learned about childcare subsidy benefits from the government, applied and was accepted. We were still receiving WIC and Medicaid benefits and the government subsidy covered most of the cost of childcare, but my husband and I knew we needed to better support our family. We made the decision to send him to finish school first. The male has a better chance at a career, right? Plus, I was at work with our child, isn't that a close second to staying at home with your child as society dictates I should? Since my husband began trade school, he could no longer work and we lost most of our childcare benefits. That was a hard blow to our little family trying to figure out life. A new scholarship programme opened up in our local county in the rural United States that supported parents with children in childcare going back to school. I applied and received enough funding to cover the cost of childcare. I continued to work while he went back to school. I was to go back to college soon enough.

With these life experiences, I found myself drawn to exploring the relationships between feminism and ECE, specifically the fourth wave of feminism that we are currently experiencing. Feminism has historically been categorized by symbolic waves to define time periods where movement occurred (Reger, 2017). These waves of feminism have been critiqued for focusing on single ideologies and then receding if not disappearing, and for being dominated by elite groups of women and essentially overlooking the experiences of marginalized groups such as women of colour, working-class women and feminist labour union organizations (Reger, 2017). The first wave from the nineteenth century mostly comprised of middle class, Western, cisgender white women and largely focused on political rights, suffrage, temperance and abolitionist movements, and ended with the 19th Amendment giving white women the right to vote (Delao, 2021; National Women's History Museum; Rampton, 2015; Reger, 2017).

The second wave began in the 1960s and focused on increasing equity for all women but still ignored social differences among women (Spelman, 1988). The third wave arose in the 1990s and was informed by postcolonial and postmodern thinking that destabilized the constructs of 'universal womanhood' (Looft, 2017; Rampton, 2015). This wave is known for critiquing the second wave's lack of attention to race, ethnicity, class, nationality and religion (McAfee, 2018) while also embracing Black feminism and focused global/multicultural perspectives (Mann & Huffman, 2005; Rampton, 2015). The fourth wave began around 2012 and is defined by technology and intersectionality. It suggests that advances in technology have created a call-out culture challenging sexism or misogyny such as the #MeToo movement (Delao, 2021; Munro, 2013). This wave gained national and international attention from mainstream press and politicians and created conditions within which there is less stigma talking about various forms of societal abuse of women such as rape on college campuses, homophobia, transphobia and unfair pay and work conditions (Delao, 2021; Looft, 2017; Rampton, 2015). Fourth-wave feminism deconstructs gender norms, systems of power, includes racial justice as an explicit goal (Delao, 2021) and embraces intersectionality within the context of the marginalization of both class and gender (Rampton, 2015).

Although fourth-wave feminism has had a significant influence on society, there is limited research on its impact on early education or the childcare workforce (Munro, 2013). Issues such as addressing how the early childhood workforce can use technology as a platform to raise the concerns of inequitable pay or the disparity in pay between women of colour and white women are rarely discussed. There are no big movements defined by the fourth wave's technology to demand more equitable practices in early childhood education. If activism is central to feminisms, we wonder why a focus on the working conditions of a predominantly female ECE workforce is not a central concern of the fourth wave? For example, the field continues to be overrun by the perception that caregiving is women's work and the belief that women are 'naturally' suited to nurturing others and that a female labour force is inferior to a male one (Lorber, 1994).

Furthermore, the caregiving 'industry' of nursing, social work and childcare are still segregated by sex. While there is an increase in females crossing over to male dominated jobs/careers, there remains little change in the opposite direction (Williams, 1993; Welna, 2020). Women account for 95 per cent of the childcare workforce (Welna, 2020). In the United States, of those women, 56 per cent are white, 15 per cent are Black and 7 per cent are Hispanic. Lower-level positions, such as teacher aides, are even more likely to be minority dominated: 42 per cent Hispanic, 33 per cent Black and 32 per cent white (Smith, McHenry, Morris & Chong, 2021). Although it has been recognized that women of colour are the proud backbone of childcare in America (National Women's Law Center, 2021), what this means for the field has been insufficiently understood.

To add insult to injury, the pay for childcare workers is among the lowest in all sectors in the United States. There are clearly 'pay penalties' for working with young children (McLean, Austin, Whitebook & Olson, 2021). Poverty rates for early childhood educators in the United States are 7.7 times higher than K-8 educators and 39 per cent of early childhood educators experience food insecurities (McLean et al., 2021). These staggering numbers are not racially neutral either. Educators of colour are paid $6,100 less per year on average than their white colleagues. When this figure is further broken down it is revealed that Black preschool educators earn $1.71 less per hour than their white peers (McLean et al., 2021). In the United States, working as a prekindergarten teacher is generally recognized as a 'pathway to poverty' (Whitebook, 2014). At the same time, early childhood accreditation agencies and policymakers have called for increased 'quality' standards. If anything, the current working conditions are a strong deterrent for highly educated educators to enter the field. Although the ECE workforce drew national attention when listed as 'essential' workers during the pandemic, this recognition was not accompanied by an improvement in the conditions highlighted or even through increased funding. In fact, the pandemic *strengthened* the gendered divisions of labour as more women than men made the sacrifice to take on the role of caregiver for their children instead of focusing on their careers. According to the US Bureau of Labor Statistics, 2.2 million fewer women were in the labour force in October 2020 than in October 2019, a phenomenon dubbed as the 'she-cession' (reference). Journalists commented that the pandemic was undoing progress made in gender equity and putting specifically women of colour at a higher risk of dropping out of the workforce (Warrell, 2021). Although early childhood educators were identified as essential during the pandemic crisis, they have unfortunately emerged from the pandemic as little more than a 'she-cession' statistic. Fourth-wave feminism alone is not enough to help us fully conceptualize these issues which is why conversations and collaborations with other feminisms are needed.

Black Feminist Thought (Flora)

> That man over there says women need to be helped into carriages, and lifted over ditches, and to have the best place everywhere. Nobody ever helps me into carriages, or over mud puddles, or gives me any best place! And ain't I a woman? Look at me! Look at my arm! I have ploughed, and planted, and gathered into barns, and no man could head me! And ain't I a woman? I could work as much and eat as much as a man – when I could get it – and bear the lash as well! And ain't I a woman?
>
> (Truth, 1992)

Sojourner Truth recognized early that her oppression lay in the contradictions of what society defined as how a woman should be praised and treated versus how they are treated in reality. During her era Black women who did domestic work 'often developed distinct views of the contradictions between the dominant group's actions and ideologies' (Collins, 2000). Truth's oppression was integrated into her existence of being Black and being a woman. Seen from within the colonial doctrine, the work and toil from her hands were never meant to be respected or held to high esteem. Black women in Sojourner's time knew this and generations of Black women that came after them would experience this contradiction of living in a society that glorified women in words but suppressed and oppressed them in deed and fought to keep their work invisible. This struggle is still present in the modern-day field of early childhood education that is dominated by women of colour (Austin et al., 2019) who remain invisible. The field of ECE pays lip service to early childhood educators through discursive 'thanks' and/or praise but this has not translated into institutional support and respect. Nevertheless, it should be recognized that the sector is a critical part of Black women's struggles for social justice.

Black Feminist Theory (BFT) which emerged in the third wave offers tools to examine intersecting gendered and racialized oppressions. BFT scholars seek resolution to those and other interlocking oppressions (Perez & Williams, 2014; Rousseau, 2013). Through poetry, counter-storytelling, advocacy and scholarly work, Black feminist thought counters the proliferation of the subordinate imagery that colonizing Western powers have placed on Black women (Collins, 2000). Even in advocacy BFT organizes itself as a form of activism that 'centers the struggles and empowerment of Black women, women of color, and those with marginalized positionalities ... it provides a theoretical framework to unveil matrices of domination' (Perez & Williams, 2014, p. 126). The work of scholars such as Pauli Murray are particularly helpful when analysing issues related to the early childhood workforce. For example, Murray, an early Black feminist legal scholar, emphasized that 'equality in employment was the cornerstone of survival and equality for African American women' (Giardina, 2018, p. 750). Her emphasis on the 'urgency of good jobs and equal wages for women of color as a central reason to fight for women's rights at the same time as civil rights' (Giardina, 2018) led to the grounding of labour issues within the BFT movement and is of particular relevance to the ECE context.

Historically, women of colour make up more of the early childhood workforce in the United States in comparison to the K-12 workforce; currently the ECE workforce is just under half women of colour as opposed to 28 per cent of the K-12 sector (Austin et al., 2019). Not coincidentally, women in the ECE workforce are paid four times less than K-12 educators, are stereotyped and stigmatized as domestic babysitters and are underpaid and work longer hours. (Pianta, 2019). From a BFT perspective, the disparities in the ECE field and the high representation of marginalized groups in the ECE workforce are connected in multiple ways. For example, according to Collins (2000), African-American women's oppression has encompassed multiple interdependent dimensions with the most critical being the exploitation of Black women's labour and its role in the US capitalism – the 'iron pots and kettles' (the labour that Black women that have historically performed that was both physically demanding as well as invisible) symbolizing Black women's long-standing ghettoization in service occupations. This represents the economic dimension of oppression (Collins, 2000) and has embedded roots in systemic racism and the progressive suppression of equity rights for women. Nicole Rousseau (2013) contends that

> Black women's labor in the U.S. cannot be fully comprehended without focusing on the historical context of Black women as instruments of production, beginning with slavery...
>
> (p. 199)

Rousseau (2013) further states that 'Black women's relationship with the United States begins with her role in a forced labor pool, it stands to reason that her continued position in society, even in generations after dissolution of the slave system would remain connected with her labor location' (p. 193). BFT can thus guide and provide critical tools that ECEs need to address the oppressive practices that have silently plagued our field through the intersections of gender, race and identity. This is particularly significant for the ECE workforce and the overall field of early childhood education that has often been overlooked, stereotyped and even silenced (Faulkner et al., 2014; Pianta, 2019). By connecting to the principles in BFT we connect to a movement that fights for solidarity, equity and sustainable progress for all people (Collins, 2000).

Postcolonial Feminism (Radhika)

My great-grandmother was the oldest of eight siblings. She married young and lost her husband not that many years later. Alone she raised two daughters both of whom were also widowed young and gravitated back to be with her as they raised their own six children (one of whom is my mother). My great-grandmother's seven siblings went on to marry and have approximately thirty children between them and family legend has it that she attended the birth of all of those children except that of my father, the son of her fourth youngest sister. When he was born in 1932, she was in prison, jailed by the British occupiers as part of the civil disobedience movement (Janaki, 1999). However, she never rebelled against the oppressive limitations placed on her by Hindu society as a widow that limited her abilities to dress as she pleased or to ever re-marry. Rather she turned into a skilled arranger of other people's marriages but also into someone who was never particularly happy when a female baby was born into the family. Yet, for the women in my family, she was the ideal we were all taught to look up to: quick-witted, strong as steel and one who kept the family together through unspeakable tragedies. I do not believe she would have considered herself a feminist, yet as her life story indicates, she embodied feminism for many. The contradictions in her story seem to illustrate the many contradictions between Western feminisms and their global counterparts as well as the tensions between colonialism and feminism, and between theorizing feminism versus living it. These themes of postcolonial feminisms and how they relate to other forms of feminism are what we would like to explore further in this section. As Rajan and Park (2005) have said, postcolonial feminisms which emerged during the third wave constitute a unique confluence of perspectives that can neither be subsumed within postcolonial studies nor within feminist studies, assuming an inherently intersectional identity that challenges the fundamental tenets of both.

Rajan and Park (2005) suggest that postcolonial feminist studies encompass two broad genres of works: those produced by feminists with origins in the so-called 'Third World' who are now part of the Western academy and 'women's movements and gender issues in many postcolonial nations which are linked with feminist studies in the academy there, as well as works originating in the First World that relate to women and women's movements in the Third World' (p. 53). Thus, the field is inherently home to theoretical works as well as to works that are rooted in the lived realities of women from across the globe. Piedalue and Rishi (2017) define postcolonial feminism as 'an explicitly transnational and globally constructed form of critical race feminism' that yields 'complex understandings of the entanglements of gender, race and sexuality in nation and empire-building as well as in resistance movements and anti-imperial struggle' (p. 550).

As is evident from this definition, the concept of location is an important consideration within the field, both as marking the multiple locations around the world from where these perspectives arise as well as in indicating the wounds engendered when universalized notions of womanhood are invoked to represent the concerns of all women. This practice, scholars contend, erases not just identities but also 'places of speaking' that 'are marked by hybridity, in-betweenness, and hyphenation' as well as 'histories of arrival' (Rajan & Park, 2005, p. 54). Postcolonial feminists thus disavow being relegated to margins that attempt to slot their voices into well-defined categories such as 'native informant' and that attempt to de-cacophonize the plurality of their voices.

Postcolonial feminisms particularly distinguish themselves from mainstream Western feminisms in that they reject the established trope of what Mohanty has titled third-world difference (Mohanty, 1988) that renders women from formerly colonized countries as perpetually oppressed. Such characterizations, Mohanty comments, not only disregard the actual realities of women's lives across time and context but also render women from outside the West into a 'signature feature of liberal humanism' (Goswami, 2020, p. 154). As Van Bussel (2014) has said for postcolonial feminists, this is epitomized by the belief that 'white women often assume that they have the knowledge and obligation to aid "other" women, whether these women need and want it or not' (p. 61). Further as Piedalue and Rishi have commented, this serves to erase the agency and experiences of women within histories of colonialism. This is particularly ironic, since as Goswami (2020) has shown, colonialism was in fact often justified as an effort to stop 'barbaric' practices against women and gradually evolved into an enterprise that attempted to re-formulate the private domestic sphere (often considered female space) as well as the public. As Piedalue and Rishi (2017) have said, 'feminist postcolonial theory has trail-blazed and evolved' a more 'relational' understanding of power that forces us to confront issues such as the lack of impact that nationalist movements of liberation have had on the labour that women are expected to consistently perform. As they would suggest, echoing, women have been left to labour in the house of the Master and to use his tools without even the hope of dismantling it.

At the same time, postcolonial feminisms and postcolonial studies also have marked areas of overlap. For one, an overall mistrust of liberal humanism is characteristic of both areas of enquiry, based on its tendency to 'flatten' experiences from outside the First World, and its convenient appropriation of geography, through which concepts such as location and distance are both defined as scientific fact and as marker of difference. We would suggest that perhaps fourth-wave feminism is the latest manifestation of this form of humanism that flattens women's experiences through technology, yet leaves the core of inequities untouched. We would suggest too that the lack of the early childhood teachers' voice in dominant discourses around early childhood education is a manifestation of this kind of obliteration. What relevance do postcolonial feminisms thus have for early childhood education? In other works, the connection between childhood and postcolonial studies has been elaborated on at length (Burman, 2016; Cannella & Viruru, 2004: Viruru, 2001). But to touch briefly on some of the main connections, it has been pointed out that the modern construction of childhood as a time of complete innocence and with almost mystical magical qualities has been equated to the exotic fantasies that the Occident came to associate with the 'Orient' (Said, 1979; Viruru, 2001). Further the characterization of children's bodies as unruly and in constant need of direction and guidance, in order for them to realize their full potential bears uncanny resemblance to colonial narratives of progress (Viruru, 2005). Postcolonial feminism would however remind us that it is not just children's bodies but women's as well that have been marked as in need of regulation. As Carty and Mohanty (2015) have pointed out, feminists across the world have been engaged in battling the effects of neoliberal ideologies, which privilege the interests of the market and free trade over human well-being (Harvey, 2005). Within such a system, women are sold the idea that 'pleasure and self-fulfillment, dreams and desires, might be acquired through the market without admitting that the very form of the market destroys our pleasures and fulfillment' (Mohanty, 2015, p. 8). Neoliberal agendas make their way into early childhood spaces by regulating the work of the (mostly) women who populate it: on the one level, the work is characterized as incredibly meaningful as in making an impact on children's lives but on the other hand, market pressures and lack of meaningful supports cause the work to take place in mostly for-profit settings while at the same time being physically demanding, underpaid and often without the possibility of benefits in the United States. Further, class divisions continue to be part of the field in the United States as has been illustrated earlier. And as Van Bussel (2014) has said, the phenomena of elite capture, 'through which women of higher social class most often hold positions of political power, leaving out voices of lower class or indigenous women' continues to haunt the field as the women who do hold positions of power tend to belong to higher social classes and thus may not represent all voices faithfully (p. 61).

Conversations

As discussed above, systemic oppressions and the experience of inequitable treatment lie at the heart of the connection between feminism and early childhood education. Now is the time for ECE advocates to ride the fourth wave and create a social movement that draws national attention to the disparities of unequal pay and sub-person treatment that has plagued the field of ECEC since its inception. ECE professionals have proven time and again that their jobs are invaluable as they nurture and support young children yet these efforts go for the most part unrecognized and underpaid. Feminist pedagogies, rooted as they are in women's liberation movements, offer alternative ways to think about supporting the early childhood workforce particularly in the United States (Lawson, 2011). Centring feminism as a core source within ECE allows women to collectively build and maintain connections as opposed to an ethic within which the morality of rights is dominant, and individuals participate in the field with little responsibility or care for the class as a whole (Shrewsbury, 1987).

What then do these three different forms of feminism have to do with early childhood educators as a sector? Together they have, we believe, underlined critical concepts to consider going forward. First, for feminisms to be representative we can neither confine ourselves to textual understandings and arguments or focus on technocracies and changes that they brought to (mostly) Western societies. To honour and respect the work of women who work in early childhood spaces, efforts must be made to listen to and honour their voices. Second, all the feminisms that we have examined coalesce around the concept of women's work being under-recognized, underpaid and mistakenly designated as unskilled. As mentioned earlier, waves of feminism arose due to both broader participation by women in the workforce as well as a belated recognition of that work, as women have always laboured (Coontz, 2016) and even though subsequent of waves of feminism have since emerged that have attempted to address current concerns in (Western) society, issues related to the early childhood workforce persist. Finally, the diverse feminist perspectives that we draw from all also caution us to be wary of casting human beings into symbols – even ones worth fighting for. Much as colonialism was often cast as a war between progress and tradition, with the female body being the terrain on which the war was waged, it behoves us to be aware that when young children are cast as contested terrain, women's bodies can become the instruments through which either competing ideologies are made concrete (as in strictly regulating what they can and cannot do) or collateral damage is done (as in when initiatives designed to improve 'quality' in ECE contexts prioritize designing environments or technology adoption over guaranteeing the workforce a living wage).

In addition, the early childhood workforce is rich with racial and ethnic diversity. In the ECE field it is easy to witness global connectedness that allows for people from all racial and ethnic backgrounds to connect as a collective in educating and caring for our youth. However, in ECE our waves of progress have consistently hit a wall due to the reciprocating of societal belief systems that perpetuate Westernized perspectives that box women of colour as people that are 'below' and their work as insignificant (Giardina, 2018; Williams, 1987).

The repression of the significance and value of the work of early childhood educators compliments the histories and experiences that suppressed women of the past and present. For many generations, the connection to 'women's work' or the professions of care were assigned to women of colour (Collins, 2000; Moloney, 2010). These associations of care and assignments of caregiving were not always presented as choice but instead as ultimatums. We cannot ignore the influence that the foundational system of forced labour has had in Westernized societies including on the early childhood workforce. The field of early childhood education can no longer ignore the connected association it has established between women of colour and economic disparities (Black, 2018). The inequitable pay, devaluing of work and Eurocentric normalizations of care have an unfortunate history in the field of ECE. Black feminisms, postcolonial feminism and fourth-wave feminism shine a light on the holes that we as a profession continue to fall through on our path to progress and awareness.

Opening up the field to the utilization of feminisms in ECE allows for us to know which tools to use to fill those holes and take the necessary steps towards equity in all aspects of the field.

References

Arndt, S., Urban, M., Murray, C., Smith, K., Swadener, B., & Ellegaard Roskilde Sygehus, T. (2018). Contesting early childhood professional identities: A cross-national discussion. *Contemporary Issues in Early Childhood, 19*(2), 97–116. https://doi.org/10.1177/1463949118768356

Austin, B. L. J. E., Edwards, B., Chávez, R., & Whitebook, M. (2019). *Racial wage gaps in early education employment. 94720* (December)

Bassok, D., Fitzpatrick, M., Loeb S. & Paglayan, A. (2013). The early childhood care and education workforce from 1990 through 2010: Changing dynamics and persistent concerns. *Education Finance and Policy, 8*(4), 581–601.

Black, F. V. (2018). Providing quality early childhood professional development at the intersections of power, race, gender, and dis/ability. *Contemporary Issues in Early Childhood, 19*(2), 206–11. https://doi.org/10.1177/1463949118778017

Burman, E. (2016). *Deconstructing developmental psychology.* Routledge.

Cannella, G. S. & Viruru, R. (2004). *Childhood and post-colonization: Power, education and contemporary practice.* Routledge.

Carty, L. & Mohanty, C. T. (2015). Mapping transnational feminist engagements: Neoliberalism and the politics of solidarity. In R. Baksh & W. Harcourt (Eds). *The Oxford handbook of transnational feminist movements* (pp.1–38). Oxford University Press.

Collins, P. H. (2000). *Black feminist thought: Knowledge, consciousness, and the politics of empowerment* (2nd ed.). Routledge.

Coontz, S. (2016). *The way we never were: American families and the nostalgia trap.* Basic Books.

Delao, M. (2021, March 4). A brief look at the four waves of feminism. *The Humanist.* https://thehumanist.com/commentary/a-brief-look-at-the-four-waves-of-feminism/.

Faulkner, M., Gerstenblatt, P., Lee, A., Vallejo, V., & Travis, D. (2014). Childcare providers: Work stress and personal well-being. *Journal of Early Childhood Research, 14*(3), 280–93. https://doi.org/10.1177/1476718X14552871

Giardina, C. (2018). MOW to NOW: Black feminism resets the chronology of the founding of modern feminism. *Feminist Studies, 44,* 736–65 https://doi.org/10.15767/feministstudies.44.3.0736

Goswami, N. (2020). *Subjects that matter: Philosophy, feminism and postcolonial theory.* SUNY Press.

Garcia, J. L., Heckman, J. J., Leaf, D. E., & Prados, M. J. (2017). Quantifying the life-cycle benefits of a prototypical early childhood program (No. w23479). National Bureau of Economic Research.

Harvey, D. (2005). *A brief history of neoliberalism*. Oxford University Press.

Heckman, J. J. (2008). Schools, skills, and synapses. *Economic Inquiry, 46*, 289–324.

Heckman, J. J. (2011). The economics of inequality: The value of early childhood education. *American Educator, 35*, 31.

Hemmings, C. (2011). *Why stories matter: The political grammar of feminist theory*. Duke University Press.

Janaki, K. (1999). *Role of women in freedom struggle in Andhra Pradesh*. Neelkamal Book Distributors.

Kagan, S. L., Kauerz, K., & Tarrant, K. (2008). *The early care and education teaching workforce at the fulcrum: An agenda for reform*. Teachers College Press.

Lash, M. & Castner, D. (2018). Stories of practice: The lived and sometimes clandestine professional experiences of early childhood educators. *Contemporary Issues in Early Childhood, 19*(2), 93–6.

Lawson, E. (2011). Feminist pedagogies: The textuality of the racialized body in the feminist classroom. *Atlantis, 35*(2), 107–17.

Looft, R. (2017). #Girlgaze: Photography, fourthwave feminism and social media advocacy. *Continuum: Journal of Media and Culture Studies, 31*(6), 892–902.

Lorber, J. (1994). *Paradoxes of gender*. Yale University Press.

Mann, S. A. & Huffman, D. J. (2005). The decentering of second wave feminism and the rise of the third wave. *Science and Society, 61*(1), 56–91.

McAfee, N. (2018). Feminist philosophy. *The Stanford Encyclopedia of Philosophy*, E. N. Zalta (Ed.). https://plato.stanford.edu/archives/fall2018/entries/feminist-philosophy/.

McLean, C., Austin, L. J. E., Whitebook, M., & Olson, K. L. (2021). *Early childhood workforce index – 2020*. Berkeley, CA: Center for the Study of Child Care Employment, University of California, Berkeley. https://cscce.berkeley.edu/workforce-index-2020/report-pdf/

Mohanty, C. T. (1988). Under Western eyes: Feminist scholarship and colonial discourses. *Feminist Review, 30*(1), 61–88.

Moloney, M. (2010). Professional identity in early childhood care and education: Perspectives of pre-school and infant teachers. *Irish Educational Studies, 29*(2), 167–87. https://doi.org/10.1080/03323311003779068

Munro, E. (2013). Feminism: A fourth wave? *Political Insight, 4*(2), 22–5. https://doi.org/10.1111%2F2041-9066.12021

Murray, S. B. (2000). Getting paid in smiles: The gendering of child care work. *Symbolic Interaction, 23*(2), 135–60. https://doi.org/10.1525/si.2000.23.2.135

National Academy of Medicine. (2015). *Transforming the workforce for children birth through age 8: A unifying framework*. The National Academies Press.

National Women's History Museum. *Feminism: The first wave*. Alexandria, VA. https://www.womenshistory.org/exhibits/feminism-first-wave-0

National Women's Law Center. (2021, May). *We are the backbone: Faces of the care nation*. https://nwlc.org/resources/we-are-the-backbone-faces-of-the-care-nation/

Nislin, M. A., Sajaniemi, N. K., Sims, M., Suhonen, E., Montero, E. F. M., Hirvonen, A., & Hyttinen, S. (2016). Pedagogical work, stress regulation and work-related well-being among early childhood professionals in integrated special daycare groups. *European Journal of Special Needs Education, 31*(1), 27–43. Doi: 10.1080/08856257.2015.1087127

Pérez, M. S., & Williams, E. (2014). Black feminist activism: Theory as generating collective resistance. *Multicultural Perspectives, 16*(3), 125–32. https://doi.org/10.1080/15210960.2014.922883

Pianta, R., Hamre, B., & Nguyen, T. (2019). Measuring and improving care in early care and education. *Early Childhood Research Quarterly, 51*, 285–7. https://doi.org/10.1016/j.ecresq.2019.10.013

Piedalue, A. & Rishi, S. (2017). Unsettling the south through postcolonial feminist theory. *Feminist Studies, 43*(3), 548–70. Doi:10.15767/feministstudies.43.3.0548

Rajan, R. S. & Park, Y. (2005). Postcolonial feminism/Postcolonialism and feminism. In H. Schwarz & S. Ray (Eds.), *A companion to Postcolonial Studies* (pp. 53–71). Blackwell Publishing.

Rampton, M. (2015, October 25). Four waves of feminism. *Pacific University*. https://www.pacificu.edu/maganize/four-waves-feminism

Reger, J. (2017). Finding a place in history: The discursive legacy of the wave metaphor and contemporary feminism. *Feminism Studies, 43*(1), 193–221. https://www.jstor.org/stable/10.15767/feministstudies.43.1.0193

Rousseau, N. (2013). Historical womanist theory: Re-visioning Black feminist thought. *Race, Gender, & Class, 20*(3–4), 191–205. https://www.jstor.org/stable/43496941

Said, E. W. (1979). *Orientalism*. Vintage Books.

Saluja, G., Early, D. M., & Clifford, R. M. (2002). Demographic characteristics of early childhood teachers and structural elements of early care and education in the United States. *Early Childhood Research and Practice, 4*, 2–21. https://ecrp.illinois.edu/v4n1/saluja.html

Shrewsbury, C. M. (1987). What is feminist pedagogy? *Women's Studies Quarterly, 15*(3/4), 6–14.

Smith, L., McHenry, K., Morris, S., & Chong, H. (2021, February 8). Characteristics of the child care workforce. *Bipartisan Policy Center*. https://bipartisanpolicy.org/blog/characteristics-of-the-child-care-workforce/

Spelman, E. V. (1988). *Inessential women: Problems of exclusion in feminist thought*. Beacon Press.

Tebes, J. K. (2019). Strengthening the child and youth serving workforce: Surveying the landscape, overcoming challenges. *American Journal of Community Psychology, 63*, 472–75. Doi 10.1002/ajcp.12340

Truth, S. (1992). Ain't I a woman. In P. C. McKissack & F. McKissack (Eds.), *Sojourner Truth: Ain't I a woman* (pp. 99–116). Scholastic.

U.S. Bureau of Labor Statistics. (2020, August 19). *Employment, hours, and earnings from the Current Employment Statistics survey (National)*. https://beta.bls.gov/dataViewer/view/timeseries/CES6562440010

Van Bussel, T. (2014). Feminism is for everybody except when it isn't: Contemporary gender theory and oppression in development. *Footnotes: University of Guelph's Undergraduate Feminist Journal, 7*, 9–18. https://journal.lib.uoguelph.ca/index.php/footnotes/article/view/5333

Viruru, R. (2001). *Early childhood education: Postcolonial perspectives from India*. Sage.

Viruru, R. (2005). The impact of postcolonial theory on early childhood education. *Journal of Education, 35*, 7–29.

Warrell, M. (2021, January 6). Women are quitting: How we can curb the 'She-Cession' and support working women. *Forbes*. https://www.forbes.com/sites/margiewarrell/2021/01/06/does-a-she-cession-loom-how-to-better-support-women-through-this-pandemic/?sh=4176ee0c3ece.

Welna, D. (2020, August 19). 1 in 5 child care jobs were lost since pandemic started. Women are affected most. *NPR*. https://www.npr.org/sections/coronavirus-live-updates/2020/08/19/903913689/1-in-5-child-care-jobs-were-lost-since-pandemic-started-women-are-affected-most

Whitebook, M. (2014, February 5). The debate about paying for preschool is a debate about income inequality. *Center for Study of Child Care Employment*. https://cscce.berkeley.edu/the-debate-about-paying-for-preschool-is-a-debate-about-income-inequality/.

Williams, C. L. (Ed.) (1993). *Doing 'women's work' men in nontraditional occupations*. SAGE Publications.

Williams, F. B. (1987). The colored girl. In M. H. Washington (Ed.), *Invented lives: Narratives of black women 1860–1890* (pp. 150–9). Anchor Press.

6

Womanist Praxis in Early Childhood Education and Care: Educators' Nourishment of Mind-Body-Spirit Relations

Nnenna Odim, Kia S. Rideaux and Michelle Salazar Pérez

Feminist theoretical framings of early childhood educators as gendered and situated subjects are diverse and expansive. Feminisms have been used to foreground vital discussions about discursive, material and socio-cultural-political dimensions of educator becomings, including research examining the governing technologies of the 'good' educator (Núñez, 2020), social inequities produced in care work (Langford et al., 2018), and ways in which educators can engage in pedagogies that affirm Black and Indigenous land relations in order to challenge settler colonialism, anti-Blackness and anthropogenic devastation (Nxumalo, 2020). We contribute to this significant body of work through a discussion on womanist, educator praxis as an enfleshed approach (Moraga & Anzaldúa, 1981) to reconceptualizing early childhood education so that it values, nourishes and celebrates the mind-body-spirit relations of young children who have been racialized as Black and Brown.

Womanism

Womanism is a dynamic worldview with myriad strands, facets and interpretations. Having strong Black and African cultural and ancestral roots (Maparyan, 2012), womanism centres the spirit (through Innate Divinity), the mystical, and the metaphysical, in order to imagine and create new ways of being in the world and in relation with other beings, both human and more-than-human. Maparyan (2012), a prominent womanist scholar, captures its essence by describing it as 'an organizing principle ... [that is] much more of a "spirit" or a "way" or a "walk" or even a "vibrational level" than it is a theory or ideology' (p. 16). Maparyan (2012) further elucidates;

> the womanist worldview... articulated primarily, but not exclusively by women of color from around the world, and now a gift to all humanity... privileges the experience of inspiration, a heightened, nonrational spiritual state that makes the seemingly impossible possible – materially, socially, politically, economically, ecologically, psychologically, and relationally – and contributes to an ongoing sense of inner well-being and power that defies, and in turn, transmutes external conditions. Womanists know this state personally and they draw from it to do their social change work.
>
> (p. 33)

As an enfleshed worldview (Moraga & Anzaldúa, 1981) that is transformative of the self (as spiritual and interconnected), humanity and the earth, these and other aspects of womanism described by Maparyan (2012) are inspired by the ideas of its 'founding foremothers', such as Alice Walker (1983), who describes womanists as 'committed to the survival and wholeness of an entire people' (p. 9). Therefore, as a social, spiritual and political framework, womanism centralizes women's lived experiences as interconnected. Through this worldview, a 'new way of talking about the relationship between women, social change, the struggle against oppression, and the quest for full humanity' (Maparyan, 2012, p. 18) is incited.

Because womanism encompasses more than just an identity, its essence, spirit, and features can be felt and made visible in moments that may not be explicitly named as such. This is central to our discussion throughout this chapter, as we unearth envisionings of a womanist educator and all that (and with whom) they are in relation.

Black Feminisms

While womanism is the primary theoretical focus of this chapter, we find it useful to thread Black feminist wisdoms into our discussion, and therefore, provide a brief background of its foundations. Black feminisms are diverse in their interpretations, yet share many aims as social theories (Collins, 2008; hooks, 2015; Lorde, 1984). Deeply influenced by Black women thinkers (Combahee River Collective, 1978/2014; Walker, 1983), Black feminisms have been birthed from enfleshed knowledges communicated through spoken, corporeal and written word in the forms of storytelling, poetry, song and art to provide accounts of the lived realities of Black women's subjugation, self/collective empowerment and liberation. By honing in on Black girls' and Black women's brilliance and resistance throughout herstory (Hill Collins, 2000; Muhammad & Haddix, 2016), Black feminisms have been crafted as a means to analyse complex social and institutional power dynamics (Collins, 2008).

Significantly, Black feminists have also conceptualized concepts to analyse the complexities of Black women's multiple identities (Collins, 2019; Dillard, 2012; Hancock, 2016; hooks, 2013; Lorde, 1984). As identities overlap and intersect, society has often attempted to label, oppress and contain Black women, producing lived realities of social and systemic inequities. To provide an analytic tool to understanding these dynamics, Kimberlee Crenshaw (1989) – influenced by a long herstory of Black women's embodied knowings and activism – theorized intersectionality to articulate how 'particular forms of intersecting oppressions, for example, intersections of race and gender, or of sexuality and nation… cannot be reduced to one fundamental type, and that oppressions work together in producing injustice' (Crenshaw, 1991 as cited in Hill Collins, 2000). Concepts such as intersectionality, in addition to numerous other Black feminist wisdoms gifted to the world, are 'invaluable in making sense of the persistence of [anti-Black] discourses in academia, in schooling contexts, and, more broadly, in society' (Nxumalo, 2019, p. 123).

In this chapter, we engage deeply with womanist ideas, while weaving in Black feminist insights, to cogitate how a womanist praxis can incite new ways to think about the subjectivity of early childhood educators.

Who We Are and Our Process to Unearth Womanist Praxis

As Black, Indigenous and Latina women with current and past experiences as early childhood educators in the United States, we have gathered over the course of several months through video conferencing to discuss and unearth insights on womanist praxis, which we share in this chapter. We have approached our process with an ethic of care for each other, nurturing well-being among us and creating spaces where we could be vulnerable, challenge our thinking, rest and tend to our spirits and our loved ones when needed, and overall, learn from each other's wisdoms, that of our ancestors, and from the womanist and Black feminist thinkers for whom we have much gratitude and draw inspiration from.

Because womanist spirituality has guided us, care has been woven into our contemplations, enacting a labour of love (hooks, 2018), eloquent rage (Cooper, 2018) and joy (Love, 2020), grounding us and being a source of support through a sisterhood. Theorizing, then, did not occur in isolation; rather, our conversations have taken place in the presence of kindred spirits and have been honest, empathetic, compassionate and fruitful. We believe that through womanism, new and nourishing imaginaries can emerge that re-envision early childhood education and early childhood educational praxis in ways that are more culturally sustaining. To provide a background of why and how these re-envisionings are imperative, we briefly discuss the context we find ourselves in as people of the global majority living in the United States, and what we believe this means for early childhood educators. Later in the chapter, we introduce two storied examples of what happens when we re-member and nourish our mind-body-spirit relations (Dillard, 2012) within ourselves as educators, with young children, and with the more-than-human.

The White Supremist Historical and Contemporary Context of the United States

Black feminists have highlighted the multiple and overlapping intersections experienced by racialized, gendered and classed communities to characterize the oppositions that occur in everyday lived experiences. That is, communities racialized as Black and Brown confront everyday strained and genocidal relationships with colonial governance that results in 'elevated rates of poverty, violence, unemployment, chronic illness, incarceration, deportation, water crises, inadequate housing' (Seeding Sovereignty, 2021, p. 1) and food insecurity which wreak unimaginable havoc. Colonization is literal, global (Tuck and Yang, 2012) and much more than an 'exploitation of the body [or land]: it achieves its ultimate success in the destruction of the human soul that results as a matter of the psychological destruction of those it seeks to enslave' (Strong-Leek, 1999, p. 149).

In the education racial project in the United States (Pérez, 2019) and other global north contexts, young children are often staged as pawns in a society to reproduce and sustain inequitable hierarchies that funnel resources and property to those considered the white elite. This amounts to an 'educational debt' (Ladson-Billings, 2006) steeped in centuries of exclusion from full access to many educational opportunities for communities racialized as Black and Brown

(Lewis, Diamond & Foreman, 2015). Grounding an early childhood analysis through a womanist and Black feminist lens unveils the forms of resistance multiple communities have employed out of necessity (Lorde, 1984) – forms of resistance that may have been made hidden or invisible – and to acknowledge and bring to the forefront historically unjust schooling structures in the United States. This highlights the actions of Black, Native and other communities who have been racialized as they negotiate power dynamics and cultivate everyday forms of resistance.

The Un/consciousness of Oppression and Womanist Offerings

As women of colour, we can feel overwhelmed at times about the socio-political context of the United States and other nations with connected histories. This can create a sense of precarity for us and others who are part of white, racialized educational spaces. Importantly, Black feminist Christina Sharpe (2016) engages precarity as structures of racism, anti-Blackness and colonial exploitation woven into spaces that impose hate. This points towards how there is still much work to be done as educators to recognize racism and anti-Blackness in educational spaces, and to confront and dismantle it. For those who embody whiteness or a proximity to whiteness, it also means learning how to secede power. We long for this larger breadth of consciousness and action for all who are educators.

Womanism helps us grapple with these and other complexities, longings and tensions, fuelling our hopes for liberation and the prospect that racist and anti-Black oppressions may not always be as prevalent. Although it is unknown whether vast shifts and changes will occur in our lifetime, womanism facilitates spiritual guidance to move towards what can be possible, even though at times a new imaginary can feel impossible (Maparyan, 2012). With a womanist worldview, we can resist and respond to the precarity in institutional and educational structures, at times masquerading as equality, by elevating the multiple forms of resistance that communities of colour exert through their humanity. A womanist spirit opens opportunities to cultivate a place to 'interrogate the gaze of the Other but also look back, and at one another, naming what we see' (bell hooks as quoted by Tavia Nyong'o, 2014, p. 70). This allows us to focus our energies on the motivations and strategies of communities as they struggle to resist oppressive and complex power matrices (Collins, 2008) that are linked and ever-changing.

During one of our initial conversations in which we envisioned a womanist praxis, we discussed whether we felt hopeful about how the world and educational spaces could engage and support the many offerings of young children, and in particular, Black children. We have reflected on how early childhood educators can learn from womanism to better understand the interconnectedness we have to each Other, spirit, and the land in order to imagine a new world. In this imagining, early childhood educators value, uplift and celebrate Black children and other children who are racialized. As a manifestation of this, Kia shares a story from an experience she had as one of three Black women working in a suburban elementary school. She then provides a reflection on how a womanist praxis was instrumental in disrupting white supremacy.

> It was a moment that I will never forget. It was almost haunting how our eyes connected in that moment; this young Black girl noticing me and me noticing her, separated by a single pane of glass. Her emotions were on full display; there was yelling, tears streaming down her face. As she stood in the glass foyer of the school building, separated from her classroom and classmates, there was an expectation that she would process this moment through her Kindergarten understanding devoid of any comfort. As the school principal stood with a walkie talkie in hand, monitoring her emotions registering in this confined space, I, an unforeseen witness to her chaos, felt so helpless. I just wanted to give her the biggest embrace, to help her come back to herself. However, at that moment, she was being disciplined... her fiery-ness was being contained without her consent.

Although Kia elected not to intervene during the encounter, there were many other instances throughout the school year when she found herself welcoming this young girl into her office space, offering her tissues, soft music or simply guiding her on how to catch her breath. Seeing herself in this young girl, or moreover, imagining her own daughter in these tense moments, illuminates how Kia incited a womanist praxis to bring a depth of care, relatability and patience that white supremacist contexts cannot.

Reflecting on Kia's profound story of a young Black girl's almost daily interactions with the school counsellor (who was also a Black woman) and administrators, we wonder what womanist praxis might incite when trauma, instability and depression rock the core foundation of a child's existence. For this young child, her home life was rapidly changing, with a parent on the verge of incarceration; pain was manifesting as anger. Yet, the consideration of depression being discussed or even acknowledged when in relation to the life of a privileged, Black woman let alone a young Black girl (Walton & Boone, 2019) is a standpoint that perhaps only a womanist stance might recognize. In her work examining the exclusionary discipline and (bad) girl performances of young

Black girls, Edwards (2020) challenges schools to reexamine how they inflict violence and are complicit in reifying deprecating notions of Black girlhood. Viewing the compulsory stories of young children who are marginalized through a womanist praxis of care (Beauboeuf-Lafontant, 2002) affords new opportunities of allyship between educators (with a range of social positions and identities) and young children who might otherwise feel disconnected within early education spaces.

Further Provocations for a Womanist Praxis

In the forthcoming, we expand on our initial insights about womanist offerings for educational imaginaries that value, nourish and celebrate childhood multiplicities. We focus our conversation on the potentials educators can foster by honouring the wholeness of who we are as mind-body-spirit beings in the world, and as contradictory and complex. In our provocations, we seek to view children and early childhood educators as spiritual beings, that when not recognized as such, can become vivisected from aspects of themselves and the more-than-human. As such, we view a womanist educator as steadfast in being conscious of and sustaining these relations.

Storytelling as a Womanist Enactment

To bring our provocations to life, we share two storied narratives of what we view as children's and educators' encounters with spirit. As a womanist enactment, storytelling in its many forms can be articulated through words, visuals, sounds and often evokes emotions (McKittrick, 2021). In this way, storytelling is an opportunity to connect, cultivate and create relationships through sharing our lived experiences. In the following, Nnenna describes her wonderings about the power of storytelling as a womanist enactment.

> Storytelling can be expressed through creations of images, photographs, drawings, words, and so much more. I listen to stories as though they are creations, seen with the eye, heard and felt with the body, and that evoke emotion. I think about visual artist and painter Kehinde Wiley who creates large-scale stained-glass images. His work situates everyday life as embodied experiences on a grand scale with vibrant and expressive colors. To me, Wiley's work draws on womanist frameworks by illustrating the way life is full of many different and sometimes conflicting moments. His work amplifies the grandeur

of cultural differences within the global majority. I see a connection to our praxis as educators in Wiley's work where young children's stories can be understood as perspectives that embody the grandeur of difference.

As Nnenna eloquently explains, storytelling through multiple aesthetic expressions incites a womanist worldview of the complexities and relationalities of childhood/s and educator subjectivities. To further elucidate these complexities, we share two stories that capture (1) young children as liberatory guides in cultivating relationships that hold spiritual and ancestral knowledges, and the ways in which honouring these relations can incite a womanist educator praxis and (2) childhood and educator more-than-human relations through water encounters.

Child Storytelling as an Expression of Woven Relations

Like the artist Kehinde Wiley, Black girlhood scholar Robin Boylorn (2013) notices the colonial boundaries placed on our experiences, and therefore, merges the words Black Girls to make them touch on paper the way they touch in everyday existence (Boylorn, 2013, p. 276). Black girlhood scholar Dominique C. Hill (2019) argues that educational spaces require a Black girl to deny elements of her identity and prioritize the objective in order to attain success; in other words, 'neglect and dismember parts and experiences that define her' (Hill, 2019, p. 276). In a similar vein, Indigenous scholar Kapua Chandler (2018) writes about her experiences in education which ask us to dismember our personalities and histories to fit into one norm of knowledges. Young children in educational spaces experience moments that might acknowledge, resist and deny the limits that colonial legacies place on them. These are important insights for educators who can also have similar lived experiences of colonial dismemberment.

To further explicate how early childhood educators can attempt to foster and co-construct educational spaces that honour young children as liberatory guides, who cultivate relationships that hold spiritual and ancestral knowledges, we share childhood stories captured by documentary filmmaker and curator Ania Freer (2018), who catalogues and archives the oral histories of Jamaica. In one moment, Ania listens to two young girls, maybe six years old, share about the fresh water mermaid who lives near Roaring River, Westmorland. The video is close up, and we see one girl's beautiful brown eyes gazing up to the sky and off into the distance as she talks, mouth chewing on pink gum, and with deep curves from dimples in her cheeks. The girl's smile is ever present while describing the rivermaid (Freer, 2018).

One night I go down to my river and I was going to bathe, when I was going to reach down there, I saw a rivermaiden on the rockstaway, and when he, when he saw, when she saw me, she jumped off.

Ania (the filmmaker) asks, you saw one! What did she look like? The girl responds, matter-of-factly: half human and half fish.

A friend joins, so we now listen to two young girls, mahogany and coconut complexions, share about the River Mamma, their faces in the mainframe. Aniah asks, is she friendly?

No.

One girl shakes her head, body follows, to emphasize

She's wicked, she's bad.

In the background, lush green, head-sized leaves canopy over her body–bushes filled with the hues of lime and yellows, signaling healthy and fertile lands. Ania asks, 'Why is she bad?'

Be… cause she's evil. She…

From the side we hear the other girl say:

She's evil. She eye right. She's evil and she a rasta. She wicked.

Ania asks, how do you know she is wicked?

Because when she singing, the whole community can hear.

The girl looks to her friend, nods her head, saying, for true.

In these moments, as the girls thought about Ania's questions, they looked at each other to tell the story. We see flashes of Alice Walker's (1983) notion of womanism as womanish, where young girls want to share the stories they know. There are notes of sisterly, communal acts of care from their smiles and glances at each other while sharing. The video tells of an interaction that is as much about their relationships together, with each other, with their families, with the water and the spirits, as it is about communicating the story to another person. This is where story holds flesh archives with the histories of our ancestors.

These descriptions bring up the power in water, like Black feminist Audre Lorde's (1984) cave. In this place, the opaqueness in a cave and the depths of water hold the confusions and emotions weaving fear, evil, wonder and joy. The young girls describe spirits of the Rivermaid as evil, shady, pretty and a friend. This depth, darkness and evil are not something to be feared but a realness that is an aspect of living in this racial colonial project intertwined with late-state capitalism. The deep darkness and Audre Lorde's cave 'roots freedom in the darkness… in that well of feeling and wisdom from which all knowledge is recreated' (Tuck and Yang, 2012, p. 36). This place offers places of possibility within ourselves [that] are dark because they are ancient and hidden; they have survived and grown strong through darkness. Within these deep places, each one of us holds an incredible reserve of creativity and power, of unexamined and unrecorded emotion and feeling. The woman's place of power within each of us is neither white nor surface; it is dark, it is ancient, and it is deep.

(Lorde, 1984, as cited by Tuck & Yang, 2012, pp. 36–7)

In this way, womanism embraces ancestral knowledges as we move through destruction, depth and darkness. These descriptions can hold the many features of water and darkness, as life, birthing evil while also cradling possibilities for change. Therefore, relations with water and darkness become family. Similarly, in Ania Freer's (2019) River Maid short videos, the young girls offered an example of respectful relationships with the spirit of the River Maid.

Engaging theories of Womanism in early childhood education opens opportunities for educators to listen to and be in community with young children who offer guidance through relationships with spirits, land, water and other living beings. With this lens, educators can better understand and foster spaces that sustain ways in which young children hold multiple truths at the same time in their core without placing a judgement on each truth, but living with each.

Childhood Relations with Water

As shared in the first story of childhood mind-body-spirit relations, womanist possibilities trouble the normative and evoke a radical authentic reading of self, others and the more-than-human. Throughout our conversations, as we further contemplated educator-child relational becomings, Kia shared a revelation she experienced while parenting her own preschool-aged daughter. Drawing inspiration from Abudullah's (2012) conception of womanist mothering 'as a particularly salient praxis through which Black mothers make the personal political' (p. 60), Kia reflected upon a recent encounter with her daughter.

> I can't keep Carter out of water. I recognize that about her... that I have to let her be with her water. It's going to be all over the house and I'm going to have to clean it up. I had so much joy watching her the other day, there was a rain shower, and this was the first time she was able to use her brand-new umbrella. As laughter filled the air, and I watched her run back and forth on the porch with her new umbrella, the simplicity of her joy in the rain solidified that her connection with water was indeed spiritual. It was the most genuinely happy

experience I have ever captured on camera. I've just come to realize that I have to let that battle go because when I was her age, I too was called to play with water.

In reflecting upon Carter and her joy with water – and letting her be in her happiness and her joy – Kia realized that any intent to regulate or control her would be detrimental to who Carter was at her core. Kia realized that there would be many other times in daughter's young, Black life that she would experience the scathing sting of dissenting voices. Kia did not want to contribute to the oppressive structures already awaiting her daughter.

We often have our own ideas as adults about how children should engage with the earth. Womanist praxis, however, inspires us to nourish children's earth relations in a way that is authentic for them, something often lacking in schools. bell hooks (2015) shared the punishments experienced in her childhood as the training grounds for her resistance, where she 'learned to be vigilant in the nourishment of my spirit, to be tough, to courageously protect that spirit from the forces that would break it' (p. 7). Similarly, in the manifestations of discipline that occurs in schools, we subjugate young children and educators by vivisecting mind-body-spirit connections, at the detriment of their well-being. Womanist praxis moves us to tap into spirit to know when these moments occur, and to know when to let go.

In a related reflection, we have pondered about the boundaries that can be placed on the introduction of water to early childhood educational spaces. With the use of water tables, sponges, and aprons, we thought about how we often adultify water experiences, potentially severing children's mind-body-spirit relations. Nnenna contemplates:

> In thinking about water, young children, and learning environments, I remember times as a classroom educator where I planned activities with tubs, buckets, sponges and pitchers. Many of the objects were meant to capture, manipulate and contain water which dictates a specific relationship with water for young children. Moreover, some classroom experiences with water are situated in a landscape of containing water and surveilling children, which places specific boundaries on how a child chooses to listen to and express their relations with water. What would it mean to think about young children and their experiences with water as spiritual connections with another living being? Engaging with womanist perspectives about water relations might offer possibilities for young children to share their many experiences with water – from community knowledge of the Rivermaid, to Carter's joy amidst negotiating boundaries and so much more. These are opportunities to forefront expressions of many senses and experiences.

The simultaneous labour of being both an early childhood educator and womanist brings visibility to nuanced regulatory practices in everyday curriculum. By thinking through these and the other contemplations that Nnenna introduces in her reflection, we ponder about how educators can nourish childhood spiritual and earth connections, such as with water, in less restrictive ways. We believe that actualizing this begins with the inner work of suturing our own mind-body-spirit splits as educators, which is intimately connected to outer transformations (Anzaldúa, 1987; Maparyan, 2012).

Returning to the notion that womanists dream beyond what many perceive as impossible, Maparyan (2012) posits that by thinking 'big' we can create new ways of being in the world. These new ways of being can shift, energetically, social and ecological relations. For educators, using such womanist tools can allow one to tap into a (renewed) spiritual consciousness, which in turn, creates a dramatically different dynamic for how one approaches curricula and what it means to be in community with young children.

Putting Womanism into Action

Womanism offers an expansion of how we might interrogate, challenge and incite a more just early childhood educational experience through educator praxis that embraces, empowers and accepts all who enter its spaces. The transformation of individual and collective consciousness is at the heart of this expansion through what Maparyan (2012) has termed a womanist methodology, or 'the transmutation of energy – mental, emotional, physical, material, social, and environmental energy' (p. 51). To enact these transformations, we must examine the dust of the ruins on our flesh by tracing the roots of social and earth oppressions, and through these iterative excavations, 'rework the ground-level platforms of human experience' (Maparyan, 2012, pp. 51–2). Maparyan (2012) explains:

> The proverbial 'changing of hearts and minds' is the basic womanist modus operandi. Changed hearts and minds then create and sustain different physical, material, institutional, and ecological structures. Womanist methodology is about being able to envision a desired outcome, then going back to the level of thought and feeling to transmute originating conditions in ways that lead to that outcome. And much of this process takes place on planes and in places that can only be described as 'spiritual' or 'invisible', and it is knowledge and wisdom that 'our grandmothers' perpetually maintained in both theory and act.
>
> (p. 52)

An entry point to the transformation of 'physical, material, institutional, and ecological structures' in early childhood education and care, is through a reimagining of educator praxis. In the storied examples we have shared throughout the chapter, we provide windows into a womanist imaginary that confronts the legacies of colonialism, anti-Blackness and racism, while concurrently offering womanist ways to 'read' childhood, incite educator inner and outer transformations, and become more attuned to relations (among each other and with the earth) as spirit infused and ancestrally connected. Our hope is that through this transformative praxis we can honour the many stories children and educator's hold as expressions of mind-body-spirit relations. By tuning into these relations, we are gifted revelations to eradicate White supremacy, in addition to cultivating spaces where childhood and educator multiplicities and relationalities are nourished, valued and sustained.

References

Abdullah, M. (2012). Womanist mothering: Loving and raising the revolution. *Western Journal of Black Studies*, 36(1), 57–67.

Anzaldúa, G. E. (1987). *Borderlands/la frontera*. Aunt Lute Books.

Beauboeuf-Lafontant, T. (2002). A womanist experience of caring: Understanding the pedagogy of exemplary Black women teachers. *The Urban Review*, 34, 71–86.

Beauboeuf-Lafontant, T. (2005). Womanist lessons for reinventing teaching. *Journal of Teacher Education*, 56(5), 436–45.

Boylorn, R. M. (2013). Blackgirl blogs, auto/ethnography, and crunk feminism. *Liminalities: A Journal of Performance Studies*, 9(2), 73–82.

Chandler, K. L. (2018). I ulu no ka lālā i ke kumu, the branches grow because of the trunk: Ancestral knowledge as refusal. *International Journal of Qualitative Studies in Education*, 31(3), 177–87.

Collins, P. H. (2008). *Black feminist thought: Knowledge, consciousness, and the politics of empowerment* (3rd ed.). Routledge.

Collins, P. H. (2019). *Intersectionality as critical social theory*. Duke University Press.

Combahee River Collective. (1978/2014). A Black feminist statement. *Women's Studies Quarterly*, 42(3/4), 271–80.

Cooper, B. (2018). *Eloquent rage: A Black feminist discovers her superpower*. Picador.

Crenshaw, K. (1989). Demarginalizing the intersection of race and sex: A Black feminist critique of antidiscrimination doctrine, feminist theory and antiracist politics. *The University of Chicago Legal Forum*, 140, 139–67.

Crenshaw, K. (1991). Mapping the margins: Intersectionality, identity politics, and violence against women of color. *Stanford Law Review*, 43(6), 1241–99.

Dillard, C. (2012). *Learning to (re)member: The things we've learned to forget, endarkened feminisms, spirituality, & the sacred nature of research & teaching*. Peter Lang.

Edwards, E. B. (2020). Toward being nobody's darling: A womanist reframing of school climate. *International Journal of Qualitative Studies in Education, 33*(7), 759–72.

Freer, A. (2019). The Goat Curry Gallery. Retrieved April 29, 2022, from http://www.goatcurrygallery.org

Freer, A. [@goatcurrygallery]. (2018, September 7). Collecting River Mumma stories in communities close to natural springs and blue holes. [Instagram video]. Retrieved from: https://www.instagram.com/p/BncF2maHTjp/?igshid=1lc4irurfi6h

Hancock, A. (2016). *Intersectionality: An intellectual history*. Oxford University Press.

Hill Collins, P. (2000). *Black feminist thought: Knowledge, consciousness, and the politics of empowerment* (2nd ed.). Routledge.

Hill, D. C. (2019). Blackgirl, one word: Necessary transgressions in the name of imagining Black girlhood. *Cultural Studies↔ Critical Methodologies, 19*(4), 275–83.

hooks, b. (2013). *Writing beyond race: Living theory and practice*. Taylor & Francis.

hooks, b. (2015). *Talking back: Thinking feminist, thinking black*. Routledge.

hooks, b. (2018). *All about love: New visions*. William Morrow.

Ladson-Billings, G. (2006). From the achievement gap to the education debt: Understanding achievement in U.S. schools. *Educational Researcher, 35*(7), 3–12.

Langford, R., Di Santo, A., Valeo, A., Underwood, K., & Lenis, A. (2018). The innovation of Ontario full-day kindergarten educator teams: Have they reproduced the split systems of care and education? *Gender and Education, 30*(5), 569–86.

Lewis, A., Diamond, J. B., & Forman, T. A. (2015). Conundrums of integration: Desegregation in the context of racialized hierarchy. *Sociology of Race and Ethnicity, 1*(1), 22–36.

Lorde, A. (1984). *Sister outsider: Essays and speeches by Audre Lorde*. Crossing Press.

Love, B. (2020). *We want to do more than survive: Abolitionist teaching and the pursuit of educational freedom*. Beacon Press.

Maparyan, L. (2012). *The womanist idea*. Routledge.

McKittrick, K. (2021). *Dear science and other stories*. Duke University Press.

Moraga, C. & Anzaldúa, G. (1981). *This bridge called my back: Writings by radical women of color*. Persephone Press.

Muhammad, G. E. & Haddix, M. (2016). Centering Black girls' literacies: A review of literature on the multiple ways of knowing of Black girls. *English Education, 48*(4), 299–336.

Núñez, X. P. (2020). Performing the (religious) educator's vocation: Becoming the 'good' early childhood practitioner in Chile. *Gender and Education, 32*(8), 1072–89.

Nxumalo, F. (2019). *Decolonizing place in early childhood education*. Routledge.

Nxumalo, F. (2020). Situating Indigenous and Black childhoods in the anthropocene. In A. Cutter-Mackenzie-Knowles, K. Malone, & E. Barratt Hacking (Eds.), *Research handbook on childhood nature* (pp. 535–56). Springer.

Nyong'o, T. (2014). Unburdening representation. *The Black Scholar, 44*(2), 70–80.

Pérez, M. S. (2019). Dismantling racialized discourses in early childhood education and care: A revolution towards reframing the field. In F. Nxumalo & C. P. Brown (Eds.), *Disrupting and countering deficits in early childhood education* (pp. 20–36). Routledge.

Seeding Sovereignty. (2021, May 3). *Capitalism media toolkit* [Instagram Post]. Retrieved 8 August 2021, from: https://www.instagram.com/p/COgjLBdrrXx/?utm_source=ig_web_copy_link

Sharpe, C. (2016). *In the wake: On Blackness and being*. Duke University Press.

Strong-Leek, L. (1999). Inverting the institutions: Ama Ata Aidoo's no sweetness here and deconstructive theory. In A. U. Azodo & G. Wilentz (Eds.), *Emerging perspectives on Ama Ata Aidoo* (pp. 145–55). Africa World Press.

Tuck, E. & Yang, K. W. (2012). Decolonization is not a metaphor. *Decolonization: Indigeneity, Education & Society, 1*(1), 1–40.

Walker, A. (1983). *In search of our mothers' gardens : Womanist prose* (1st ed.). Harcourt Brace Jovanovich.

Walton, Q. L. & Boone, C. (2019). Voices unheard: An intersectional approach to understanding depression among middle-class black women. *Women & Therapy, 42*(3–4), 301–19.

Additional Authors Who Inspired Our Thinking

Abu El-Haj, T. R. (2007). 'I was born here, but my home, it's not here': Educating for democratic citizenship in an era of transnational migration and global conflict. *Harvard Educational Review, 77*(3), 285–316.

Kelley, R. D. G. (1993). 'We are not what we seem': Rethinking Black working-class opposition in the Jim Crow south. *The Journal of American History, 80*(1), 75.

Lipsitz, G. (1995). *A life in the struggle: Ivory Perry and the culture of opposition* (Vol. 79). Temple University Press.

7

Decolonizing Feminisms: Provocations for Early Childhood Educators in Aotearoa/New Zealand

Jenny Ritchie

Decolonizing Feminisms as Part of a Wider Project of Social, Cultural and Ecological justice

In this chapter, a range of decolonizing feminisms are canvassed, situating feminist movement within a wider project of social, cultural and ecological justice. Decolonizing feminisms are positioned as tools for challenging the patriarchal, colonial, hyper-capitalist, neoliberal exploitation of not only women (including those working in the early childhood education sector which is predominately staffed by women), but also of Indigenous people, children, those people who are socio-economically marginalized, and those who face challenges caused by the way our society ignores their disabilities. Overarching all of these oppressions and now imperilling all of humanity is the jeopardy caused by human exploitation of the planet and its biodiversity in the current Anthropocene epoch. Within this context, I provide an overview of how a range of key feminist thinkers have influenced my own praxis as an early childhood educator, teacher educator and scholar.

Exploration of the oppression of women, including those in the early childhood education sector, cannot sit outside consideration of wider social forces and constructs of social hierarchies and positionings. Gaile Cannella and Radhika Viruru (2004) consider that all Western knowledges and discourses are imbued with colonial assumptions of entitlement (of white, male and monied privilege) while othering those who are discounted (women, children, Indigenous people, people of colour, working-class people). And, of course, our planet Earth is part of the domain exploited by those in power. This is illustrated in the Enlightenment paradigm of the 'Great Chain of Being' which positioned 'God at the apex followed by archangels and angels, divine kings, the aristocracy and successive ranks of human beings, from "civilised" to savage', followed by animals, plants and minerals and the earth in descending order' (Salmond, 2017, p. 35). As Anne Salmond (2017) explains:

> Those at the top of the Great Chain exercised power and authority over those lower down, who in turn were required to offer up deference and tribute. In this cosmic model, men ruled over women and children, free men over slaves, and 'civilised' people over 'barbarians' and 'savages'.
>
> (pp. 35–6)

Indigenous story-teller Thomas King (2005) highlights how the stories we tell are fundamental to our worldviews. He contrasts Indigenous creation stories with that of Genesis, fundamental to the Christian doctrine, writing that 'the elements in Genesis create a particular universe governed by a series of hierarchies – God, man, animals, plants – that celebrate good government, while in our Native story, the universe is governed by a series of co-operations' (King, 2005, p. 23).

As the recent report of the Intergovernmental Panel on Climate Change (2021) has reinforced, education has a key role in supporting societies to transition to sustainable ways of living that no longer contribute to the increasingly urgent climate crisis through a focus on action for climate empowerment (United Nations Framework Convention on Climate Change, 2021). Early childhood education is fundamentally important in this regard, as the early years of learning establish foundational dispositions, such as an ethic of care for oneself, others, and the environment (Ritchie, Duhn, Rau & Craw, 2010). As will be outlined in a later section, ecofeminist analysis enables critique of the pervasiveness of discourses and practices that are currently contributing to the convergent crises of the climate emergency, the Covid-19 pandemic, and the recognition of the ongoing, Covid-exacerbated legacies of racism in the form of slavery and colonization. The late Australian critical environmental scholar Val Plumwood offered a prescient critique when she ended the acknowledgements to her (1993/2003) book, *Feminism and the mastery of nature*, with this quote from bell hooks (1989):

> Feminism, as liberation struggle, must exist apart from and as a part of the larger struggle to eradicate domination in all forms. We must understand that

patriarchal domination shares an ideological foundation with racism and other forms of group oppression, that there is no hope that it can be eradicated while these systems remain intact.

(p. 22, as cited in Plumwood, 1993/2003, p. x)

Māori Activism, Mana Wāhine

In Aotearoa[1] Māori women's theorizing has been at the forefront of counter-colonial activism and heavily influential in furthering the project of Māori language revitalization, for example, through the establishment of kōhanga reo, a Māori immersion early childhood language movement. This activism, in turn, heavily influenced through the National Te Kōhanga Reo Trust appointed writers Tilly and Tamati Reedy, the first Aotearoa early childhood curriculum, *Te Whāriki. He whāriki mātauranga mō ngā mokopuna o Aotearoa* (Ministry of Education, 1996). Māori women activist visionaries such as Hilda Halkyard (1982), Donna Awatere (1984), Ripeka Evans (1994), Ani Mikaere (1994, 2011) and Linda Tuhiwai Smith (Smith, 1999/2012, 2019) responded to the rise of the Western feminist movement in the 1970s with critique of many of the assumptions that these feminists were making, often from a privileged white middle-class perspective, including the presumption of the 'white women's assumption that feminism is for all' (Jenkins & Pihama, 2001, p. 299).

As Kuni Jenkins explained, whilst Pākehā feminists focused on male oppression, Māori women's realities were in solidarity with the Māori collective inclusive of men. Jenkins states: 'What the feminist discourse was dealing with was the oppression of women by men'. So that's the gender struggle. What was wrong with the feminist struggle is that they were actually fighting Pakeha men and then they expected Māori women to join and fight Māori men. Both Donna Awatere and Ripeka Evans said that our women's struggle is not against Māori men because they are more oppressed than Māori women (Jenkins & Pihama, 2001, p. 300).

For Māori women, their primary identity was to their family and tribal affiliations through their *whakapapa*, or genealogical ties. Linda Tuhiwai Smith (2019) explained that, 'one of the difficulties in subsuming our struggle as Māori women under existing feminist analyses is that we deny the centrality of our identity and the specific historical and cultural realities which we endure' (p. 41). The struggle for Māori women was of necessity primarily focused on the forces of colonization which through the imposition of patriarchal practices had impacted severely on Māori women and children by denying their mana wāhine (power, prestige, esteem, authority as Māori women). This is not to assume that Māori women had quietly acceded to these impacts as Simmonds (2011) explains:

> Māori, in fact indigenous peoples the world over, have never merely been passive recipients of 'colonisation' and have always engaged in the struggle over how to live in the multiple worlds created by our colonial history. Indeed, Māori women have been involved in the struggle to retain and regain their sense of self from the very moment colonial discourses and hierarchies reached our shores. Mana wahine, as an extension of Kaupapa Māori [Māori political and educational philosophy] is located in the wider indigenous struggle that has emerged because 'we' were unwilling to continue to try and 'find' ourselves in the words, texts and images of others.
>
> (p. 13)

In 1993, concerned about the impacts of colonization on their people as exemplified, for example, in the negative health statistics of Māori women,[2] a group of Māori women leaders took an urgent claim to the Waitangi Tribunal, which was a Crown initiative to enable historical treaty grievances to be heard and provide recommendations for redress. Legal scholar Ani Mikaere (1994) explained that 'colonisation is not a finite process; for Māori, there has been no end to it. It is not simply part of our recent past, nor does it merely inform our present. Colonisation is our present' (p. 142). The claim intended to establish that successive governments had failed to uphold the status of Māori women as had been promised in Article Two of the 1840 Tiriti o Waitangi, the treaty that had allowed for British colonization of Aotearoa. In early 2021, almost three decades since the original claim was lodged, the Mana Wāhine WAI 381 pre-hearing finally began, with one of the original claimant Ripeka Evans highlighting 'the colonial frame in which the colonising culture that looked to men as leaders and chiefs – this caused the negation of wāhine Māori mana motuhake and rangatiratanga [Māori women's authority and self-determination] over their whenua [lands], taonga [everything of value], mātauranga [Māori knowledge], hearts, bodies, minds and beliefs' (as cited in Dunlop, 2021, para. 13).

In 1981, out of political expedience and in defiance of international condemnation of the extremely repressive South African apartheid system, the New Zealand government allowed the South African Springbok rugby team to tour New Zealand. Māori women, including Donna Awatere, Ripeka Evans and Mereana Pitman MZMN (Laing, 2019) were at the forefront of activism during the widespread protests, in which many Pākehā New Zealanders marched against the tour. These wāhine toa (Māori women leaders) strategized that this was an opportunity to leverage change from Pākehā New Zealanders by challenging us to recognize that we also needed to address racism in our own country (Hana Jackson, in Awatere, 1982b; Evans, 1982). This was a provocation that, as a convicted Springbok tour protestor, I have continued to address in my teaching and research.

Māori women's activism was evident in service of education and the revitalization of the Māori language as seen in the instigation of the kōhanga reo movement, and in advocacy for the return of their lands (Hana Jackson, in Awatere, 1982b; Halkyard et al., 1982). As Hilda Halkyard explained, 'When we fight for land, we fight for ourselves, we fight for our identity, we fight for what rightfully belongs to Māori people. It is us' (as cited in Halkyard et al., 1982, p. 32).

As a kindergarten teacher in the 1980s in predominately Māori communities, this activism was salient for me. Educational psychologist Donna Awatere (1982a) explained in her powerful 'Māori Sovereignty' analysis:

> The education system is the major gate which keeps the Maori out. There is an invisible sign over every kindergarten, playcentre, school, and university. That sign reads: 'Maori Keep Out: For White Use Only'. White people can't see this sign, you have to identify or be identified as a Maori before you can see it. Kindergartens are the first educational gate. A bastion of white power. Kindergartens have frightened Māori people off pre-school education. As He Huarahi, the report on Maori education pointed out, the percentages of Māori children getting pre-school education is way below that of whites. In Otara, kindergartens have falling rolls. In an area chock full of pre-schoolers. Māori parents, in particular, won't take their children there, not because they don't want to, but because kindergartens in particular and play centres to a lesser extent don't meet their needs. One could tell kindergartens to take down the sign warning Maoris to keep away, but the Kindergarten Association won't listen. As far as they are concerned, because they can't see the sign, it doesn't exist.
>
> (p. 41)

This quote from Donna Awatere remains a painful illumination of the ways that the monocultural colonial education system in Aotearoa continued to exclude Māori families. This resonated deeply with my own experiences as a kindergarten teacher, when many Māori families were not comfortable to enter the kindergarten grounds. In responding to the racism, I experienced from colleagues in the kindergarten arena in the 1980s, I was privileged in receiving support from Rangimārie Rose Pere (1983, 1988, 1991), who was then a Māori education advisor for the local Education Board. Rose Pere's work has provided significant understandings of *te ao* Māori (a Māori worldview) which have been hugely influential in Aotearoa as we struggle to address the racism inherent in our colonial education system.

Theorizing by North American Black and Latinx Feminists

I have been also profoundly influenced by the feminist analyses of US women writers such as Audre Lorde (2017), bell hooks (1984, 1989) and Gloria Anzaldúa (1987, 2009, 2015). As with the Māori scholarship discussed above, these writers complexified the over-simplified analysis of patriarchy by their white Western feminist contemporaries, adding texture to understandings of the multi-layered oppressions of those working in the early childhood sector in Aotearoa. Gloria Anzaldúa shared an understanding of collectivist inter-relationality that includes a spiritual, healing agenda:

> We each are our sisters' and brothers' keepers; no one is an island or has ever been. Every person, animal, plant, stone is interconnected in life and death symbiosis. We are each responsible for what is happening down the street, south of the border or across the sea. And those of us who have more of anything – more brains, more physical strength, more political power, more money, or more spiritual energies – must give or exchange with those who don't have these energies but may have other things to give. It is the responsibility of some of us who tap the vast source of spiritual/political energies to heal others, to put down a drawbridge; at the same time we must depend more and more on our own sources for survival.
>
> (Anzaldúa, 2015, p. xxviii)

In her transformational feminist envisioning, Anzaldúa (2002) used the term 'nepantla'. She explains how this term provokes movement beyond conventional boundaries, 'to theorize liminality and to talk about those who facilitate passages between worlds, whom I've named nepantla. I associate nepantla with states of mind that question old ideas and beliefs, acquire new perspectives, change worldviews, and shift from one world to another' (Anzaldúa, 2002, p. 1). This construct has relevance for those teaching and researching in the early childhood sector, as we seek to challenge legacies of historical hierarchical discourses such as colonization. Anzaldúa also used the metaphor of bridges to encourage movement beyond conventional constraints:

Bridges are thresholds to other realities, archetypal, primal symbols of shifting consciousness. They are passageways, conduits, and connectors that connote transitioning, crossing borders, and changing perspectives. Bridges span liminal (threshold) spaces between worlds, spaces I call nepantla a Nahuatl word meaning tierra entre medio. Transformations occur in this in-between space, an unstable, unpredictable, precarious, always-in-transition space, lacking clear boundaries.... I think of how feminist ideas and movements are attached, called unnatural by the ruling powers, when in fact they are ideas whose time has come, ideas as relentless as the waves carving and later eroding stone arches. Change is inevitable, no bridge lasts forever.

(Anzaldúa, 2002, p. 1)

As early childhood educators and scholars, we can take inspiration from such metaphors, which provide a source of strength and vision to accompany our decolonizing analysis and action.

In her book, *Feminist Theory: From Margin to Center*, bell hooks (1984) critiqued Betty Friedan's (1963) book, *Feminine Mystique*, for its blindness to the white privilege that it exemplified in describing the 'one-dimensional' dilemma of well-educated white middle-class married, heterosexual bored housewives, portraying an embarrassing ignorance of racism and social class issues (hooks, 1984, p. 3). hooks (1984) wrote further: 'privileged feminists have largely been unable to speak to, with, and for diverse groups of women because they either do not understand fully the inter-relatedness of sex, race and class oppression or refuse to take this inter-relatedness seriously' (p. 14). In response, hooks (1984) considered Black women's analyses as vital in contributing to the collective responsibility of 'liberatory feminist theory and praxis' (p. 15). A key challenge therefore for those who educate future early childhood teachers in Aotearoa (and elsewhere) is to foster a critical consciousness of the intersectionality of racism, feminism, and other oppressive ideologies (Mikuska & Lyndon, 2021).

Since the late 1980s, I have run workshops for early childhood teaching students, the wider early childhood education sector, and groups from the health sector. These focus on commitments to Māori stated in the 1840 Tiriti o Waitangi that allowed for British colonization, and understanding the racism underpinning the colonial history of Aotearoa which disregarded these obligations. Such work aligns with a commitment of our first early childhood curriculum, *Te Whāriki*, which stated that 'The early childhood curriculum actively contributes towards countering racism and other forms of prejudice' (Ministry of Education, 1996, p. 18). It also responds to hooks' (1984) challenge to white women to critique the pervasiveness of the impacts of the ideology of white supremacy and racist socialization on their attitudes and behaviour. hooks also identified that men should play a key role as 'comrades' in this anti-racist and anti-sexist struggle:

> After hundreds of years of anti-racist struggle, more than ever before non-white people are currently calling attention to the primary role white people must play in anti-racist struggle. The same is true of the struggle to eradicate sexism – men have a primary role to play ... in the area of exposing, confronting, opposing and transforming the sexism of their male peers.
>
> (hooks, 1984, p. 81)

hooks (1984) further calls for community-based childcare, pointing out that this is often the case in Black and Indigenous communities where care for children is not seen as the sole domain of the mother as is so very often still the case within a Western 'nuclear' family construct. Instead, care of young children is shared by women and men and across generations, horizontally as well as vertically, aunts and uncles, cousins and grandparents of both genders, the latter providing intergenerational transmission of ancestral knowledges. It is timely that we take inspiration from such traditional modes of shared responsibility and care. Instead of individualized for-profit atomized services, we might organize for provision that offers localized communities of care, valuing contributions from elders and family members, in de-institutionalized not-for-profit models of community-based care.

hooks' later work focuses on re-centring community *and* love as fundamental educational aspirations (hooks, 2000, 2003). She quotes Paulo Freire in naming love as foundational for human inter-relationships:

> Dialogue cannot exist, however, in the absence of a profound love for the world and for people. The naming of the world, which is an act of creation and re-creation, is not possible if it is not infused with love. Love is at the same time the foundation of dialogue and dialogue itself. It is thus necessarily the task of responsible Subjects and cannot exist in a relation of domination. Domination reveals the pathology of love: sadism in the dominator and masochism in the dominated. Because love is an act of courage, not of fear, love is commitment to others. No matter where the oppressed are found, the act of love is commitment to their cause – the cause of liberation. And this commitment, because it is loving, is dialogical.
>
> (Freire, 1972, as cited in hooks, 1984, p. 161)

The expectation that early childhood teachers foster te ngākau aroha, the loving heart, is prominent in the 'refreshed' version of *Te Whāriki* (New Zealand Ministry of Education, 2017). Dialogical pedagogies that resonate a commitment to love for ourselves, others and the environment and generate critical consciousness are critical tools for challenging the hegemonic power dominant paradigm of the 'racial, political economic, social, epistemological, linguistic, and gendered hierarchical orders' imposed through globalized coloniality and neoliberalism (Richardson, 2020, pp. 3–4).

Another important US feminist theorist is Audre Lorde (2017). Her work aligns with that of hooks in calling for recognition of emotions as a central platform of decolonizing feminisms. In her 1985 essay, *Poetry is not a luxury,* she called for a vision that moved away from Western cognitivism, stating that:

> as we become more in touch with our own ancient, black, non-european view of living as a situation to be experienced and interacted with, we learn more and more to cherish our feelings, and to respect those hidden sources of our power from where true knowledge and, therefore, lasting action comes.
>
> (Lorde, 2017, p. 2)

Audre Lorde (2017) urged recognition of feelings and of difference as sources of creativity, encouraging women who were excluded from conformist society to stand tall and in solidarity:

> It is learning how to stand alone, unpopular, and sometimes reviled, and how to make common cause with those other identified as outside the structures, in order to define and seek a world in which we can all flourish. It is learning how to take our differences and make them strengths. For the master's tools will never dismantle the master's house. They may allow us temporarily to beat him at his own game, but they will never enable us to bring about genuine change. And this fact is only threatening to those women who still define the master's house as their only source of support.
>
> (pp. 18–19)

This metaphor of dismantling the (white, Western) master's house has had huge resonance across time and space. Lorde (2017) called for a visionary feminist collective solidarity that integrated personal and political commitment:

> In a world of possibility for us all, our personal visions help lay the groundwork for political action. The failure of the academic feminists to recognize difference as a crucial strength is a failure to reach beyond the first patriarchal lesson. Divide and conquer, in our world, must become define and empower.
>
> (p. 19)

The national and global dominance of oppressive exploitative economic, industrial and technological structures have led to the current convergent crises of the climate emergency, diminishing biodiversity and the global pandemic, along with exacerbated social injustice. Whilst the onslaught of these nested crises can seem monolithic, as educators we can draw hope and inspiration from the wisdom of such feminist elders to generate 'new conditions of possibility' for ourselves, the children and the families with whom we work (Kaukko et al., 2021, p. 1).

Early Childhood Decolonizing Feminisms

In this section, I discuss scholars whose writings on feminisms and decolonizing early childhood have significantly influenced my own work. Training in childcare in the 1970s, I had questioned the uncritiqued assumptions of universalized Western male-dominated child development theory such as Piaget's stages of cognitive development and Kohlberg's categories of moral development. This led me to explore the work of Carol Gilligan (1982) and later that of Nel Noddings (1994) which provided alternative, feminist conceptualizations privileging an ethic of care over cognitivist developmentalist goals. Such theorizing confirmed my tendency towards scepticism regarding the 'appropriateness' of child development theory. This dominant early childhood discourse has been critiqued for its imposition of universalized narrowly defined Western norms, which then stigmatize children and families who do not reflect these expectations (Fleer, 1995; Genishi, 1994; Lubeck, 1994; MacNaughton, 1995; Ritchie, 2019). Furthermore, these models position the teacher as the expert, reflecting a hierarchical authoritarian model which is the cornerstone of white patriarchal paradigms dominant not only within families and schools, but also underpinning the historical and ongoing colonization of Indigenous peoples.

The in-depth qualitative research of Bronwyn Davies and colleagues (Davies, 1989; Fernie, Davies, Kantor & McMurray, 1993) confirmed for me the value of multiple researcher lenses, including feminist poststructural analysis, to understand the ways in which young children negotiate gendered positionings in early childhood classrooms. Davies (1989, p. 4) pointed out that 'children are defined as *other* to adults in much the same way that women are other to men'. She explained that 'children learn to see and understand in terms of the multiple positionings and forms of discourse that are available to them [and] learn the forms of desire and of power and powerlessness that are embedded in and made possible by the various discursive practices through which they position themselves' (p. 4). Children's experiences and experimentation with multiple, fluid and contradictory possible ways of being are in tension with the 'liberal humanist concept of the person as fixed and unitary' that are the Western societal expectation (Davies, 1989, p. 140). Supporting children to critically grapple with the complexities of discourses and positionings can foster decolonizing dispositions.

The work of Glenda MacNaughton (1993) extended this analysis of gender to consider the intersection of racialized/gendered children's play. In her 1993 study in Melbourne, Australia, the role of 'Mother' in family play was a powerful positioning for a white girl, Shelley, who was able to draw on it to continually dominate her two Black Afro-Caribbean Australian female classmates, Natalie and Tanya:

> Shelley, as 'mum' directly benefited from her position of power in all of the play observed – her storylines and her desires were privileged. Thus in these specific domestic play episodes distinctly different power effects were evident for each child involved. These different power effects were racially distributed. The net result of this was that being 'mum' enabled Shelley to set policy, allocate resources and define what the acceptable ways of being and acting were in the children's play society.
>
> (MacNaughton, 1993, p. 14)

Interestingly, when for many years I showed early childhood teacher education students a clip from a US video which depicted a white girl fiercely dominating Black children in the family corner, and then asked them to tell me what they thought was going on, white students were unable to identify racism as a dynamic underpinning the white girl's behaviour. This points to the invisibility of racism to those who have yet to question the privilege of whiteness.

The analysis of Valerie Walkerdine (1993) highlighted the way that gendered discourses disempower early childhood teachers in their capacity to respond to inappropriate sexist harassment of girls and teachers by young boys. Walkerdine (1993) explained the exchanges she had observed:

> The resistance of the boys to their female teacher can be understood in terms both of their assertion of their difference from her and their seizing of power through constituting her as the powerless object of sexist discourse. Although they are not physically grown men they can take the positions of men through language and in doing so gain power which has material effects. Their power is gained by refusing to be constituted as the powerless objects in her discourse

and recasting her as the powerless object of theirs. In their discourse she is constituted as 'woman as sex-object' and as that object she is rendered as the powerless object of their oppression. Of course, she has not in a sense ceased to be a teacher, but what is important is that she has ceased to signify as one: she has been made to signify as the powerless object of male sexual discourse. The boys' resistance takes the form of a seizure of power in discourse such that despite their institutional positions they achieve power in this instance.

(p. 209)

The progressive liberal pedagogy of these teachers meant that they consider the behaviour of the boys as a 'natural' expression of their emotions, and therefore they decline to challenge it. As noted above, children commonly assume the positionality of the role of 'Mother' in order to control the play, this positioning conferring some dominance in the domestic sphere (Fernie et al., 1993; Walkerdine, 1993).

The significant work of Gaile Cannella and Radhika Viruru (Cannella, 1997, 1999, 2000; Cannella & Viruru, 2004; Viruru, 2000) focused on deconstructing the discursive influence of the 'quintessential', developing individual male Western child, opening up possibilities for recognition of multiple, culturally and historically located paradigms for understanding the positioning of children, and of the predominately female early childhood education workforce. Gaile Cannella's words from 1997 still resonate:

> Early childhood educators continue to advocate for recognition and respect for younger human beings and the work of those who share their lives. We all recognise that the general public and even those in other fields of education at times refer to work with young children as 'babysitting' or 'play'.
>
> (Cannella, 1997, p. 137)

Cannella (1997) provided insights into the ways the field of early childhood education in the West reflected deeply embedded patriarchal power relations that result in a feminized profession of 'good mothers' and that perpetuate dominant discourses of 'professional truths' resulting in the silencing, power and control over young children, disguised in liberal discourses of free play. She highlights the dilemma of early childhood professionals, whereby in seeking to gain status and respect, conformity to external pressures and discourses that re-perpetuate hierarchies of oppression of both women and younger human beings is necessary.

> Our pursuit of professionalism as a way of gaining respect and empowering the field may actually result in a false empowerment. In our attempts to improve the lives of younger human beings, we may actually perpetuate power over them and ourselves. We may even generate the desire and expectation to be told what to do and how to do it. We may create the wish to be regulated, to need to judge ourselves and to make judgements through standards created by others.
>
> (Cannella, 1997, p. 155)

It is therefore key that early childhood education resists pressures to situate teachers, children and families as educational problems, rather than recognizing the wider societal structures and conditions that impose these discourses (Cannella, 1997).

In their later work, Cannella and Viruru (2004) critique the economic oppression of neocolonial, neoliberal globalized markets that 'have been built on the backs of slaves, women, poor people' and immigrant labour (p. 18). They consider how postcolonial critique can assist in addressing ongoing oppressive systems, acknowledging that:

> As feminists, our bias is that Western thought is grounded in patriarchy. The logic of Enlightenment/modernism that has been forced on the colonized is a linear, male-constructed form of reason and hierarchical power that reinforces the notion that one group is superior to another.
>
> (Cannella & Viruru, 2004, p. 21)

They caution that even when patriarchy is not directly referenced in their work, 'the assumptions of patriarchal discourse and practice are prevalent throughout colonialism and imperialism' (Cannella & Viruru, 2004, p. 21). Cannella and Viruru consider how the pursuit of 'social transformation for liberation', involving 'critical specific activism as collective transformational power' requires challenging 'the will to truth and power that legitimizes control for particular privileged peoples' and the marginalization of those who are 'othered' (pp. 148–9). Integral to this project of social transformation in our work as early childhood teachers and teacher educators is to model and foster an anti-oppressive critical disposition that challenges such power constructions through 'political, decolonialist actions' determined by children and young people in consultation with their communities (Cannella & Viruru, 2004, p. 155). In this way, early childhood educators can work to decolonize oppressive power structures within our spheres of influence.

Ecofeminisms

As indicated in the opening section of this chapter, decolonizing feminisms must take account of the ways in which the ongoing patriarchal, hyper-capitalist hegemony is causing inestimable damage to humans along with earth's biodiversity, through its exploitative, extractive treatment of both people and planet. Early childhood educators have an important role to play in fostering in young children a disposition of an ethic of care for the environment. A number of visionary ecofeminists have provided valuable critique in this regard. Val Plumwood (2002) presciently highlighted the failure of the global economic and political systems to react to the ecological crisis that was already apparent at that time. Her critique included the reliance on the construct of 'sustainability' which she felt obscured the seriousness of the situation. She wrote in her introduction that it was evident that a culture that had set in motion and normalized 'massive processes of biospheric degradation' and then failed to address this situation, could 'not hope to survive for very long' (Plumwood, 2002, p. 1). Plumwood (2018) explained that 'Surviving the environmental crisis thus presents the dominant culture with two linked historic projects of cultural transformation: the task of situating the human in ecological terms and the task of situating the more-than-human in ethical and cultural terms' (p. 101).

To address the ecological crisis, Plumwood (2006) identified a range of 'counter-hegemonic stances' that can maximize both the ethical sensitivities of early childhood care and education communities to other members of our ecological communities as well as our 'openness to their agency' (Plumwood, 2006, p. 194). These include the need for humans to recognize our interdependence with/in our environments and to foster a more inclusive inter-species ethic; to counter the dualistic construction of human/nature difference; to adopt a non-hierarchical conception of more-than-human difference; to foster openness and listening to the more-than-human other as an intentional and communicative being; as well as attend to the other's complexity whilst recognizing the limitations of our knowledge (p. 194). In synergy with the calls of hooks and Freire's for dialogue, Plumwood calls for a cultural shift away from human-centric monological and dualistic relationships to a 'spirituality with place' (p. 231). Such ecofeminist ethics can assist us in decolonizing our relationships with/in the more-than-human realm, through modelling such commitments in early childhood services and fostering dispositions of care in the young children with whom we engage (Alcock & Ritchie, 2018).

To Conclude

This chapter has traversed a range of feminisms that contribute to a weaving together of counter-hegemonies that can serve in the cultural shift of decolonizing current monolithic Western, white, neoliberal political and economic structures. As we become aware of the damage that these systems have imposed on our planet's capacities to sustain life, these alternative conceptualizations require our urgent attention. Early childhood care and education settings are uniquely positioned to offer significant learning opportunities for both young children and their families. Dispositions established in these early years may provide a platform for ongoing commitments and influence that extends well beyond the experiences provided during attendance at an early childhood setting. In Aotearoa, we are currently piloting a nationwide programme, Te Hurihanganui (Ministry of Education, 2021). The aim is an education system-wide antiracist transformation, in effect a counter-colonial initiative. One of the key pou (pillars) of this programme is critical consciousness, explained as follows: 'Building critical consciousness means reflecting critically on the imbalance of power and resources in society, and taking anti-oppressive action to do something about it for the better' (Ministry of Education, 2021, section four). The decolonizing analyses of the feminist theorists as outlined in this chapter serve as inspiration for such endeavours.

Notes

1 Aotearoa is a Māori term for New Zealand. Whilst highly skilled Polynesian navigators had explored the Pacific and eventually settled these south Pacific islands from around 1300 CE (Anderson, 2016), the name 'New Zealand' resulted from the later 'discovery' of these lands by Dutch explorer Abel Tasman in 1642 CE. It is thus a problematic colonialist emblem.

2 High death rates for Māori women are seen in the following quote: 'Some of the negative indicators ... include the lung cancer death rate (3.6 times higher for Māori women than for non-Māori women), the likelihood of death from coronary heart disease (3.5 times higher for Māori women in the 25–44 year age group than for non-Māori women in that age group) and the likelihood of death from respiratory disease (4.6 times higher for Māori women in the 25–44 year age group than for non-Māori women)' (Mikaere, 1994, pp. 143–4).

References

Alcock, S. & Ritchie, J. (2018). Early childhood education in the outdoors in Aotearoa New Zealand. *Journal of Outdoor and Environmental Education, 21*(1), 77–88. Doi: 10.1007/s42322-017-0009-y

Anderson, A. (2016). *The first migration: Māori origins 3000BC – AD1450*. Bridget Williams Books.

Anzaldúa, G. (1987). *Borderlands. La frontera. The new mestiza*. Spinsters | Aunt Lute.

Anzaldúa, G. (2002). Preface. (Un)natural bridges, (Un)safe spaces. In G. E. Anzaldúa & A. Keating (Eds.), *This bridge we call home. Radical visions for transformation* (pp. 1–5). Routledge.

Anzaldúa, G. (2009). Let us be the healing of the wound. The Coyolxauhqui imperative – la sombra y el sueño. In A. Keating (Ed.), *The Gloria Anzaldúa reader* (pp. 303–17). Duke University Press.

Anzaldúa, G. (2015). Acts of healing. In C. Moraga & G. Anzaldúa (Eds.), *This bridge called my back. Writings by radical women of color* (4th ed., pp. xxvii–xxviii). State University of New York Press.

Awatere, D. (1982a). Donna Awatere on Māori sovereignty (part 1). *Broadsheet. New Zealand Feminist Magazine* (100), 38–42.

Awatere, D. (1982b). Wahine ma, korerotia – Hana Jackson. *Broadsheet. New Zealand Feminist Magazine* (101), 24–5.

Awatere, D. (1984). *Maori sovereignty*. Broadsheet.

Cannella, G. S. (1997). *Deconstructing early childhood education: Social justice and revolution*. Peter Lang.

Cannella, G. S. (1999). The scientific discourse of education: Predetermining the lives of others – Foucault, education, and children. *Contemporary Issues in Early Childhood, 1*(1), 36–44.

Cannella, G. S. (2000). Critical and feminist reconstructions of early childhood education: Continuing the conversation. *Contemporary Issues in Early Childhood, 1*(2), 215–21.

Cannella, G. S., & Viruru, R. (2004). *Childhood and postcolonization. Power, education and contemporary practice*. RoutledgeFalmer.

Davies, B. (1989). *Frogs and snails and feminist tails. Preschool children and gender*. Allen & Unwin.

Dunlop, M. (2021). Mana wāhine inquiry: Original claimant Ripeka Evans gives evidence. https://www.rnz.co.nz/news/te-manu-korihi/435730/mana-wahine-inquiry-original-claimant-ripeka-evans-gives-evidence

Evans, R. (1982). Rebecca Evans. *Broadsheet. New Zealand Feminist Magazine* (103), 12–17.

Evans, R. (1994). The negation of powerlessness: Maori feminism, a perspective. *Hecate: An Interdisciplinary Journal of Women's Liberation, 20*(2), 53–65.

Fernie, D., Davies, E., Kantor, B. R., & McMurray, P. (1993). Becoming a person in the preschool: Creating integrated gender, school culture, and peer culture positionings. *Qualitative Studies in Education*, 6(2), 95–110.

Fleer, M. (Ed.) (1995). *DAP centrism: Challenging developmentally appropriate practice.* Australian Early Childhood Association.

Friedan, B. (1963). *The feminine mystique.* Norton.

Genishi, C., Dyson, Anne Haas, & Fassler, Rebekah (1994). Language and diversity in early childhood: Whose voice is appropriate? In B. Mallory & R. New (Eds.), *Diversity and developmentally appropriate practice* (pp. 250-68). Teachers College Press.

Gilligan, C. (1982). *In a different voice: Psychological theory and women's development.* Harvard University Press.

Halkyard, H., Hawke, R., & Hawke, S. (1982). Women of the land. Reni and Sharon Hawke interviewed by Hilda Harawera. *Broadsheet. New Zealand Feminist Magazine* (101), 32–4.

Hooks, b. (1984). *Feminist theory: From margin to center.* South End Press.

hooks, b. (1989). *Talking back: Thinking feminist, thinking black.* South End Press.

hooks, b. (2000). *All about love. New visions.* Harper Collins.

hooks, b. (2003). *Teaching community. A pedagogy of hope.* Routledge.

Intergovernmental Panel on Climate Change. (2021). AR6 climate change 2021: The physical science basis. https://www.ipcc.ch/report/ar6/wg1/

Jenkins, K., & Pihama, L. (2001). Matauranga wahine: Teaching Maori women's knowledge alongside feminism. *Feminism & Psychology*, 11(3), 292–303.

Kaukko, M., Kemmis, S., Heikkinen, H. L. T., Kiilakoski, T., & Haswell, N. (2021). Learning to survive amidst nested crises: Can the coronavirus pandemic help US change educational practices to prepare for the impending eco-crisis? *Environmental Education Research*, 1–16. Doi: 10.1080/13504622.2021.1962809

King, T. (2005). *The truth about stories. A Native narrative.* University of Minnesota Press.

Laing, D. (2019). Mereana Pitman MNZM – Long campaign recognised, *NZ Herald.* https://www.nzherald.co.nz/hawkes-bay-today/news/mereana-pitman-mnzm-long-campaign-recognised/QWRULNSTYEBKRAGJNFXM7P4JOY/

Lorde, A. (2017). *The master's tools will never dismantle the master's house.* Penguin Random House.

Lubeck, S. (1994). The politics of developmentally appropriate practice: Exploring issues of culture, class, and curriculum. In B. L. Mallory & R. S. New (Eds.), *Diversity & developmentally appropriate practices: Challenges for early childhood education* (pp. 17–43). Teachers College Press.

MacNaughton, G. (1993). Gender, power and racism: A case study of domestic play in early childhood. *Multicultural Teaching*, 11(3), 12–15.

MacNaughton, G. (1995). A post-structuralist analysis of learning in early childhood settings. In M. Fleer (Ed.), *DAPcentrism: Challenging developmentally appropriate practice* (pp. 35–54). Australian Early Childhood Association.

Mikaere, A. (1994). Maori women: Caught in the contradictions of colonised reality. *Waikato Law Review, 2*, 125–50.

Mikaere, A. (2011). *Colonising myths. Maori realities. He rukuruku whakaaro*. Huia Publishers and Te Tākupu, Te Wānanga o Raukawa.

Mikuska, E., & Lyndon, S. (2021). Co-constructions, co-performances and co-reflections in early years qualitative research. *Journal of Early Childhood Research*, https://journals.sagepub.com/doi/abs/10.1177/1476718X211020048

Ministry of Education. (1996). Te Whāriki. He whāriki mātauranga mō ngā mokopuna o Aotearoa: Early childhood curriculum. https://www.education.govt.nz/assets/Documents/Early-Childhood/Te-Whariki-1996.pdf

Ministry of Education. (2021). Te Hurihanganui. https://www.education.govt.nz/our-work/overall-strategies-and-policies/te-hurihanganui/

New Zealand Ministry of Education. (2017). *Te Whāriki. He whāriki mātauranga mō ngā mokopuna o Aotearoa. Early childhood curriculum*. Ministry of Education. https://www.education.govt.nz/assets/Documents/Early-Childhood/Te-Whariki-Early-Childhood-Curriculum-ENG-Web.pdf.

Noddings, N. (1994). An ethic of caring and its implications for instructional arrangements. In L. Stone (Ed.), *The education feminism reader* (pp. 171–83). Routledge.

Pere, R. R. (1983). *Ako. Concepts and learning in the Māori tradition. Working Paper No 17*. University of Waikato.

Pere, R. R. (1988). Te wheke: Whaia te maramatanga me te aroha. In S. Middleton (Ed.), *Women and education in Aotearoa* (pp. 6–19). Allen and Unwin: Port Nicholson Press.

Pere, R. R. (1991). *Te wheke*. Ao Ake.

Plumwood, V. (1993/2003). *Feminism and the mastery of nature*. Routledge.

Plumwood, V. (2002). *Environmental culture. The ecological crisis of reason*. Routledge.

Plumwood, V. (2006). *Deep sustainability as cultural work*. Contribution to CRES forum on Sustainability. https://valplumwood.wordpress.com/category/vals-papers/.

Plumwood, V. (2018). Ecofeminist analysis and the culture of ecological denial. In L. Stevens, P. Tait, & D. Varney (Eds.), *Feminist ecologies: Changing environments in the anthropocene* (pp. 97–112). Springer International Publishing.

Richardson, E. T. (2020). *Epidemic illusions. On the coloniality of global public health*. MIT Press.

Ritchie, J. (2019). A brief historical overview of curriculum in early childhood care and education. In T. Fitzgerald (Ed.), *Handbook of historical studies in education: Debates, tensions, and directions* (pp. 1–18). Springer.

Ritchie, J., Duhn, I., Rau, C., & Craw, J. (2010). *Titiro Whakamuri, Hoki Whakamua. We are the future, the present and the past: Caring for self, others and the environment in early years' teaching and learning. Final Report for the Teaching and Learning Research Initiative*. http://www.tlri.org.nz/sites/default/files/projects/9260-finalreport.pdf.

Salmond, A. (2017). *Tears of Rangi. Experiments across worlds.* Auckland University Press.

Simmonds, N. (2011). Mana wahine: Decolonising politics. *Women's Studies Journal, 25*(2), 11–25.

Smith, L. T. (1999/2012). *Decolonizing methodologies. Research and Indigenous Peoples.* Zed Books Ltd and University of Otago Press.

Smith, L. T. (2019). Māori women: Discourses, projects and mana wahine. In L. Pihama, L. T. Smith, N. Simmonds, S-P, Joeliee & K. Gabel (Eds.), *Mana Wahine Reader | A Collection of Writings 1987–1998, Volume I* (pp. 39–52). Te Kotahi Research Institute. https://www.waikato.ac.nz/__data/assets/pdf_file/0010/508879/Mana-Wahine-Volume-1.pdf.

United Nations Framework Convention on Climate Change. (2021). Action for climate empowerment guidelines. https://unfccc.int/topics/education-and-outreach/resources/ace-guidelines

Viruru, R. (2000). Subjugated knowledges as the foundation for reinvention. In Canella, Gaile S. Critical and feminist reconstructions of early childhood education: Continuing the conversation. *Contemporary Issues in Early Childhood, 1*(2), 215–21.

Walkerdine, V. (1993). Sex, power and pedagogy. In M. Alvarado, E. Buscombe, & R. Collins (Eds.), *The screen education reader.* Palgrave. https://doi.org/10.1007/978-1-349-22426-5_15

Commentary 2

Brooke Richardson and Rachel Langford

In this second group of chapters, we engage with what Flora Harmon, Erica Ritter and Radhika Viruru refer to as the third and fourth 'waves' of feminism. As pointed out by these authors, there was a conceptual shift in the third and fourth wave in which feminisms were both about attending to the differences between men and women and about grappling with the multiple, intersecting differences within the category of 'woman'. Authors in these chapters are carefully attuned to the insights offered by Black feminist scholars such as bell hooks, Audre Lorde, Patricia Hill Collins and Kimberle Crenshaw who problematized how first- and second-wave feminisms overlooked the experiences, ways of being and ways of knowing of racialized women. While chapters in the first group discuss intersections of oppression, this cluster of chapters brings closer attention to Black feminist scholars' development of the concept of intersectionality. As Hekman (2014) notes:

> It is not a stunning insight that identities are complex, that not only gender but race, sexuality and a myriad of other factors constitute identity. What intersectionality has done is to bring this insight to the fore and give it a name.
>
> (p. 145)

Paying attention to Collins' (2000) matrix of domination which makes visible the 'social organization within which intersecting oppressions originate, develop, and are contained' (p. 228) is also central to each chapter. In this commentary, we explore how the authors connect intersectionality to possibilities for the subject construction of the early childhood educator. We learned from Newberry's chapter and her language of 'womenandchildren' that it can be difficult to centre and locate alternative ways of thinking about the early childhood educator subject. With the essential shift to an intersectional lens in third- and fourth-wave feminisms, the search for the ECE subject amidst the layering of many possible ways to theorize about subjectivity and identity is even more complex. In this commentary, we begin to distil how the key themes from each chapter open up possibilities for the educator herself/themselves as well as how the concepts and ideas presented in each chapter overlap and interplay with each other.

Similar to Newberry in the last group of chapters, Harmon, Ritter and Viruru bring a clear focus to the ECE as a labouring subject while, along with Bruce and Powell, they give 'voice' to early childhood educators. Harmon, Ritter and Viruru each focuses specifically on how one feminism has been instrumental in interpreting and/or understanding their experiences as ECE subjects and now scholars. For example, Harmon describes her experiences through fourth-wave feminism which 'deconstructs gender norms, systems of power and includes racial justice as an explicit goal' (p. 85). Ritter's reflections are shaped by Black feminist thought which she feels offers the 'tools to examine intersecting gendered and racialized oppressions' (p. 87). She makes explicit how the exploited labour of Black women, rooted in slavery, continues to drive the undervaluing of Black women's care labour in the United States. Leaning on a postcolonial lens, Viruru's narrative untangles the complexities of feminism in a colonial context in which dominant ways of thinking about feminism leave little to no space for the plurality and 'cacophony' of voices that resist colonial structures. While Viruru has expressed concern about the construction of children's bodies as 'unruly and in constant need of direction' through a postcolonial perspective elsewhere (see Cannella & Viruru, 2004; Viruru, 2001), here she challenges us to consider how gendered, racialized educator bodies and beings may be subjected to the same violent, oppressive, regulatory colonial structures. In doing so, she creates the opportunity for educators to name and resist these structures – though she recognizes this is work that must be done in a movement for racial justice. What all these three authors make clear is that ongoing, active resistance to dominant, hegemonic norms in ECEC is foundational to an ECE subjectivity that engages with fourth wave, postcolonial feminism as well as Black feminist thought. In their own words, the authors articulate how these feminisms 'shine a light on the holes that we continue to fall through' (p. 93).

Nnenna Odim, Kia Rideaux and Michelle Salazar Peréz take a similar approach to structuring their chapter, developing the concept of a womanist praxis in early childhood education drawing on womanism and Black feminist thought and feminist storytelling. These authors extend our theorizing about ECE subjectivity to the 'spirit (through Innate Divinity), the mystical, and the metaphysical, in order to imagine and create new ways of being in the world and in relation with other beings, both human and more-than-human' (p. 99). To illustrate the possibilities for this imagining and creating, they describe their writing process whereby they met frequently to explore their own and each other's thinking and experiences, honouring each other and the process. Through a focus on the mind-body-spirit connection, interconnectedness to each other, enfleshed knowledge, storytelling and active resistance to hegemonic social structures, Odim, Rideaux, Odim and Salazar Pérez argue that a womanist praxis offers 'a depth of care, relatability and patience White supremacist contexts cannot' (p. 104). For these authors, a womanist praxis has the potential to open doors for all early childhood educators who are currently forced to operate within structures that systematically silence the embodied experiences of Black women and children (Rideaux's story of witnessing the Black girl's pain is a profound example of this). This chapter makes clear that holding space to dream or imagine seemingly unimaginable possibilities is a necessary component of resistance, and indeed survival, for groups who face perpetual, systemic oppression.

Similar to other chapters in this group, Jenny Ritchie draws on a number of third and fourth-wave feminist scholars (i.e. hooks, Lorde, Davies, Anzaldúa, Naughton) that have come to influence her thinking rhizomatically over time. Ritchie's focus on these decolonizing feminisms raises an important question about how other feminisms do or do not offer the critical tools for decolonizing theory. Countering oppressive colonial discourses, Ritchie introduces us to Gloria Anzaldúa's concept of '*nepantla*' – a construct defined as a 'states of mind that question old beliefs, acquires new perspectives, changes worldviews and shifts from one world to another' (Anzaldúa, 2002 as quoted by Ritchie, p. 120). *Nepantla* offers a way of being that operates outside of hegemonic colonial structure and discourses, embodying an anti-racist, anti-colonial ethos. This concept is thus relevant to much of the thinking presented throughout this book. Like the womanist praxis described by Odim, Rideaux and Salazar Pérez in Chapter 6, *nepantla* honours the spiritual, building bridges to new ideas, people and worlds. Nepantla similarly captures Arndt and Tesar's thinking about subjects being in motion, always in the process of coming to know oneself, others and the world in new ways. On a very practical level, *nepantla* offers the intellectual and emotional space to critique the 'womenandchildren' construct Newberry problematizes, opening up possibilities to see and understand women – including early childhood educators – in relation to, but not defined by, others. Looking ahead to Meagan Monpetit's chapter on posthuman feminisms and to Gunilla Dahlberg and Ann Merte Otterstad's use of the concept of thresholds,

Ritchie points to how *nepantla* offers an opportunity to decolonize relationships not only within ourselves and between other humans, but also with/in the more-than-human realm.

The implications of *nepantla* for the subjective possibilities for early childhood educators are significant. An educator who thinks with *nepantla* positions herself outside of existing hegemonic practices rooted in white, colonial, developmental frameworks. Theoretically, she is able to let go of, and be let go from, the oppressive, highly regulated, demoralizing structures that in many ways dictate who she is and how she should be (i.e. the nurturing, self-sacrificing female educator who applies technocratic knowledge to children's learning). There instantly becomes space for creativity, imagination, uncertainty and relationality between humans and the-more-than-humans. But again, exploitative structures, like the early childhood education systems in the majority of the world, systematically silence and divide educators. In this book, and consistent with Bruce and Powell's call for caring about, for and with ECEs, we try to hold space for both: an urgent need to address the material inadequacies of existing early childhood education systems alongside the burning desire to imagine/explore connected (mind-body-spirit) ways of being with ourselves, others and the more-than-human.

References

Anzaldúa, G. (2002). Preface. (Un)natural bridges, (Un)safe spaces. In G. E. Anzaldúa & A. Keating (Eds.), *This bridge we call home. Radical visions for transformation* (pp. 1–5). Routledge.

Cannella, G. S. & Viruru, R. (2004). *Childhood and postcolonization. Power, education and contemporary practice*. RoutledgeFalmer.

Collins, P. H. (2000). *Black feminist thought: Knowledge, consciousness, and the politics of empowerment* (2nd ed.). Routledge.

Hekman, S. J. (2014). *The feminine subject*. Polity Press.

Viruru, R. (2001). *Early childhood education: Postcolonial perspectives from India*. Sage.

8

Queer Bodies in Early Childhood: Gender and Sexuality Disruption(s) and Impure Feminisms to 'Get Us Free'

Janice Kroeger

In this chapter, I propose that feminist theories have gone through a series of overlapping and situated movements that have allowed feminist scholars (and others) to influence teachers and practitioners as they take steps to accommodate sexuality and gender disruptions in early childhood education. Queer feminism matters because it allows early childhood practitioners to support 'queer' bodies in schools and classrooms. By understanding gender diversity and moving beyond developmental frameworks, one can better position themselves and children or families as ally and advocate for LGBTQ persons. I did this as an ally and writer in my own work as a lesbian-identified bisexual teacher, by deconstructing the challenges of including lesbian family identity in a homophobic context for the mothers of a child in my classroom (Kroeger, 2001). Although I did not use queer theory at that time, its abiding presence has sustained scholarship in early childhood matters for decades.

Queer theory emerged, following gay and lesbian and feminist studies of the 1990s, when the AIDs crisis and human rights violations of LGBTQ people, especially those with transgender and intersex identities, came to the forefront in public life (Halberstam, 2018a; Jagose, 2009). The word and identity of 'queer' have been reclaimed from its negative meaning and reused as a source of analyses, and the means to counter dominant and oppressive norms. Queer theory aims through predominantly poststructural concepts to deconstruct (or to queer) norms of gender and explore the harm they cause to those individuals who cannot or do not wish to conform to these norms. Feminist theorist Judith Butler (1990) viewed sexuality and gender as discursive social constructions that are 'fluid, plural and continually negotiated rather than a natural fixed core identity' (pp. 17–18). Thus, Queer and third-wave feminism share common goals:

> Similar to how queer activists and theorists have insisted that "queer" is and should be open-ended and never set to mean one thing, third wave feminism's complexity, nuance, and adaptability become assets in a world marked by rapidly shifting political situations.
>
> (Kang et al., 2017, p. 123)

In early childhood education, theorists such as Kerry Robertson, Jonathan Silin, Mindy Blaise, Affrica Taylor, as well as Alexandria Gunn and Nicole Surtees have brought attention to how constructs of 'queerness', such as gender, sexuality and family diversity are understood and addressed (or not) by practitioners. The work of these scholars shows that queer feminism matters greatly in early childhood education because it can provide the tools for early childhood practitioners to support 'queer' bodies in their programmes and become advocates and allies. Just as importantly, queer feminism opens up possibilities for thinking differently about queer early childhood educators and early childhood pedagogy. Each of these ideas will be explored in this chapter.

The Rise of Queer Feminism(s)

Many feminist scholars argue that mid- and late-twentieth century feminisms arose because Marxist theory, a starting place to study broad constructs like social stratification and social inequity from an economic perspective, did little to examine stratified society from a gender, race, or sexuality perspective (Braidotti & Butler, 1997; Butler, 1990; Jagose, 2009; Rubin & Butler, 1997). Early feminisms lacked the kind of nuance expected by women of colour, lesbians, and transgender individuals necessary to understand, apply and critique lived experiences of these individuals (The Combahee River Collective, 2013; Halberstam, 2018a & b; Feinberg, 2013; Jagose, 2009). Black, Latino as well as lesbian feminists protested against a universalized feminism viewed as hegemonic, heteronormative and Eurocentric and argued that second-wave feminism was inattentive to the economic and social problems experienced uniquely by the gay and lesbian population (healthcare denials, hospitalization rights of non-married partners, marriage equality, housing and employment protections, etc.).

In academia, early gay and lesbian studies scholars (and later queer scholars) argued that second-wave feminism did not address issues of sexual variation to a complex enough degree, and that simply adding sexualities to considerations of feminism did not address sexual persecution(s) (harassment, employment and housing discrimination, homelessness, murder, hate crimes) or the idea that almost anything beyond heterosexual activity was considered deviant. Moreover, the merging of 'gay and lesbian experiences' was considered a problem because gay men and lesbians function in different cultural fields. While gay men are 'othered' in a society that privileges heterosexuality, they are accorded privileges as men that lesbians cannot access (Rubin & Butler, 1997). In the late 1990s, queer scholars intensified critiques of compulsory heterosexuality and the role societies, communities, institutions and families play in shaping normative gender and sexuality identities. Scholars, such as Rubin and Butler (1997), argued that gay and lesbian communities and cultures were transforming family and kinship arrangements, subverting dominant heterosexual power and thus reconfiguring Freudian derived forms of thinking on sexuality, gender and the psyche (Rubin & Butler, 1997).

The earliest traces of the term 'queer' in academia consider that the constructs of gender, sexuality, race and class intersect and manifest in social relations differently for gays, lesbians, straight woman and straight men (Butler, 1997, 2013). In early critical feminist scholarship, lesbian feminist scholars, such as Anzaldúa, Butler, and Rubin, drew on postfoundational concepts to bend categories of normality, using constructs such as subjectivity, identity, discursive formation, borderlands and analytical tools such as the deconstruction of binaries. Each scholar studied aspects of the social formation(s) of gender and sexual identities that arise within particular cultures and communities. Rubin's work, for example, offered a more nuanced understanding of queer communities as unique anthropological units with their own rituals; stylized enactments of desire and inclusion, which contribute to both sexual identity formation; unique economic formation(s); and familial and community relations (Rubin & Butler, 1997).

Butler argued, in her formative 1997 essay, that the 'formation of a gender' identity is always tenuous in time and is 'constituted by a stylized repetition of bodily acts' which can be understood as the mundane way(s) in which 'gesture, movement, and enactments of various kinds constitute the illusion of an abiding gendered self' (p. 462). This construct of gender as *performative* became a central idea in Butler's work and was later employed as a move to 'queer' gender, by queer feminists. Butler's work, informed by Foucault, Freud, Lacan, Wittig and others, helped feminists see how gender *performativity* gave individuals the ability to *overthrow* the category of 'sex' as a fixed, permanent or enduring subject (position) (Butler, 1990). Expressions of subverting the *heterosexual matrix* provided queer subjectivities room to move within gender identities. Additionally, Butler noted (2020) how audiences responded to *Gender Trouble*, with both anticipation and hope, at a time in which conservative attacks on gender ideology prevailed. *Gender Trouble* took on a kind of life of its own, with particular relevance to the emerging field of queer studies in both the continental United States and globally. The cultural relevance of subverting gender allowed progressive audiences to interpret performances of the body in new ways (as applied to classrooms for example), but a right-wing response to *Gender Trouble* merited reactions, claiming the work might be 'end of the heteronormative family' and the 'destruction of civilization' (Butler, 2020, p. 969).

Butler did not especially use the term 'queer' in her early work, even if her work was central to advancing the aims of gay and lesbian and queer movements. Rather, Butler drew upon Gloria Anzaldúa's (1987/2012) writing and *performance* as *mestiza*. For Anzaldúa (2012), the *mestiza* reflected her experiences with border crossing between México and the Texas Southwest bringing insights into a *third world* culture in which 'vague but forbidden identities such as Chicano, Indian, or Black' were disallowed (p. 25). But she saw herself and others in a rich, queerly reconfigured border culture, in which some 'maimed, mad, and sexually different people were believed to possess supernatural powers by primal cultures' magico-religious thinking' (p. 41). Such trespassers (*la travesía*) were contained in the *borderlands* of even their own homelands, not particularly occupying normal territories and thus recreating spaces, identities and cultures of their own from the residue of rejection from the mainstream. Anzaldúa expressed this more fully in a passage about her experiences; 'Los Atraesados live here: the squint-eyed, the perverse, the queer, the troublesome, the mongrel, the mulato, the half-breed, the half dead; in short those who cross over, pass over, or go through the confines of the "normal"' (Anzaldúa, 1987/2012, p. 25).

Since its early developments, gay and lesbian feminism was critiqued for exclusions of other queerness(es) such as trans or transgender identities (formerly called transsexual or transvestite) as well as intersex individuals (Halberstam, 2018b). Queer scholars, studying the desire to cross gender or change sex, point to transgender identities' long and complex history. Feinberg argued in 1992, for example, that early history is replete with examples of individuals who chose to express themselves beyond the gender they were born into, but that the notion of 'passing' (having to hide) is new. She maintains that with the rise of industrial capitalism and male-dominated households what is considered acceptable/normal masculine behaviour became increasingly narrowed. Those individuals whose expressions of gender transcended strict divisions of male and female or celebrated forms of sexuality outside of heterosexuality were labelled heretic and suppressed (Feinberg, 1992/2013). Halberstam (2018b) further maintains that modern-day terminologies such as 'intersex', 'gay' or 'lesbian', and 'transgender' are incapable of mapping accurately onto historical categories of human gender and/or gender subjectivities. For Halberstam, the use of today's term 'trans' captures the provisional nature of 'a wide variety of bodies with varying relations to cross-gender identification' (Halberstam, 2018b. p. 25).

Mass public mobilizations of the LGBTQ community resisting conservative forces in human rights have included the 'cross-relational promise' of queer identities. This promise has brought gays, lesbians, bisexuals, transgender, questioning individuals, intersex persons, and their allies to the fore of public life (Weed, 1997, pp. viii–xi). Queer is used across identities (gay, lesbian, bi- and intersex, transgender individuals and those who are questioning) as a reclaiming, and in response to exclusively gay and lesbian interests (which might have previously omitted many of their concerns). Queer theory, as well as queer feminism, therefore is an attempt to challenge the norms of gender and sexuality, moving against intellectual movements and social activism(s) which have not historically included those non-binary, provisional or indeterminate constructs of sexuality and gender expression within broader categories of minority race or ethnic groups, who arguably may experience oppression more severely than others (Ahmed, 2016; Butler, 2020; Halberstam, 2018a).

The Queering of Early Childhood

The queering of early childhood became more visible in the 1990s with an important article, in the *Harvard Educational Review*, authored by Virginia Casper, Harriet Cuffaro, Steven Schultz, Jonathan Silin and Elaine Wickens. These educators, each with their own corpus of contributions to the literature, hoped that their exploration of the intersections between teacher education, sexual orientation and the 'coming out' of educators and parents would help pre-service and in-service teachers understand their own perspectives on their own (and others') gender, sexuality, and schooling (Casper & Schultz, 1995; Wickens, 1993).

In the United States, and across the globe, gay and lesbian parents were establishing a foothold as a legitimate family unit and early childhood scholars responded with affirming research. Such work expanded non-traditional explorations of sexuality and young children, feminist readings of children's agency, poststructural explorations of classroom and family life, and critical ethnographic portraits of gender identities in classrooms (Boldt, 2011; Davies, 1989/2003; Francis, 1998; Gunn et al., 2004; Kroeger, 2001; MacNaughton, 2008; Robinson, 2003; Taylor & Richardson, 2005; Thorne, 1993; Yelland, 1998).

Historically, the gender development of children in families and in schools has been regulated and socially produced along binary lines of what are acceptable masculine and feminine identities and studied mostly from Freudian or Piagetian perspectives (Gunn & MacNaughton, 2007; Maccoby, 1988, 1990). Moreover, a gender identity, consistent with the sex category assigned at birth was seen as the desired outcome of healthy development. Most teachers were taught that the early socialization and cognitive milestones for children should include such things as an understanding of gender permanence (the idea that one's gender does *not* change) and a child's positive identification with an adult of the same gender as ideal and desirable (Maccoby, 1988, 1990). In early childhood, gender is seen to be primarily learned through heterosexual marriage, family life and schools, but feminist influences remind us that all three are dominant carriers of heteronormativity, homophobia and normative gender conformity.

Queer theory and queer feminism have brought to early childhood theoretical tools, and analyses, that challenge the dominant discourses of gender and sexuality and their intersections in childhoods. By using queer theory, with its roots in poststructuralist feminism, and postcoloniality, early childhood scholars are able to make arguments that gender is never fixed or stable, but rather constructed within dominant discourse systems (Blaise, 2005; Blaise & Taylor, 2012; Davies, 1989/2003; Kitchen, 2014). Performing gender under and within dominant gender, sexuality and heterosexual norms can be upstaged by looking at gender *queerly*. Looking or thinking queerly allows one to question if 'normal' genders actually exist(s) and are instead created in gesture and ritualistic acts of performances (Blaise & Taylor, 2012; Butler, 1990). Queer feminism(s) helped teachers to recognize that children have a complex and developing knowledge of sexuality and gender (and their intersections) before they come to school and that they practice these knowledges expertly, even when they are urged not to (Kroeger & Regula, 2017). Additionally, queer feminism(s) helped teachers to think about how children are being 'gendered' through everyday experiences in classrooms. Butler's concept of the heterosexual matrix, has been used to upend binary gender categories, even if that matrix remains challenging to us (as adults) because it is largely invisible, normalized, and accepted as part of our larger systems of dominant discourses (Blaise, 2005; Butler, 1990; Davies & Robinson, 2013; Davies & Semann, 2013; Osgood & Robinson, 2017; Paechter, 2017; Surtees, 2005; Thorne, 1993). Blaise and Taylor (2012), for example, suggest that early childhood teachers need to critically examine their own priorities in sustaining heteronormativity, and doing this will help to create opportunities for children to enact inclusive gender relations more fully in classrooms (Blaise & Taylor, 2012).

Queer feminisms have also allowed educators to consider children as powerful in as many ways as *the myriad of diverse* gender performance(s) makes possible. Scholars such as Betsy Cahill and Rachel Theilheimer (1999) maintained that children whose behaviours and activities fall outside of the conventional heterosexual matrix (including their attractions to same gender peers, or an expression of gender attributes and performances which are perceived as persistently unusual for their biological gender category) should be considered part of the fabric of classroom life, mirroring everyday life (Blaise & Taylor, 2013; Kroeger, Recker & Gunn, 2019; Kroeger & Regula, 2017). For example, Kroeger and Regula (2017) described instances of very young children, who recognize what is typically expected for their gender (dress, play activities and social grouping), yet display gender non-conformity and resist schools' and parents' efforts to regulate their gender expressions (Alegria, 2016; Ehrensaft, 2014; Kroeger & Regula, 2017; Terreni, Gunn, Kelly & Surtees, 2010). Drag Queen Story Hour, an early childhood programme in which drag artists channel many forms of literacy and artistry, promotes positive expressions of a queer aesthetic (Keenan & Hot Mess, 2021). Queer feminisms in all of these many instances can help teachers question their conventional sense of normality, and allow gender or sexual identities which are 'bent' (rather than straight) to upstage heterosexual becoming(s) as the only right and true becoming(s) (Kitchen, 2014). At the same time, teachers can encourage conversations about exclusions and acceptance of queer identities so that they are integral to life in schools.

More recently, scholars have urged teachers and other professionals to take up concerns of the transgender movement, and further conceptualize(s) how the end-point gonadal sex (commonly used to determine gender based on body appearance) *does not keep pace* with the complex gender fluid or transgender options available to young children and families (Ehrensaft, 2014; Kroeger & Regula, 2017; Mosso-Taylor, 2016; Nutt, 2015). For example, poststructural, feminist and queer sensibilities allowed Davies and Robinson (2013) to argue that foster care, adoption, reproductive technologies and alternative kinship arrangements *queerly conceived* would further push the early childhood field to manage and change their notions of conception and family life beyond the given heterosexual relationship. In turn, recent changes in family structures and trans identity development have pushed the early childhood field to support the emergent identity of trans students in schools and to make better sense of how children's peer relationships can be positively mediated by teachers and when students have a trans parent (Kroeger & Regula, 2017; Mosso-Taylor, 2016; Sullivan & Urraro, 2019).

Queer theory values a political commitment to open up singular gender and sexuality discursive formations that serve to constrain individuals (Kitchen, 2014; Sedgwick, 1993). Educators who value their students recognize the intense social pressure LGBTQ individuals experience to conform to heteronormativity and gender congruence, which often leads to negative mental health and physical safety outcomes in schools as young children grow into middle school and adulthood (DePalma & Atkinson, 2009; Gunn, 2015; Kosciw et al., 2009; Sullivan and Urraro, 2019; Toomey, McGuire & Russell, 2012). Sullivan and Urraro illuminated the perspectives of transgender adults. In collaboration with the researchers, they recalled and reflected on their persistent transgender desires and painful sanctions in school in physical spaces (like restrooms, gyms, locker rooms, playgrounds and principal offices) often leading to alienation, anxiety and despair (Sullivan & Urraro, 2019). Conversely, they also conveyed that classroom experiences in the arts, music and literature as well as experiences in libraries and studios *with* individual teacher allies provided liberation and safety. Sullivan and Urraro's important work (2019) highlights the ways in which early childhood spaces, curriculum opportunities and teacher behaviour can support or thwart children's efforts at authenticity and congruence with their 'transgendered' selves.

The Queer Early Childhood Educator

While there is increasing literature on how early childhood educators can support non-gender conforming children, there is less literature focusing on the vulnerability and invisibility of queer early childhood educators themselves. Perhaps this is where there is a problem. DeJean (2010) quotes Kissen (1996) who describes the experiences of queer educators:

> To be a lesbian or gay teacher, in most schools, is to walk a constant line between safety and honesty. The very qualities of trust and authenticity that lie at the heart of all good teaching are often incompatible with their physical and emotional well-being. [Often]acknowledging a gay identity means rethinking the whole notion of being a teacher.
>
> (p. 16)

DeJean (2010) further describes how educators with queer identities regularly negotiate dominant discourses of fixed genders, childhood innocence and compulsive heterosexuality that vigorously circulate in early childhood settings. Based on his study of the experiences of a queer preservice teacher, openly queer teacher educators can play a part in providing positive role modelling, for negotiating the vulnerability, and potential isolation surrounding homogeneous settings in schools and universities (DeJean, 2010).

Reimers (2020) argues that schools are discursive sites, in which heterosexuality becomes desexualized as the normal position, while simultaneously, homosexuality becomes exposed. In seeking the perspectives of out and queer educators who articulated the benefits and rewards of their queer identities, Reimers discovered that they articulated the strengths of their queer identities, creating transformations in schools. Reimers' informants saw themselves as powerful disruptors of desexualized heteronormativity, leaders of gender equality networks and important supporters of gender non-conformity in children. Reimers (2020) regards her research results as contributing to a shift 'in the tale(s) about LGBTQ teachers so that they are presented as subjects rather than victims' and as important pedagogical resources (p. 112). Reimers concludes more broadly that queer bodies and queer moments in early childhood programmes create 'interruptions, disruptions, subversions, and unease' (p. 124). Thus, she argues:

> The core of queer pedagogy is not to make colleagues, children/students familiar with and accepting of LGBTQ persons and lives. Stopping at that would not disturb the desexualized heterosexual norm in education. In order for queer moments to emerge, it is necessary to embody affective queerness, that is, a queerness that creates uncertainty and uneasiness, a queerness that demands responses. It is to put both the teacher and the students at risk, not knowing what will emerge. The presence of queer bodies in classrooms interrupts the dominant heterosexual norm.
>
> (p. 122)

The Challenge and Promise of Feminist Queer Advocacy in Early Childhood Education

One of the challenging aspects of reviewing a corpus of gender identity, feminist and queer feminist literature which intersects with early childhood literature, is that early childhood scholars do not always self-identify as feminist, gay, lesbian, bisexual, activist or queer, even if the work they are producing and publishing makes references to these ideas. Similarly, it's completely possible that scholars can contribute to queer movements even if their scholarship is not labelled as such.

While it would seem that DeJean (2010) and Reimers (2020) are arguing for queer early childhood educators to take an 'out' and proud position within their own research and teaching, there is no conclusive evidence to support the idea that such a move would make the world better for young children – even if the move reframes the vulnerable position of the queer educator into one of authenticity, strength and challenge to mainstream thinking (Kitchen, 2014). This is clearly a queer advocate's quandary. The sexuality of the educator is often considered private terrain both in higher education and in early childhood classrooms. But as the literature reviewed above indicates, it is worth further considering the role that openly queer educators, including University faculty, have played in leading early childhood thinking. As I read and re-read many of the formative early childhood articles for this chapter, I found that only some of the scholars within the early childhood field self-identify as queer, use queer theory or feminist theory in their writing to advocate for gender and sexuality diversity. The articles which do use explicit queer or queer feminist theoretical frameworks do so with scenarios that problematize gender exclusions between boys and girls or amplify binary and heterosexual becoming(s) of identity. Additionally, those articles which seem to support gender-nonconformity often do not explicitly lay claim to feminist or queer theories at all. This signals to me as a reader that it is easier to use queer or queer feminist theory with less controversial scenario(s) about the young child than it is to use queer theory to argue for children's queer becoming(s) which challenge the heterosexual matrix. Clearly, publishing, must supersede fear of sanctions within settings (such as being fired or acting in opposition to other more powerful tenured colleagues), but publishing in conservative and mainstream venues comes at a cost of literary compromise.

Queer feminism is concerned with both theory and action, putting teachers in a forceful position to critique life in schools, subvert dominant heteronormative discourses and interpret transgressions as a strength (Keenan & Hot Mess, 2021; Kitchen, 2014; Sedgwick,1993). Despite the growth of literature that seeks to queer notions of gender and sexuality in early childhood classrooms, it seems that advocacy for sexual and gender minority children, and their families remains difficult for some people to do. Teachers appear to find it easier to undertake equity work around racism and other social issues rather than around homophobia and transphobia (DePalma & Atkinson, 2010). Strong curricular and education guidelines and policy mandates do exist to support teachers in thinking about gender diversity and using non-discrimination strategies, especially in early and elementary education in many countries across the globe (DePalma & Atkinson, 2010; NASP, 2014; Surtees, 2005). However, teachers and many parents are still uncomfortable with LGBTQ families, and children who they perceive as having gay or lesbian, bisexual, non-binary and transgender identities. Scholarship also demonstrates that in many countries where LGBTQ rights have flourished, advocacy for young children is still not perceived as safe for teachers (DePalma & Atkinson, 2010; Gunn & MacNaughton, 2007; Payne & Smith, 2014; Kroeger & Regula, 2017). Early childhood educators may deny their responsibilities to affirm the gender and sexual diversity of young children or elementary students by omission, heteronormative silencing or through perceptions of curriculum irrelevancy (DePalma & Atkinson, 2010; Gunn & MacNaughton, 2007; Robinson, 2003; Surtees, 2005). This is despite the fact we know that children who are supported to perform their gender in ways consistent with their gender identity (i.e. those who are living cis-normatively or who have experienced social transition to match gender performance with identity experience) exhibit better mental health and social outcomes (NASP, 2014; Olson, 2016; Olson et al., 2016; Sherer, 2016).

Advocacy and safe space creation requires teachers to explore and recognizing where their values about including LGBTQ children and families and their understanding of gender nonconformity reside (Casper & Schultz, 1999). Some early years teachers recognize the struggle of young children who perform their gender differently because of their own relationships to gay and transgender member(s) of their own families, or more broadly in relation to other oppressions and intersections (Casper & Schultz, 1999; Kroeger & Regula, 2017; Kroeger, 2006). Early childhood literature routinely turns to anti-bias approaches as a way to demonstrate ally behaviour, but those approaches are context dependent (Davies & Robinson, 2013; Earles, 2010; Gunn & Surtees, 2011). For example, a lesbian or bisexual teacher (or family ally) may or may not advocate by placing feminist literature or books with LGBTQ imagery and story lines in the classroom because of community safety concerns. Yet, discursively, that same teacher might be exploring other options, like reaffirming the primacy of LGBTQ parenting relationships within that particular family, or affirming relationships and the right of the LGBTQ family unit to secure a place in the school among heterosexual parents (Kroeger, 2001). A supervisor or director of an early childhood education programme may demonstrate whole community advocacy by ensuring that the moral values of an organization are congruent with the welcoming of a child who is transitioning, as they reinforce existing affirmative policies in their community and communications, thereby bypassing bullying (Mosso-Taylor, 2016). Teachers as advocates witness and affirm children's gender discussions about who can marry in the dramatic play centre and encourage as a child's right the fuller exploration of adornments, clothing, and pretending as valid and acceptable forms of gender play (Cahill & Theilheimer,1999; Kroeger, Recker & Gunn, 2019; Osgood & Robinson, 2017). Additionally, it is often the case with the ally behaviours of straight and LGBTQ communities that procedural and policy changes in school safety, teacher protection and gay straight organizations occur to make whole schools and whole districts (including elementary schools) safer for LGBTQ individuals (Kroeger, 2006, 2019; Sullivan & Urraro, 2019; Toomey et al., 2012). Thus, it may similarly be that LGBTQ and straight allies together will make early childhood spaces safer for young children, their families and teachers.

Conclusion: Maintaining Affective Vulnerability through Queer Feminisms

Feminist Queer theory helps early educators know that children are being gendered (by schools and by families) continuously, and gives openings to acknowledge and honour that process. When young children learn that gender and sexuality diversity is acceptable in classrooms, then they can exercise greater autonomy over their developing identities. Paechter argues that although they are surrounded by heterosexual relationships, they are also 'always striving to become parties in the social contract by virtue of their desire to have more control over their lives' (2017, p. 286). Getting their gender right, getting their sexuality right, queerly or otherwise matters to them and is arguably one of their most basic rights (Paechter, 2017). Conversely, our ability as early educators to respect children and families and learn from them as they construct their unique gender and sexual configuration(s) has as much to teach us about them as it might ourselves (Kitchen, 2014; Robinson & Davies, 2014). Our work, and moral obligation to support those who might be unfairly mistreated because of their indeterminant, still evolving, and yet-to-be fully-understood or -expressed gender identity or sexuality remains critically important. Affectively, this means that early childhood educators must willingly engage with unease as they face vulnerability, reaction or resistance from the field (Kroeger, Recker, Gunn, 2019; Reimers, 2020). As feminists, early childhood educators, or queer others, queer theory allows us to overthrow the category of sex and gender, providing opportunity for children and early childhood educators to cross over, to pass over, to go through or even surpass the confines of heterosexual normality. Affectively, our obligation, in relation to queerness, is to 'get them free' to allow children, teachers and families to construct their identities, and their queer bodies in ways that make the most sense to them as humans.[1]

Note

1 I wish to thank Alexandria Gunn, Deniz Akyel and Sabastian Ochoa-Kaup for conversations and supports which contributed to this manuscript.

References

Ahmed, S. (2016). Interview with Judith Butler. *Sexualities, 19*(4), 482–92. http://doi.org/10.1177/1363460716629607

Alegria, C. A. (2016). Gender nonconforming and transgender children/youth: Family, community, and implications for practice. *Journal of the American Association of Nurse Practitioners, 28*(10), 521–7. http://doi.org/10.1002/2327-6924.12363

Anzaldúa, G. (2012). *Borderlands: La Frontera: The New Mestiza*. Aunt Lute Books. (Original work published 1987).

Boldt, G. M. (2011). One hundred hotdogs or performing gender bending in an elementary classroom. In T. Jacobson (Ed.), *Perspectives on gender in early childhood* (pp. 77–93). Redleaf.

Blaise, M. (2005). *Playing it straight! Uncovering gender discourses in the early childhood classroom*. Routledge.

Blaise, M. & Taylor, A. (2012). Using queer theory to rethink gender equity in early childhood education. Research in review. *Young Children, 67*(1), 88–98.

Braidotti, R. & Butler, J. (1997). Feminism by any other name: Interview. In E. Weed & N. Schor (Eds.), *Feminism meets queer theory* (pp. 31–67). Indiana University Press.

Butler, J. (1990). *Gender trouble: Feminism and the subversion of identity*. Routledge.
Butler, J. (1997/2013). Performative acts and gender constitution: An essay in phenomenology and feminist theory. In C. R. McCann and S-K. Kim (Eds.), *Feminist theory reader: Local and global perspectives* (pp. 462–73). Routledge.
Butler, J. (2020). Reflections on gender trouble thirty years later: Reply to Hershatter, Loos, and Patel. *The Journal of Asian Studies*, 79(4), 969–76.
Cahill, B. & Theilheimer, R. (1999). Stonewall in the housekeeping area: Gay and lesbian issues in the early childhood classroom. In W. J. Letts IV & J. Sears (Eds.), *Queering elementary education: Advancing the dialogue about sexualities in schooling* (pp. 39–48). Rowan & Littlefield.
Casper, V., Cuffaro, H. K., Schultz, S., Silin, J., & Wickens, E. (1996). *Harvard Educational Review*, 66(2), 271–93. https://doi.org/10.17763/haer.66.2.h44831447873261p
Casper, V. & Schultz, S. B. (1999). *Gay parents straight schools: Building communication and trust*. Teacher College Press.
Clark, T. C., Lucassen, M. F. G., Bullen, P., Denny, S. J., Fleming, T. M., Robinson, E. M., & Rossen, F. V. (2014). The health and well-being of transgender high school students: Results from the New Zealand Adolescent Health Survey (Youth'12). *Journal of Adolescent Health*, 55(1), 93–9. https://www.jahonline.org/article/S1054-139X1300753-2/fulltext
Davies, B. (1989/2003). *Frogs, snails and feminist tales: Preschool children and gender* (Revised edn). Hampton Press.
Davies, B. (1993). *Beyond dualisms and towards multiple subjectivities*. Falmer Press.
Davies, C. & Robinson, K. H. (2013). Reconceptualising family: Negotiating sexuality in a governmental climate of neoliberalism. *Contemporary Issues in Early Childhood*, 14(1), 39–53. https://journals.sagepub.com/doi/pdf/10.2304/ciec.2014.14.1.39
Davies, C. & Semann, A. (2013). In conversation with Jonathan Silin. *Contemporary Issues in Early Childhood*, 14(1), 1–7. https://journals.sagepub.com/doi/pdf/10.2304/ciec.2014.14.1.1
DePalma, R. & Atkinson, E. (2010). The nature of institutional heteronormativity in primary schools and practice-based responses. *Teacher and Teacher Education*, 26, 1669–1676. https://doi.org/10.1016/j.tate.2010.06.018
DeJean, W. (2010). The tug of war: When queer and early childhood meet. *Australasian Journal of Early Childhood*, 35(1), 10–14.
Earles, J. (2017). Reading gender: A feminist, queer approach to children's literature and children's discursive agenda. *Gender & Education*, 29(3), 369–88. https://doi.org/10.1080/09540253.2016.1156062
Ehrensaft, D. (2014). Found in transition: Our littlest transgender people. *Contemporary Psychoanalysis*, 50(4), 571–92.
Fienberg, L. (1992/2013). Transgender liberation: A movement whose time has come. In C. R. McCann & S-K, Kim (Eds.), *Feminist theory reader: Local and global perspectives* (pp. 148–60). Routledge.
Francis, B. (1998). *Power plays: Primary school children's constructions of gender, power and adult work*. Trentham.

Gunn, A. C. (2011). Even if you say it three ways, it still doesn't mean it's true: The pervasiveness of heteronormativity in early childhood education. *Journal of Early Childhood Research*, *9*(3), 280–90. https://journals-sagepub-com.proxy.library.kent.edu/doi/pdf/10.1177/1476718X11398567

Gunn, A. C. (2015). The potential of queer theorizing in early childhood education. In A. C. Gunn & L. Smith (Eds.), *Sexual cultures in Aotearoa New Zealand Education* (pp. 21–34). Otago University Press.

Gunn, A. C., Child, C., Madden, B., Purdue, K., Surtees, N., Thurlow, B., & Todd, P. (2004). Building inclusive communities in early childhood education: Diverse perspectives from Aotearoa/New Zealand. *Contemporary Issues in Early Childhood*, *5*(3), 293–308. https://journals.sagepub.com/doi/pdf/10.2304/ciec.2004.5.3.4

Gunn, A. C. & MacNaughton, G. (2007). Boys and boyhoods: The problems and possibilities of equity and gender diversity in early childhood settings. In H. Hedges & L. Keesing-Styles (Eds.), *Theorising early childhood practice: Emerging dialogues* (pp 121–36). Pademelon Press.

Gunn, A. C. & Surtees, N. (2011). Matching parents' efforts: How teachers might resist heteronormativity in early education settings. *Early Childhood Folio*, *15*(1), 27–31.

Halberstam, J. (2018a). Interview with J.J. Halberstam. *Paragraph*, *41*(3), 388–91.

Halberstam, J. (2018b). *A quick and quirky account of gender variability*. University of California Press.

Jagose, A. (2009). Undisciplined: Feminism's queer theory. *Feminism & Psychology*, *19*(2), 157–74. http://doi.org/10.1177/0959353509102152

Kang, M., Lessard, D., Heston, C., & Nordmaken, S. (2017). *Introduction to women, gender and sexuality studies*. Women, Gender, Sexuality Studies Educational Materials, 1. https://doi.org/10.7275/R5QZ284K

Keenan, G. & Hot Mess, L. M. (2021). Drag pedagogy: The playful practice of queer imagination in early childhood. *Curriculum Inquiry*, *50*(5), 440–61.

Kissen, R. (1996). *The last closet: The real lives of lesbian and gay teachers*. Heinemann.

Kitchen, J. (2014). Inqueerings into self-study: Queering the gaze of teacher educator identity and practice. In M. Taylor & L. Coia (Eds.), *Gender, feminisms, and queer theory in the self-study of teacher education practices* (pp. 127–41). Sense Publishers.

Kosciw, J. G. & Diaz, E. M. (2008). *Involved, invisible, ignored: The experiences of Lesbian, Gay, Bisexual and Transgender parents and their children in our nation's K-12 schools*. Lesbian and Straight Education Network (GLSEN), Spencer Foundation.

Kosciw, J. G., Greytak, E. A., & Diaz, E. M. (2009). Who, what, where, when, and why: Demographic and ecological factors contributing to hostile school climate for lesbian, gay, bisexual, and transgender youth. *Journal of Youth and Adolescence*, *38*(7), 976–88. http://dx.doi.org/10.1007/s10964-009-9412-1

Kroeger, J., Recker, A. E., & Gunn, A. (2019). Tate and the pink coat. *Young Children*, *74*(1), 83–93.

Kroeger, J. & Regula, L. (2017). Queer decisions in early childhood teacher education: Advocating for gender and sexual minority young children and families. *The*

International Critical Childhood Policy Studies Journal: Special Issue Confronting and Countering Bias and Oppression through Early Childhood Policy and Practice, 6(1), 106–21. http://journals.sfu.ca/iccps/index.php/childhoods/article/view/59

Kroeger, J. (2001). A reconstructed tale of inclusion for a lesbian family in the early childhood classroom. In S. Grieshaber & G. Cannella (Eds.), *Shifting identities in early childhood education* (pp. 773–86). New York: Teachers College Press.

Kroeger, J. (2006). Stretching performances in education: Gay activism and parenting impacts identity and school change. *The Journal of Educational Change, 7*, 319–37. http://doi.org/10.1007/s10833-006-9000-x

Kroeger, J. (2019). School community partnerships for full inclusion(s) of LGBTQI youth and families. In S. Sheldon & T. Taylor-Vorbeck (Eds.), *The Wiley handbook of school-family-community partnerships* (pp. 117–38). Wiley Blackwell.

Maccoby, E. E. (1988). Gender as social category. *Developmental Psychology, 24*(6), 755–65.

Maccoby, E. E. (1990). Gender and relationships: A developmental account. *American Psychologist, 45*(4), 513–20.

MacNaughton, G. (2008). *Rethinking gender in early childhood education*. Paul Chapman.

Mosso-Taylor, S. (2016). Humanity, heart, & praxis: Foundations of courageous leadership. In S. Long, M. Souto-Manning & V. M. Vasquez (eds.), *Courageous leadership in early childhood education* (pp. 150–62). Teachers College Press.

National Association of School Psychologists (NASP). (2014). *Safe schools for transgender and gender diverse students* [Position statement].

Nutt, A. E. (2015). *Becoming Nicole: The transformation of an American family*. Random House.

Olson, K. R. (2016). Prepubescent transgender children: What we do and do not know. *Journal of the American Academy of Child and Adolescent Psychiatry, 55*(3), 155–6. http://doi.org/10.1016/j.jaac.2015.11.015

Olson, K. R., Durwood, L., DeMeules, M., & McLaughlin, K. A. (2016). Mental health of transgender children who are supported in their identities. *Pediatrics, 137*(3), 1–8. http://doi.org/10.1542/peds.2015-3223

Osgood, J. & Robinson, K. H. (2017). Celebrating pioneering and contemporary feminist approaches to studying gender in early childhood. In K. Smith, Alexander K., Campbell S. (Eds.), *Feminism(s) in early childhood, Perspectives on Children and Young People, 4*, Springer. http://doi.org/10.1007/978-981-10-3057-4_4

Paechter, C. (2017). Young children, gender and the heterosexual matrix. *Discourse: Studies in the Cultural Politics of Education, 38*(2), 277–91. http://doi.org/10/1080/01596306.2015.1105785

Payne, E. & Smith, M. (2014). The big freak out: Educator fear in response to the presence of transgender elementary school students. *Journal of Homosexuality, 61*(3), 399–418. http://doi.org/10.1080/00918369.2013.842430

Reimers, E. (2020). Disruptions of desexualized heteronormativity: Queer identification(s) as pedagogical resources. *Teaching Education*, *31*(1), 112–25. https://doi.org/10.1080/10476210.2019.1708891

Robinson, K. H. (2003). Making the invisible visible: Gay and lesbian issues in early childhood education. *Contemporary Issues in Early Childhood*, *3*(3), 415–34. https://doi.org/10.2304/ciec.2002.3.3.8

Robinson, K. H. & Davies, C. (2014). Doing sexuality research with children: Ethics, theory, methods and practice. *Global Studies of Childhood*, *4*(4), 250–63.

Rubin, G. & Butler, J. (1997). Sexual traffic: Interview. In E. Weed & N. Schor (Eds.), *Feminism meets queer theory* (pp. 68–108). Indiana University Press.

Sedgwick, E. K. (1993). *Tendencies*. Duke University Press.

Sherer, I. (2016). Social transition: Supporting our youngest transgender children. *Pediatrics*, *137*(3), 1–2. http://doi.org/10.1542/peds.2015-4358

Smith, L., & Gunn, A. C. (2015). Challenging the pervasiveness of heteronormativity. In A. C. Gunn & L. Smith (Eds.), *Sexual cultures in Aotearoa New Zealand education* (pp. 226–39). Otago University Press.

Sullivan, A. L. & Urraro, L.L. (2019). *Voices of transgender children in early childhood education: Reflections and resiliency*. Palgrave/Macmillan.

Surtees, N. (2005). Teacher talk about and around sexuality in early childhood education: Deciphering and unwritten code. *Contemporary Issues in Early Childhood*, *6*(1), 19–29. https://doi.org/10.2304/ciec.2005.6.1.5

Taylor, A. & Richardson, C. (2005). 'Queer-ing home corner'. *Contemporary Issues in Early Childhood*, *6*(2), 163–73.

Terreni, L., Gunn, A., Kelly, J., & Surtees, N. (2010). In and out of the closet: Successes and challenges experienced by gay- and lesbian-headed families in their interactions with the education system in New Zealand. In V. Green & S. Cherrington (Eds.), *Delving into diversity: An international exploration of issues of diversity in education*. (pp. 151–61). Nova Science Publishers.

Toomey, R. B., McGuire, J. K., & Russell, S. T. (2012). Heteronormativity, school climates, and perceived safety for gender nonconforming peers. *Journal of Adolescence*, *35*(1), 187–96. http://dx.doi.org/10.1016/j.adolescence.2011.03.001

The Combahee River Collective (1977/2013). A Black feminist statement. In C. R. McCann & S-K Kim (Eds.), *Feminist theory reader: Local and global perspectives* (pp. 116–22). Routledge.

Thorne, B. (1993). *Gender play: Girls and boys in school*. Rutgers University Press.

Weed, E. (1997). Introduction. In E. Weed and N. Schor (Eds.), *Feminism meets queer theory* (pp. vii–xiii). Indiana University Press.

Wickens, E. (1994). Penny's question: 'I will have a child in my class with two moms; What do you know about this?' *Young Children*, *48*(3), 25–8.

Yelland, N. (1998). *Gender in early childhood*. Routledge.

Posthuman Possibilities for the Early Childhood Educator

Meagan Montpetit

In this chapter, I think with posthumanism as a possible way to intervene in the anthropocentric and developmental logics that govern early childhood spaces. Initially, I offer a brief introduction to my conceptualizations of posthuman theory, acknowledging posthumanism is broad and taken up in many different ways. My purpose in this chapter is not to offer a comprehensive telling of what posthuman feminism is but to think specifically how the early childhood educator subject is constructed within posthuman feminism. I then revisit two moments from my doctoral research in which, alongside educators and children, I experiment with attuning to more-than-human relations by foregrounding posthuman and earth-based feminist spiritual relations with the world. In these moments, educators, children and I bump up against the tensions and difficulties of shifting from human/child-centred logics prevalent in early childhood education and experiment with how we might embody posthuman subjectivities.

Why Posthumanism?

Posthumanism challenges the nature/culture divide that positions the human as separate and often above other more-than-human constitutes of our world and which obscures human accountability in ecological devastation (Braidotti, 2013, 2017, 2019). Posthumanism responds to the conditions of the geological period, the *Anthropocene* in which human involvement in the natural world has resulted in ecological devastation (Crutzen, 2002; Steffen, Crutzen & McNeill, 2007). For me, to think about ways in which we might begin to pull apart the logics that have resulted in the Anthropocene, we must consider the interrelations between climate devastation and patriarchal, racist and colonial power relations (Braidotti, 2019). Posthuman subjectivities engage affirmative ethics to challenge the dominance of these insidious power relations. Braidotti (2013, 2019) asserts that posthuman subjectivities requires a shift from thinking about *anthropos*, which focuses only on *bios* – exclusively human life, to *zoe* – 'the life of animals and other nonhuman entities' (Braidotti, 2017, p. 26). However, posthumanism does not do away with the human, as it is sometimes mistakenly critiqued. Instead, it proposes relational ontologies that respond to the violences that have been done in the name of universalized human subjectivity (Braidotti, 2013, 2017, 2019) by thickening the contexts of what matters in the world.

In childhood studies, research and theory has been done that challenges the construction of the child subject through human-centric dominant discourses such as developmentalism and its histories of racism, sexism, colonialism and ableism (Burman, 2017; Hancock, Morgan & Holly, 2021; Nxumalo, 2018; Pacini-Ketchabaw & Nxumalo, 2015). Because the early childhood educator is intricately related to the child, specifically through practices that centre the child in early childhood education, the educator often too constructed through these discourses. Therefore, the early childhood educator is constructed as mainly one who ensures the child develops into an 'appropriate' adult human. Posthuman early childhood educator subjectivities challenge this singular construction of the educator, by acknowledging and centring the relations between educators with the larger more-than-human world.

The definition of what it is to be human is insidiously grounded in the assumption that the human subject is masculine, white, heterosexual and able-bodied (Braidotti, 2013, 2017, 2019; Burman, 2001, 2017; Dahlberg and Moss, 2005). Narrow conceptualizations of whom the human is and is supposed to be, continuously position feminized, racialized and disabled bodies as less than human. The consequences of being made less than human are the oppression and exploitation of these nonhuman humans (Mies & Shiva, 2014). Posthuman feminisms radically reconvene subjectivity, shifting away from the definable unified human subject to subjects that are always in a state of becoming, which is always in negotiation with human and more-than-human presences (Braidotti, 2019). Posthuman subjectivity is multiple and fluid and moves through complex relational webs of being (Tsing, 2015). By destabilizing the universal subject, through human/more-than-human relationality, 'it is impossible to speak in one unified voice about any category, including women' (Braidotti, 2017, p. 24). Posthumanism, despite misguided criticisms as possibly negating marginalized people's lived experiences, has the capacity for a radical restructuring on how we come to understand relations with the world that make an onto-epistemological stance in which one group of humans is superior to another, fundamentally incommensurable (Braidotti, 2017, 2019). Posthumanism allows us to work towards subjectivities that reflect the current complexities of the twenty-first century and to create affirmative ethical responses that help us to be *worthy of our times* in ways in which we acknowledge anthropocentric historical and political contexts are the building blocks of current oppression and ecological crisis (Braidotti, 2019).

Posthuman subjectivities are emergent, complex human/more-than-human assemblages (complex webs of interconnectivity) that create possibilities to respond to and be in the world in ethically responsive ways. To attend to complex collaborative more-than-human assemblages requires a specific type of attunement in which we must pay attention to the way humans and more-than-humans come together in ways that are more than simply the sum of their parts that which are never fully knowable and therefore contain multitudes of possibilities (Tsing, 2015). Acknowledging that nothing or no one is ever fully knowable makes impossible the categorizations of traits that make up a universal human subject. Thinking with more-than-human assemblages refuses understandings of the world that promote individual and humancentric extractive relations with the more-than-human world and instead engages with the partial, messy, shifting entangled relations (Tsing, 2015) to stay with the trouble of our more-than-human worlds (Haraway, 2008, 2016). To stay with the trouble means dwelling in the uncomfortable tensions of human and more-than-relations rather than searching for quick, universal solutions to complex realities of our times. In posthumanist thinking, there is a shift from only humans as having agency to noticing the agency of all more-than-human others.

Thinking Early Childhood Education with Posthumanism

When I began my doctoral research with a group of educators and children in a local childcare the educators and I hoped to create spaces that shifted from objective-based engagements with children to sites of possible pedagogical engagements with the complex worlds of children. Also, the educators and I, like many others, felt acutely the effects of our time. Social injustice and climate change seemed to increase even as early childhood educators engaged in interventions to respond to them. I realized that the humancentric, rational, capitalist logics that shaped the neoliberal educational landscape did not create spaces to engage with the complexities of the twenty-first-century life, and in fact, they continued to reproduce the logics that led to the problems in the first place. In addition to not doing much to restructure how we engaged with the world, I was beginning to notice how early childhood education spaces promoted subjectivities that narrowly defined who the ideal child was and, in turn, positioned the responsibility of good early childhood educators as ensuring that children developed into ideal human subjects. I was introduced to posthumanism through the Common Worlds Research Collective (http://commonworlds.net/). Common worlds frameworks helped me to think otherwise about human/more-than-human relationality in early childhood education. Common worlds frameworks and pedagogies enact a posthuman stance by acknowledging twenty-first-century children's and educator's complex and multi-layered lives as being a part of a larger interconnected more-than-human world (Pacini-Ketchabaw, Khattar & Montpetit, 2019; Taylor, 2013, 2017). To engage this frameworks and pedagogical practices require a 'reconvening of all of the constituents of our worlds, including non-human life forms, forces and entities' (Pacini-Ketchabaw & Kummen, 2016, p. 432) and respond to humancentric logics that shape that individualist and capitalist thinking that is so prevalent in the neoliberal education system. Because common worlds frameworks and pedagogies are localized and situated, thinking with them requires and enables educators to experiment with doing early childhood outside the rigid boundaries of predetermined curriculum (Jobb, MacAlpine &Pacini-Ketchabaw, 2019). For me, and the educators I was working with, common worlds perspectives provided us with different theoretical perspectives, that create space for us to craft pedagogical questions outside of the humancentric leanings of much early childhood education curriculum and that also engaged our own interests and curiosities. Thinking with common worlds frameworks, we began to question children's and our own relations with the more-than-human world and to broaden and complexify who we were as early childhood educators and researchers. We wondered how engaging in non-innocent experimental pedagogical practices might disrupt humancentric and developmental underpinnings of early childhood education.

Like the broader theory of posthumanism, commons worlds frameworks are not universal, and many early childhood scholars have engaged with common worlds frameworks in a variety of ways to challenge anthropocentric (Nxumalo, 2017; Pacini-Ketchabaw and Nxumalo, 2015; Pacini-Ketchabaw, Taylor and Blaise, 2016; Taylor, 2017), colonial (Nelson, 2019; Nxumalo, 2015, 2016, 2019; Pacini-Ketchabaw, 2013; Taylor, 2019; Taylor, Pacini-Ketchbaw, de Finney & M.

Blaise, 2016) and developmental (Hodgins, 2019; Jobb, MacAlpine & Pacini-Ketchabaw, 2019; Land et al., 2020a; Taylor & Pacini-Ketchabaw, 2018) doings of early childhood. However, because both posthuman and common worlds theories challenge Euro-Western ontologies that centre the rational man, and the singular construction of the universalised male subject (Braidotti, 2017; Hodgins, 2019), when put to work in early childhood education, they both make possible the construction of a feminist posthuman. Both common worlds frameworks and posthumanisms, in general, pay attention to the multiple more-than-human relations, such as with other species and place, which is the focus of the research I briefly outline in this chapter, as well as the agency of materials (Kind & Argent, 2019; Kind, Vintimilla & Pacini-Ketchabaw, 2018; Pacini-Ketchabaw & Boucher, 2019; Pacini-Ketchabaw, Kind & Kocher, 2016) and the complex relations of technology (Land et al., 2020a, b) in early childhood spaces. These important reconfigurations in which other species, materials and technologies are not positioned as either good or bad but as the constituents of the lives of educators and children offer important points of divergence for who the early childhood educator can be within early childhood spaces. Within common worlds frameworks, instead of the role of educators as delivering curriculum designing to orient children towards future success, educators become co-researchers and engage in methodological processes not bounded by future-orientated logics of development. These processes enable educators to ask different questions, ones that are not limited to what defines good or bad practices for early childhood care and curriculum but how humans come together with more-than-humans and how educators may enact these relationalities towards more liveable futures. Within these common worlds configurations, the posthuman educator subject is then 'embodied and embedded, and its relational affectivity produces a shared sense of belonging to, and knowledge of, the common world we are sharing' (Braidotti, 2019, p. 47).

My intention is not to create a binary between good practice or bad early childhood practice but instead to share insight into what I think posthuman subjectivities may offer to educator/child/more-than-human coming together. I propose that resisting the 'good educator' subjectivity as inscribed through humanistic discourses such as capitalism, neoliberalism and developmentalism, there are possibilities for pedagogical engagements that create otherwise possibilities. Because pedagogical practices within common worlds frameworks respond to the specificities of the time and place of the educators and children, they offer the possibility of enacting posthuman affirmative ethics. Affirmative ethics are 'a collective practice of constructing social horizons of hope, in response to the flagrant injustices, the perpetuation of old hierarchies, and new forms of domination' (Braidotti, 2019, p. 156). For me, enacting affirmative ethical subjectivities is how I began to address my itchy desire to do something different in early childhood education, that I mentioned earlier and enabled me to engage in joyful experimentation with the possibility to shake loose some of the dominant practices that I was feeling overwhelmed by. In practice, experimenting with affirmative ethical responses to children and the more-than-human enabled educators to engage with possibilities of more-than-human relations, through the construction of themselves as posthuman subjects. To centre affirmative ethical practices, educators and myself followed not only our own curiosities, but also our complex relations for the world, both human and more-than-human. What guided us in our enactment of affirmative ethical practices was a commitment to address common concerns in early childhood while taking seriously an understanding that we do not experience these concerns in the same way, or as Braidotti (2019) so eloquently puts it '"we, posthuman subjects", who are in *this* particular project together, but "we are not One and the same"' (p. 153). For example, the educators and I shared concerns about the climate crisis, and a desire to want to think with children about climate relations, but we each had different specific concerns, and each felt the effects of the climate crisis differently because we were each embedded in the specific particularities of our individual lives. Bringing together these different positionalities allowed us, as posthuman early childhood educator subjects, to come together in ways that did not universalize or simplify our own relations to the more-than-human world but carried the possibilities of new and exciting interconnectivities and relationalities. In the following two examples from my research, I outline how educators and I worked at embodying posthuman subjectivities. This process was both difficult and generative and offered us small, but important possibilities to engage in methodological processes that subvert the violences often done in the name of the universalized human.

The shift from humancentric subjectivity to posthuman subjectivity is not easy. Many early childhood educators, myself included, were trained in ways that positioned developmental psychology as *the* way to do early childhood education. Developmental psychology offers an ideal universalized human subject, which, as mentioned at the beginning of this chapter, excludes and pathologizes feminized, racialized and disabled bodies. This singular theoretical orientation narrowly defines the purpose of early childhood education as preparing children to be successful, functioning adults and consequently positions the primary responsibility of educators as guides to bring children in enjoyable child-friendly ways along to this idealized state (Brown, 2015; Vintimilla, 2014). I want to be careful to position subjectivity as something one can choose to step into but rather as the shaping of who one can be in the world. Dahlberg and Moss (2005) define subjectification as 'the shaping of a certain kind of subject who will govern herself or himself, replacing the need for coercive force' (p. 20), and as discussed above, the human subject is often positioned as 'rational, knowing, stable, unified, self-governing, and freed of obligation – also, by implication, adult, male and white' (Dahlberg & Moss, 2005, p. 2). Early childhood spaces, the places in which children are educated and cared for, can be considered institutions for subjectification (Dahlberg et al., 2007), meaning that these spaces are sites of potential both reproduction and disruption of capitalistic, neoliberal subjectivities for both children and educators.

Meeting Common Worlds Frameworks

In my doctoral research, I worked as a pedagogist[1] on the traditional lands of the Anishinabek, Haudenosaunee, Lūnaapéewak and Attawandaron peoples in what is colonially known as London, Ontario, Canada. This research was part of a larger SSHRC-funded research project led by Dr Veronica Pacini-Ketchabaw, *Climate Action Network: Exploring Climate Change Pedagogies with Children* (http://www.climateactionchildhood.net/). At my specific research site, we wanted to rethink energy relations through posthuman understandings and to do this we needed to embody posthuman subjectivity. Weekly, educators, children, and I walked to a local cemetery that was rife with more-than-human others: animals, trees, rocks (both natural and unnatural in the form of tombstones), bacteria, decaying bodies, weather, soil, grass, sun, and so on and so on). Specifically, I wanted to think about how we could move past discussions about whether the cemetery was an *appropriate* place for children or what children could learn from the cemetery to think about how the cemetery was a place where we might come to know our relations with the more-than-human world differently. I was curious about what possibilities enacting affirmative more-than-human ethical relations might generate towards enacting climate change pedagogies that did more than reinstate human exceptionalism. As posthuman subjects we needed to craft pedagogical practices that resisted positioning ourselves and children at the centre of the more-than-human world. This required an acknowledgement that we are in relation with the world, and not acting upon the natural world, as is often perpetuated in environmental education initiatives with children (Cole & Malone, 2019).

I had been thinking about how I might bring my interest in earth-based feminist spirituality to our work with common worlds frameworks as a way to intervene in the anthropocentric logics that have caused the current ecological crisis. However, I knew that this was the particular ontological way in which I experienced the world, and that to actually embody posthuman subjectivities, the educator's world views mattered as well. In other words, we needed a place to start, a way into thinking with common worlds and posthuman frameworks and we might begin to engage in our work with children as posthuman educator subjects. We decided to read Pacini-Ketchabaw, Taylor and Blaise's (2016) chapter *Decentring the Human in Multispecies Ethnography*, in which the authors offer vignettes about their relations with more-than-human others. Each vignette offers complex insight into more-than-human relations and importantly refuses to offer ways in which these relations in which children are at the centre. the thickness of these multispecies encounters outrightly denies the readers the ability to translate these stories into teachable moments for children or reproducible educational practices. The vignettes offer tellings of encounters with worms, raccoons, dogs and dead kangaroos. At first, the educators were disturbed by the piece, confused and frustrated with why an article about early childhood dwells in the stink of death, urine and faeces instead of the romanticized child/animal stories they were familiar with. The propositions of the chapter were unfamiliar and quite uncomfortable, precisely because they refused to use the tools of human exceptionalism (Pacini-Ketchabaw, Taylor & Blaise, 2016) to configure child relations with the more-than-human, or anthropomorphism to teach children about morality. I share this little story, not as a criticism of the educators, caring and dedicated folks, who I am very grateful to have learned alongside, but to gesture towards how thinking with more-than-human relationality demands a radically different subjectivity than what most educators are trained in and familiar with enacting. At first uncomfortable by the chapter's refusal to centre the child, as we continued to read it together over many weeks while continuing regular visits with the cemetery, the educators and I began to explore what kinds of questions and practices they might begin to engage in, if the child's development (the human perspective) needn't be the sole focus. Thinking with the concepts presented in *Decentring the Human in Multispecies Ethnography* offered possibilities for us not only to think about human/more-than-human relations in radically different ways than what we were used to in early childhood education, but also to wonder who we might be as educators and researchers if we embraced these concepts.

Enacting Earth-Based Feminist Spirituality

Indebted to the posthuman conceptualizations of children's relations with other species offered to us by Pacini-Ketchabaw, Taylor and Blaise, the educators and I began to think about how we could experiment with ways of knowing the cemetery that decentred children, and the human. I slowly started to introduce earth-based feminist spirituality as a possible way to reconfigure the human/more-than-human relations we embodied in our weekly walks to the cemetery. Earth-based feminist spirituality is a broad term but is often associated with neo-pagan beliefs such as Wicca. Ecofeminists acknowledge that many women's ways of knowing were eradicated in the name of the rise of patriarchy (Starhawk, 1982), capitalism (Federici, 2004, 2018; Skott-Myhre, 2017), and science (Ehrenreich & English, 2010). Many of these ways of knowing, and certainly the ones I focus on in my research, propose a deeply connected, mutually reciprocal relation between the human and the more-than-human. With the literal and figurative murder of the 'witches', knowledges that many women had about relationality with nature have been destroyed (Mies & Shiva, 2014). Ecofeminists and others who seek to reanimate these knowledges propose reclaiming of these purposefully erased ways of being in the world as experimental modes of intervening in human-caused ecological disaster. Ecofeminists Mies and Shiva (2014) note that the current climate crisis has significant effects on the bodies of women and other marginalized groups. In other words, the climate crisis affects bodies differently, and women and other marginalized groups suffer these effects more materially than others. Reclaiming these feminist embodied ways of knowing are a possible entry point to craft refrains (Stengers, 2008) that respond to the 'vast disconnection, an abyss of ignorance that becomes apparent whenever an issue involving the natural world arises' (Starhawk, 2004, p. 7). Refrains are responsive and contingent as they move away from applying dogmatic categorizations of understanding of what is happening in the world to engage with partial and situated truths to create democratic practices, ask speculative questions that assemble and reassemble subjectivities (Stengers, 2008) and are speculative practices that help us embody feminist posthuman subjectivities. Enacting these subjectivities constitutes a radical reconvening of the world in which the assemblages of human and more-than-humans flow and reflow through each other to create happenings (Tsing, 2015) which make possible onto-epistemologies that are flexible and embrace multiplicity. These complex understandings of the world no longer position spirituality and scientific beliefs as incommensurable and so educators and myself are able to sit with both scientific and spiritual knowledges to think outside the dogmatic compartmentalizations of what is true and that which is not rational (Starhawk, 2004). In our work at the childcare setting, through embracing concepts related to how earth-based feminist spirituality challenged universal constructions of the human, we were able to begin to think of ourselves as different educator subjects because we didn't have to choose *one* way of being with children in the world. This shift allowed us to experiment with ways in which our work with children could matter in ways that went beyond the individual development of the child.

To usurp logics of human exceptionalism and thinking alongside philosopher of science Isabelle Stengers and Witch and ecofeminist Starhawk, the educators and I began experimenting with how we might actively reclaim earth-based feminist knowledges as modes to engage in posthuman pedagogical practices. Reclaiming, which Stengers (2015) borrows from neo-pagan contemporary witch activists, is to experiment 'with the possibilities of manners of living and cooperating that have been destroyed in the name of progress' (p. 12). It is important to note that reclaiming is not rooted in nostalgia for simple, more natural pasts, or a return to more 'innocent' times, but rather is a way of reconnecting with that which we have been separated from through subjectivities that position the human as rational, with rationality being directly correlated with objective Science[2] and universalized conceptualizations of the human. Reclaiming earth-based feminist spirituality then is a way to enact posthuman feminist subjectivities, as early childhood educators, because it allows us to bring knowledges that not only focus on more-than-human relationality, but have been 'lost' in the name of masculinist scientific knowledges. Building on Starhawk's (1982) assertion that the legacies of the eradication of spiritual feminist-based knowledges, through infamous witch burnings and continued oppression and punishment of women who don't go along with that which is rational, still shapes how women move through the world, Stengers (2017) is not making an argument for a universal shift to feminist spirituality which would be misaligned with the affirmative ethics at the centre of posthuman theory. Instead, her point is to interrogate why these knowings are 'relegated to the dustbin of culturally situated beliefs' (Nocek, 2018, p. 101) and to experiment with how reclaiming these knowledges in our current times might make possible subjectivities that begin to puncture the violence of human exceptionalism. Alongside Stengers' (2008) propositions, I wonder what might emerge when engaging with pedagogies of reclaiming with children and educators in early childhood education spaces and how this might work to construct feminist posthuman early childhood educator subjects. My understanding of feminist earth-based spirituality draws on neo-pagan and ecofeminist understandings of human/more-than-human relations 'to liberate women and nature from patriarchal destruction' (Mies & Shiva, 2014, p. 17). I want to strongly reiterate that earth-based feminist engagements are how I go about thinking more-than-human relations and subjectivities, and I am not offering these modes of engagement as a switch to or the new way to do early childhood education. I also acknowledge the deep spiritual relations with more-than-human others of Indigenous Peoples,[3] and I am grateful for this scholarship and the reminder that the posthuman turn in academia owes a great deal to these onto-epistemologies (Todd, 2016), and that as a White settler on colonized lands, I have an obligation to tread carefully and respectfully, as I discuss more-than-human spiritualities to resist offering my specific conceptualization of spirituality as privileged.

In addition to our weekly walks with children to the cemetery, educators and I frequently met to read, discuss what was happening on our walks, and experiment with ways to document our enquiry with the cemetery. We began to read *The Earth Path: Grounding Your Spirit in the Rhythms of Nature* by Starhawk as a possible way to begin enacting feminist earth-based spiritual posthuman subjectivities in our pedagogical work. We wondered how alongside this book, we might begin to notice our engagements with the more-than-human outside the paradigms of child development. We wanted to notice what was happening in the cemetery versus thinking only about what children could learn from it. In her book, Starhawk (2004) proposes observation as a mode to attune to more-than-human presences and build relationality with the more-than-human world. The type of observation proposed by Starhawk is vastly different from the positivistic, objective mode of observation prominent in early childhood education spaces (Woodhead & Faulkner, 2008). In early childhood education, the scientific underpinnings of developmentally focused observation reinforce the nature/culture divide and position the observer, most frequently the educator, as separate from that which she observes, and positions children and more-than-human others as knowable subjects (Holt, 2004). In this positioning, the educator appropriates what she observes into abstract ideals, reproducing the ideal human subject by determining when what she observes does not fall into the 'natural' developmental order. Haraway (1998) refers to this type of observation as the God-Trick, a masculinist practice in which the observer sees everything from nowhere. Much like Starhawk, she advocates instead for a more situated approach in which the observer, in the case of my research, the early childhood educator acknowledges the material, local and partial accounts of the world are as what is necessary for interrelated webs of connection to flourish. Starhawk (2004) proposes that to engage with observation in ways that transcend the reproduction of already known facts about the world, we must let go of the stories about what we *know* to be true and instead pay attention to the more-than-human world differently. Tsing (2015) offers similar propositions, which she names *arts of noticing*. Arts of noticing foreground the observers' embodied and embedded relations with the more-than-human assemblages to pay attention to the messy and often ignored stories in traditional observation techniques. These nuanced ways of noticing construct the early childhood educator subject as complex and as always in fluid relation with the more-than-human world, by challenging the types of observation that are dominant in early childhood education.

Similar to our beginnings with reading posthuman common world perspectives, this shift in modes of observation was not easy. We were not able to just put aside the ways we had been trained and practiced observing children. We needed some help along. This brought another tension to our work, how do we think with, be inspired by others, but not reproduce what they have offered? We returned to Starhawk and found her *nine ways of observing* to be a generative guide to how we might begin to experiment with observation differently. The first way of observing she offers is to start with the proposition *I wonder…* Prior to our next weekly walk to the cemetery, the educators and I chose something we wondered about, aligning with affirmative ethical practices, we had a shared interest of paying attention to the more-than-human world differently, with the hope of reconvening not only how we see these spaces, but how in noticing how we are always in deep relation with the more-than-human, we could construct early childhood posthuman subjectivities by purposely choosing to not focus on the children's relation with the cemetery. Guided by our shared interest, we each spent time thinking about what we were personally curious about and why. Knowing that it would be challenging to observe differently, we each chose something that did not have to do with the children, particularly focusing our curiosities on the more-than-human. Some wonderings included: I wonder if the grass will be dewy? I wonder if we will encounter cicada exuviae? Prepared with these wonderings, we were able to pay attention to more-than-human presences in ways that made them integral to our knowings of the place. Our wonderings came from our own curiosities and allowed us to enact posthuman subjectivities that were fluid and in relation with more-than-human presences. We were able to pay attention differently to the cemetery through these wonderings, and our curiosity invigorated more wonderings, and we continued to deepen the conceptualizations of our observations. For example, we did find cicada exuviae, which inspired the educator who was wondering about these abandoned shells to spend some time researching the life span of the cicada and sharing this information with children and families in the childcare centre. Observing outside the familiar developmental models allowed us to bring ourselves to our pedagogical work. Careful not to recentre the human through focusing on the self-fulfilment of the educators, I do want to propose that through this posthuman engagement, educators were able to enact subjectivities that positioned them as active participants in their relations with children (and the more-than-human) rather than passive facilitators of reproductive curriculums.

A Provocation for Meeting and Enacting Posthuman Possibilities

The stories I shared above tell about the particular experiences educators and I had in engaging in affirmative ethics to enact posthuman subjectivities. However, they are not reproducible, which is a tricky but fundamental aspect of posthuman pedagogical work. Posthuman subjectivities must always be in response to the specificities of the time and place in which they are enacted and are always constructed in relation to the more-than-human world. For me, thinking with earth-based feminist spiritualities allows me to bring erased feminist knowledges to how I conceptualize more-than-human relationalities, but this is just one way that posthuman subjectivity can be explored in early childhood spaces. As demonstrated by the vast common worlds scholarship, posthuman subjectivities provide multiple possible entry points to disrupt anthropocentric logics that uphold patriarchal, colonial and capitalist power relations that define a particular universalized human subject. Rupturing the ideal human subject through engaging with posthuman subjectivities makes possible an early childhood educator subject who is not bound to taken-for-granted, reproductive developmentalism.

Notes

1 A role in Ontario and British Columbia, Canada. Pedagogists work alongside educators and children to 'envision pedagogical connections and projects to provoke educational processes that, through interdisciplinary and provocative questions, ideas, theories, materials, relationships... deepen and complexify strong, situated pedagogical work in early childhood contexts' (Land, Vintimilla, Pacini-Ketchabaw & Angus, 2020: 2).

2   Following Subramaniam and Willey's (2017) thinking with Sandra Harding's (1997) distinction between Science and science I capitalize science in instances in which I wish to draw attention to knowledge that is recognized by EuroWestern institutions as 'official knowledge'.
3   See Hall, L. (2008). The Environment of Indigenous Economies: Honouring the Three Sisters and Recentering the Haudenosaunee Ways of Life; Kimmerer, R. (2013), Braiding Sweetgrass: Indigenous Wisdom, Scientific Knowledge and the Teachings of Plants; Todd, Z. (2017), Fish, Kin, and Hope: Tending to Water Violations in Amiskwaciwâskahikan and Treaty 6 Territory; Watts, V. (2013). Indigenous place-thought & agency amongst humans and non-humans (First Woman and Sky Woman go on a European world tour!); Whyte, K. (2018). Settler Colonialism, Ecology, and Environmental Injustice.

References

Braidotti, R. (2013). *The posthuman*. Polity Press.
Braidotti, R. (2017). Four theses on posthuman feminism. In R. Grusin (Ed.), *Anthropocene feminism* (pp. 21–48). University of Minnesota Press.
Braidotti, R. (2019). *Posthuman knowledge*. Polity Press.
Brown, C. P. (2015). Conforming to reform: Teaching pre-kindergarten in a neoliberal early education system. *Journal of Early Childhood Research*, *13*(3), 236–51.
Burman, E. (2001). Beyond the baby and the bathwater: Postdualistic developmental psychologies for diverse childhoods. *European Early Childhood Education Research Journal*, *9*(1), 5–22.
Burman, E. (2017). *Deconstructing developmental psychology* (3rd ed.). Routledge.
Cole, D. R. & Malone, K. (2019). Environmental education and philosophy in the Anthropocene. *Australian Journal of Environmental Education*, *35*(3), 157–62.
Crutzen, P. (2002). Geology of mankind. *Nature*, *415*, 23.
Dahlberg, G. & Moss, P. (2005). *Ethics and politics in early childhood education*. RoutledgeFalmer.
Dahlberg, G., Moss, P., & Pence, A. (2007). *Beyond quality in early childhood education and care: Languages of evaluation* (2nd ed.). Routledge.
Ehrenreich, B. & English, D. (2010). *Witches, midwives & nurses: A history of women healers* (2nd ed.). The Feminist Press.
Federici, S. (2004). *Caliban and the witch*. Autonomedia.
Federici, S. (2018). *Witches, witch-hunting, and women*. PM Press.
Hall, L. (2008). The environment of Indigenous economies: Honouring the Three Sisters and recentering the Haudenosaunee ways of life. In L. Simpson (Ed.), *Lighting the eighth fire: The liberation, resurgence, and protection of Indigenous nations* (pp. 149–60). Arbeiter Ring.

Hancock, C. L., Morgan, C. W., & Holly, J. Jr (2021). Counteracting dysconscious racism and ableism through fieldwork: Applying DisCrit classroom ecology in early childhood personnel preparation. *Topics in Early Childhood Special Education*, *41b*(1), 45–56.
Haraway, D. (1998). Situated knowledges: The science question in feminism and the privilege of partial perspective. *Feminist Studies*, *14*(3), 575–99.
Haraway, D. (2008). *When species meet*. University of Minnesota Press.
Haraway, D. (2016). *Staying with the trouble: Making kin in the chthulucene*. Duke University Press.
Haraway, D. (2017). Symbiogenesis, sympoises, and art science activisms for staying with the trouble. In A. Tsing, H. Swanson, E. Gan, & N. Bubandt (Eds.), *Arts of living on a damaged planet* (pp. M25–M50). University of Minnesota Press.
Harding, S. (1997). Comment on Hekman's 'truth and method: Feminist standpoint theory revisited': Whose standpoint needs the regimes of truth and reality? *Signs: Journal of Women in Culture and Society*, *22*(2), 382–91.
Hodgins, B. D. (2019). Caring: Method as affect, obligation and action. In B. D. Hodgins (Ed.), *Feminist research for 21st-century childhoods: Common worlds methods* (pp. 171–8). Routledge.
Holt, L. (2004). The 'voices' of children: De-centring empowering research relations. *Children's Geographies*, *2*(1), 13–27.
Jobb, C., MacAlpine, K. & Pacini-Ketchabaw, V. (2019). Educators experimenting with common worlds pedagogies. In L. Gibbs & M. Gasper (Eds.), *Challenging the intersection of policy with pedagogy* (pp. 35–48). Routledge.
Kimmerer, R. (2013). *Braiding sweetgrass: Indigenous wisdom, scientific knowledge and the teachings of plants*. Milkweed Editions.
Kind, S. & Argent, A. (2019). Fabricating: Fabric fluidities and studio encounters. In B. D. Hodgins (Ed.), *Feminist research for 21st-century childhoods: Common worlds methods* (pp. 35–42). Bloomsbury Academic.
Kind, S., Vintimilla, C. D., & Pacini-Ketchabaw, V. (2018). Material choreographies: Fabric as a living language of exchange. *Innovations in early education: The International Reggio Emilia exchange* (pp. 40–51). Spring.
Land, N., Vintimilla, C. D., Pacini-Ketchabaw, V., & Angus, L. (2020). Propositions toward educating pedagogists: Decentering the child. *Contemporary Issues in Early Childhood*, 1–13.
Land, N., Hamm, C. Yazbeck, S., Brown, M., Danis, I., & Nelson, N. (2020a). Doing pedagogical intentions with facetiming common worlds (and Donna Haraway). *Global Studies of Childhood*, *10*(2), 131–44.
Land, N., Hamm, C. Yazbeck, S., Brown, M., Danis, I., & Nelson, N. (2020b). Facetiming common worlds: Exchanging digital place stories and crafting pedagogical contact zones. *Children's Geographies*, *18*(1), 30–43.
Mies, M. & Shiva, V. (2014). *Ecofeminism*. Zed Books Ltd.
Nelson, N. (2019), Tracking: Cultivating the 'arts of awareness' in early childhood. In B. D. Hodgins (Ed.), *Feminist research for 21st-century childhoods: Common worlds methods* (pp. 102–10). Bloomsbury Academic.

Nocek, A. J. (2018). On the risk of Gaia for an ecology of practices. *SubStance, 47*(1), 96–111.

Nxumalo, F. (2015). Forest stories: Restorying encounters with 'natural' places in early childhood education. In V. Pacini-Ketchabaw & A. Taylor (Eds.), *Unsettling the colonial places and spaces of early childhood education* (pp. 21–42). Routledge.

Nxumalo, F. (2016). Towards 'refiguring presences' as an anti-colonial orientation to research in early childhood studies. *International Journal of Qualitative Studies in Education, 29*(5), 640–54.

Nxumalo, F. (2017). Geotheorizing mountain–child relations within anthropogenic inheritances. *Children's Geographies, 15*(5), 558–69.

Nxumalo, F. (2018). Stories for living on a damaged planet: Environmental education in a preschool classroom. *Journal of Early Childhood Research, 16*(2), 148–59.

Nxumalo, F. (2019). Presencing: Decolonial attunements to children's place relations'. In B. D. Hodgins (Ed.), *Feminist research for 21st-century childhoods: Common worlds methods* (pp. 159–67). Bloomsbury Academic.

Pacini-Ketchabaw, V. (2013). Frictions in forest pedagogies: Common worlds in settler colonial spaces. *Global Studies of Childhood, 3*(4), 355–65.

Pacini-Ketchabaw, V. & Boucher, K. (2019). Claying: Attending to earth's caring relations'. In B. D. Hodgins (Ed.), *Feminist research for 21st-century childhoods: Common worlds methods* (pp. 25–34). Bloomsbury Academic.

Pacini-Ketchabaw, V., Taylor, A., & Blaise, M. (2016). De-centring the human in multispecies ethnographies. In C. Taylor and C. Hughes (Eds.), *Posthuman Research Practices in Education* (pp. 149–67). Palgrave MacMillan.

Pacini-Ketchabaw, V. & Nxumalo, F. (2014). Posthumanist imaginaries for decolonizing early childhood praxis. In M. N. Bloch, B. B. Swadener, & G. S. Cannella (Eds.), *Reconceptualizing early childhood care and education: A reader* (pp. 131–42). Peter Lang Publishing.

Pacini-Ketchabaw, V. & Nxumalo, F. (2015). Unruly raccoons and troubled educators: Nature/culture divides in a childcare centre. *Environmental Humanities, 71*(1), 151–68.

Pacini-Ketchabaw, V., Kind, S., & Kocher, L. (2016). *Encounters with materials in early childhood education*. Routledge.

Pacini-Ketchabaw, V. & Kummen, K. (2016). Shifting temporal frames in children's common worlds in the Anthropocene. *Contemporary Issues in Early Childhood, 17*(4), 431–41.

Pacini-Ketchabaw, V., Khattar, R., & Montpetit, M. (2019). Reconfiguring early childhood education: Common worlding pedagogies. In S. Jagger (Ed.), *Early years education and care in Canada: A historical and philosophical overview* (pp. 191–206). Canadian Scholars.

Skott-Myhre, K. (2017). *Feminist spirituality under capitalism: Witches, fairies, and nomads*. Routledge.

Starhawk (1982). *Dreaming the dark: Magic, sex & politics*. Beacon Press.

Starhawk (2004). *Earth path: Grounding your spirit in the rhythms of nature*. HarperOne.

Steffen, W., Crutzen, P., & McNeil, J. I. (2007). The Anthropocene: Are humans now overwhelming the great forces of nature? *Ambio, 36*(8), 614–21.

Stengers, I. (2008). Experimenting with refrains: Subjectivity and the challenge of escaping modern dualism. *Subjectivity, 22*(1), 38–59.

Stengers, I. (2015). *In catastrophic times: Resisting the coming barbarism.* (A. Goffey, Trans.). Open Humanities Press.

Stengers, I. (2017). Autonomy and the intrusion of Gaia. *The South Atlantic Quarterly, 116*(2), 381–400.

Subramaniam, B. & Willey, A. (2017). Introduction: Feminism's sciences. *Catalyst: Feminism, Theory, Technoscience, 3*(1), 1–23.

Taylor, A. (2011). Reconceptualizing the 'nature' of childhood. *Childhood, 18*(4), 420–33.

Taylor, A. (2013). *Reconfiguring the natures of childhood.* Routledge.

Taylor, A. (2017). Beyond stewardship: Common world pedagogies for the Anthropocene. *Environmental Education Research, 23*(10), 1448–61.

Taylor, A. (2019), Rabbiting: Troubling the legacies of invasion. In B. D. Hodgins (Ed.), *Feminist research for 21st-century childhoods: Common worlds methods* (pp. 111–18). Bloomsbury Academic.

Taylor, A. & Pacini-Ketchabaw, V. (2018). *The common worlds of children and animals: Relational ethics for entangled lives.* Routledge.

Taylor, A., Pacini-Ketchbaw, V., de Finney, S., & Blaise, M. (2016). Inheriting the ecological legacies of settler colonialism. *Environmental Humanities, 7*(1), 129–32.

Todd, Z. (2016). An Indigenous feminist's take on the ontological turn: 'Ontology' is just another word for colonialism. *Journal of Historical Sociology, 29*(1), 4–22.

Todd, Z. (2017). Fish, kin, and hope: Tending to water violations in Amiskwaciwâskahikan and Treaty 6 Territory. *Afterall: A Journal of Art, Context, and Enquiry, 43*(1), 102–7.

Tsing, A. (2015). *The mushroom at the end of the world: On the possibility of life in capitalist ruins.* Princeton University Press.

Vintimilla, C. D. (2014). Neoliberal fun and happiness in early childhood education. *Canadian Children, 39*(1), 79–87.

Watts, V. (2013). Indigenous place-thought & agency amongst humans and non-humans (First Woman and Sky Woman go on a European world tour!). *Decolonization: Indigeneity, Education, & Society, 2*(1), 20–34.

Whyte, K. (2018). Settler colonialism, ecology, and environmental injustice. *Environment and Society, 9*(1), 125–44.

Woodhead, M. & Faulkner, D. (2008). Subjects, objects or participants? Dilemmas of psychological research with children. In P. Christensen, & A. James (Eds.), *Research with children: Perspectives and practice* (2nd ed., pp. 26–55). Routledge.

10

Early Childhood Pedagogues, Thresholds and the Potentialities of Feminisms and New Materialism

Gunilla Dahlberg and Ann Merete Otterstad

Returning and Starting

This chapter is an ongoing process in the middle of Gunilla and Ann Merete's conversations about feminism and early childhood education in Norway and Sweden, two countries that are part of the Nordic territory. Looking back fifty years (towards the political era of the 1970s), we are specifically interested in the combinations of how our political standpoints were embedded in feminism, working-class backgrounds and a social democratic political orientation. While these three aspects of our upbringing and early years careers are still working bodily on and with us, we seek here to question why we both seem to have taken-feminism-as-bodily-granted, since we seldom have stated feminism as an academic writing position. In the 1970s, there were several feminist movements which we were part of as were many others living in different social locations. We collectively demonstrated, made posters, critically argued, were part of ongoing social justice movements as activists, and cared professionally about ethics and democracy for all. We also have a two decades-long professional relationship facilitated through the international Reconceptualizing Early Childhood Education (RECE) community, an academic critical network group that offers opportunities for supportive and collective exchanges of ideas.

Due to our Scandinavian egalitarian values and a politics of democracy, our countries have been leaders in the development of the modern family, affirmative gender policies and the establishment of public systems of early childhood education and care (ECEC). Scandinavia has also been recognized as a location that has the most gender-equal labour markets in the world. Both countries were among the first to grant women the right to vote. Since the 1960s, social democratic politics in these small countries have been actively concerned with the 'women question' and the 'child question'.

Some would say that as state policies responded to these questions instrumentally the deeper, feminist nuances of them got lost. However, attunement to these questions did lead to family politics that recognized a woman's right to meaningful work, combined with good care and education for their young children. In Sweden, a 1968 National Commission on Child-Care, (Barnstugeutredningen), stressed that *all* children should have the right to a pedagogical institution characterized by a curriculum approach that prioritizes listening, exploration, dialogic relations and attitudes alongside a transdisciplinary focus on society, nature and culture. These principles were regarded as necessary for children to experience concrete forms of democracy (Hammarström Lewenhagen, 2013). From our perspective, these government actions were creative, sensible and transformative. The commission's work in Sweden was joyfully embraced by pedagogues and children at the local level and subsequently influenced childcare policy directions[1] in the Scandinavian countries.

This historical overview might romanticize our Scandinavian political ECEC field and might be a contrast to how professional lives have been practiced during the pandemic particularly when neoliberal political individualized values have infiltrated ECEC pedagogical practices during the last decades. We want this chapter to present a variety of feminist thinkers with the hope that the Scandinavian early childhood pedagogue can become bodily attuned to a future to come. We argue for the necessity of feminist ethical commitment to each other, creating networks and collective connections in ECEC in Scandinavia. However, it is important to point out that feminist perspectives cannot be incorporated into one epistemological category. There are many feminisms including new materialisms that have influenced our knowledge in ECEC for many years already.

Our Thinking/Writing Processes

Our cooperative thinking/writing has involved dialogues on Zoom, literature searches, reading, writing and more Zooming to think about feminisms, early childhood pedagogues, children and politics in the Scandinavian field of early childhood education and care. Our dialogues included a search for ideas, thresholds and storytelling to think otherwise about feminisms and early childhood pedagogues in Scandinavia. We were inspired by 're-reading the past' (Grosz, 2010, p. 48; Haraway, 2016) to evoke present futures alongside Barad's (2014) concept of 're-turning' for possibilities for the yet not known. We also 'returned' to and 're-read the past' with Hekman (2014), and with Manning and Massumi (2014) which opens for thinking and exploring with the 'what more' and 'what if'.

We have organized our chapter in three directions; first we discuss early childhood theorists who have influenced our thinking; second, we look more broadly to how feminist thinkers have taken up the question of the woman subject; and third, we consider how feminist new materialism in early childhood studies could open up new ways of thinking about the early childhood pedagogue.[2]

In this chapter, we take a middling position. According to Manning and Massumi (2014), the concept of threshold encourages thinking and acting from the middle. They write that in this middle, 'the threshold shifts. It vibrates. It is not figure or form. Not this or that history, this or that memory. It resonates with all it touches. But it cannot quite be seen' (p. 64).

Manning (2019) describes thresholds as doorways we cross every day and as crossings into thought, imagination and valuation. In writing this chapter, we wondered how feminisms as thresholds might open up to new crossings and ways to consider how worlds of childhood education shift and what meanings these shifts carry. We thought about how some feminist thresholds can be more challenging to cross than others and how they traverse or travel over spaces and time. For example, a threshold to cross and change can be related to how the construction of gender continuously recruits women into the early childhood labour force and shapes their understandings of the work. We recognized that there are differences in how individuals cross thresholds, which we think is dependent on how theoretical concepts and analysis of everyday practices can be intensely productive and life-giving encounters.

We also connect to feminist storytelling (Haraway, 2016) to critically view how our lives in Scandinavia might have contributed to taking feminisms for-granted. Through our dialogues, we reflected on stories that explored connections over time between feminisms, particularly new materialism and pragmatism, early childhood pedagogues and children in our two locations. We wondered why feminisms have not historically had a clear impact in our field despite being dominated by women with a rich history of social activism (Bloch, 1992).

We began our writing with the understanding that we need to be critical, collective, active and affirmative by creating networks and alliances between multiple groups of humans and the more-than-human world. To open to new materialism, we build on Hekman (2014) who describes new materialism as embracing feminism and the philosophy of science, cultural studies, animal studies and the posthuman (p. 148). Drawing on Tuana (2001), Hekman further explains that new materialism 'complicates our understanding of reality' (p. 148) by seeing that 'everything is always in flux: the human, more-than-human, material, and discursive are interacting in a complex mix. The result is a transformation of our understanding of knowledge and the world that is revolutionary' (p. 150).

We also embraced an attitude of critiquing beyond criticism (Foucault, 1997) whereby critique communicates hope for a world-making that is otherwise. We acknowledged the range of feminisms and theories – intersectionality, Black feminist thought, women of colour feminisms, transnational feminism, queer theory and disability studies – that enrich our thinking and that have circulated in the Scandinavian feminist fields. Like Hekman (2014), our concern here is not to get 'woman', 'the pedagogue', 'child' or 'feminisms' right but, rather, to explore what shapes and produces feminist knowledges in ECEC with specific interest in a future to come. We want to explore with feminisms and the potential already inherent and immanent in how pedagogues affect children and schools through unexpected processes and life-giving encounters that at a given moment take place and are in the making. Like Stenger (2018), we are reminded to search for 'more than' and to be sensitive to 'what comes':

> We don't know what the strange adventure of the modern sciences could have been, or could yet be, but we know that doing 'better' that we are already in the habit of doing will not be sufficient for learning. It is a matter of unlearning an attitude or more or less cynical ('realist') resignation, and becoming sensitive once again to what we perhaps know, but only as in a dream.
>
> (p. 81)

The Era of the 1970s and Following Years

In the 1970s, the number of early childhood educational students at Swedish and Norwegian universities and university colleges greatly expanded. Many students from a working-class background were recruited and became the first women in their family with higher education. Ann Merete was part of this movement, starting her preschool education programme and finishing as a preschool pedagogue in 1977. Feminist collective activism was part of the social life of university students and we both signed on to these movements. In the 1980s and

1990s, we began to connect with international critical feminist researchers who reflected our own thinking on the upbringing of children and the early childhood pedagogue. In this chapter, we refer to four of these feminist thinkers who have been important for us and our own research milieus: Valerie Walkerdine, Erica Burman, Gaile Cannella and Lynn Fendler.

Valerie Walkerdine

Walkerdine (1993) viewed developmental psychology as one of the grand modern metanarratives of science that universalizes the rational, the masculine and European thinking so that women and, by extension early childhood pedagogues, become 'the Other' and marginalized subjects reduced to pathology and abnormality. Walkerdine's postmodern critique of developmental psychology offered early childhood pedagogues an awareness of discursive oppressive processes and the analytical tools to politicize governmental documents and show how they upheld categorizations of 'the Other'. Gunilla who met Walkerdine in a feminist study-group in London in the late 1970s was inspired by her critique. In the 1980s, Gunilla drew on Walkerdine's critique to argue in her own work that interpretations of children's development do not exist independently of and/or separate from our own participation in the interpreting; rather interpretations are subjective and contextual constructions.

Erica Burman

Walkerdine's critique was followed by Erica Burman's book, *Deconstructing Developmental Psychology* (1994), which provided a critical feminist response to dominant theories of child development. Burman argued that developmental psychology discursively serves to regulate family behaviour and marginalize working-class and ethnic minority families. Burman further described how the European early childhood pedagogue came to hold a representation or an image of the child consistent with developmental psychology. Burman argues that this representation has been exported around the world and particularly to 'developing' countries.

Gaile Cannella

In 1997, Gail Cannella's book, *Deconstructing Early Childhood Education: Social Justice and Revolution,* started to spread across the Scandinavian early childhood education and care field. In this book, Cannella critically questioned dominant discursive power practices in connection to children's and women's lives and to prejudices, stereotypes and the privileging of certain groups over others.

Lynn Fendler

Later Lynn Fendler (2001), with inspiration from Michel Foucault's ideas of 'governmentality', described the continuing prominent aim of developmental psychology in ECEC as:

> Finding a universal and scientific guide for who the child is, can be and should be by representing, classifying and normalizing the child through the concepts of "developmentality" as well as directing how to govern the child's development and progress.
>
> (p. 120)

Combined with our own work, these authors' critical perspectives showed how the child and pedagogue subject are discursively constructed, weaving knowledge and power into a coercive structure that regulates through classifications and categorizations originating from the positivist social sciences. Here we recognized the normalized child, 'the deficit and lacking child', the non-normal, based on universal stages of development. Such a lacking child-creation, marked by deficits, implies a repeated asking: What is a child? What is a pedagogue? And what is a parent? Universalizing discourses that assert something as 'typical for this child' or state that 'this teacher always does this like that' or 'we can't expect more from these parents' are narrowing potentialities. This leads to feminism without possibilities where we seldom ask the much-needed 'what else' or 'what if' questions (Manning, 2016).

Pedagogy in a Changing World – The Stockholm Project

Through reading and collective networking with early childhood practices in Sweden, Gunilla became increasingly aware of how we, as researchers and pedagogues, are ourselves part of power/knowledge regimes that privilege and value certain truths about 'good education', 'good knowledge', 'good methods' and 'good care' (Popkewitz, 1984). This awareness compelled Gunilla to engage in the questions of how power works in subtle ways and how power and knowledge are intertwined and shape the early childhood pedagogue as a certain subject.

In 1992, during her second visit to the communal preschools in Reggio Emilia, Gunilla became aware that Loris Malaguzzi, the philosopher and head of

Reggio Emilia preschools and the pedagogues of the preschools shared this kind of thinking. With fascism as a living experience, Malaguzzi and the pedagogues had made a crucial choice to create the schools as democratic meeting places. Since the early 1960s, together with activist women in the city, they had border-crossed, 'brick by brick', taken-for-granted constructions of knowledge and learning, categorizations of the child and the pedagogue, and normalizing techniques and practices. This experience in Reggio Emilia and the encounter with Malaguzzi's thinking, combined with feminist theories, and the theories of Michel Foucault, Jacque Derrida, Gilles Deleuze and Felix Guattari inspired the 1993 Stockholm project, 'Pedagogy in a Changing World' (see Dahlberg, Moss & Pence, 1999/2013; Dahlberg & Moss, 2005).

This project embraced Loris Malaguzzi's ideas of the hundred languages and entanglement, which connected to the Deleuzian idea of rhizomatic thinking and its multiple functionings through connections and heterogeneity with no given construction. It opened thinking about the becoming-woman and the becoming-child, and hence, the becoming-early childhood pedagogue. These vivid ideas have, since then, been central to collaborative continuations (Gunilla Dahlberg, Hillevi Lenz Taguchi and Jeanette Rhedding-Jones) of the Stockholm project and its focus on pedagogical changes and transformations (e.g. Dahlberg & Lenz-Taguchi, 1994; Elfström, 2013; Halvars-Franzén, 2010; Lenz Taguchi, 2010; Lind, 2010; Nordin Hultman, 2004; Olsson, 2009; Unga, 2013).

Nevertheless, despite feminist influences in Nordic ECEC, looking back we now notice there was an absence of feminism in our own writing from 2000 on. Previous to this, feminism was more central in our work and the Nordic ECEC context. For example, Gunilla arranged a two-day conference in the early 1980s, bringing together a group of feminist researchers and early childhood educational researchers who did not use a feminist framework. Bloch in the United States (1991, 1992, in De Lair & Erwin, 2000) suggested that ECEC's 'close alliance to psychological and child developmental perspectives, with its strong influence by the positivist tradition' (p. 153) had contributed to the lack of alliances between feminism and ECEC in Western countries.

We think this is very fair to say. However, looking back to our own work, our resistance to the influence of developmental psychology and its research models of that time, had made us move towards Bernstein's sociology of education and to thinkers such as Lundgren, Løvlie, Popkewitz, Foucault, Derrida, Levinas and Deleuze. These critical theories and philosophies had made a break from modernism and thus opened up analyses of power/knowledge regimes, expressed in neoliberalism and new quality management (Dahlberg & Åsén, 1994; Dahlberg, Moss and Pence, 1999/2013). Given that we were drawn to these thinkers, 'what else' could feminist theories offer early childhood pedagogues and how can they be taken up and enacted locally in ECEC? In the 2000s, De Lair and Erwin (2000, pp. 156–9) articulated four feminist assumptions that resonated with us:

1. teaching[3] is a *political act*
2. gender, ethnicity, culture, language, social class, and sexual orientation are *part of the educational context*
3. *societal inequalities and oppression* are reflected in education and educational institutions
4. good teaching requires *active commitment* to and involvement in *working for social change and social justice*.

We argue that these assumptions are still important considerations for feminist and collective activist networking and for thinking about the early childhood pedagogue in Nordic ECEC. The theoretical drive for these assumptions comes from a range of feminist and philosophical theories to which we now turn. We begin with Simone de Beauvoir and continue shortly with Judith Butler and then Erin Manning. These three women build on philosophical thinking and the first two also take a clear feminist standpoint. We read Manning between the lines as a feminist philosopher affected by vitalities, intensities, bodies and movements. Lately, she has also focused on decolonial perspectives and more-than-human entities in her work.

Simone de Beauvoir

For Beauvoir, questions about the category of 'woman' did not fit into the vocabularies of any of the philosophical positions that were available to her in the late 1940s. Thus, Hekman, 2014, p. 26) argues that Beauvoir stepped outside the philosophical canon of that time, radically redefining 'woman' in her influential book, *The Second Sex* (1949). According to Hekman (2014), 'Beauvoir agrees that woman, like man, is her body, but claims that her body is something other than herself' (p.15). Beauvoir concluded, therefore, that 'Women is not a fixed reality, but a becoming' (Hekman, 2014, p. 15), and that 'the identity of woman as a complex mix of cultural and material factors' (Hekman, 2014, p. 24). These ideas were, at that time, in direct opposition to the fixed, biological and essentialized category of woman asserted in Western philosophy.

Judith Butler

According to Hekman's description of Butler's work, particularly her influential postmodern books, *Gender Trouble* (1990) and *Undoing Gender* (2004), Butler continued to destabilize the category of 'woman'. Hekman (2014) summarizes Butler's position: 'gender is a becoming, not a being. It follows that if *to be* a woman is to become a woman, then this process is not fixed, and it is possible to *become* a being who is neither "man" nor "woman"' (Hekman, 2014, p. 119). Butler further maintains that in this 'becoming', gender is performed through available socially constructed norms assigned to one's sex. Butler's theory of performativity suggests that gender is inherently interactional, whereby individuals enacting gender with an awareness that others will assess and potentially shape the gendered performance.

Erin Manning

We now move onto the work of Erin Manning and her exploratory and process-oriented way of working which border-crosses the strong emphasis on 'the self' (e.g. the child and the pedagogue) as the site of change. Her work with Brian Massumi in *Thought in the Act* (2014) explores a collaborative mode of thinking at the intersection of art, philosophy and science. Manning begins with ideas of movement, perception and experience. In the book *Always More-Than-One: Individuations Dance* (2013), she continues to deepen this exploration. In further work, *The Minor Gesture* (2016), Manning explores the processes of interdependency between organic and non-organic bodies through introducing the concepts of *affect*, *more-than-human* and *the minor gesture*. Her writing is inspired by the Dutch seventeenth-century philosopher Baruch Spinoza's idea that we never know what a body can do, as we become affected and we affect. Following Massumi (2015), affects in Spinoza's definition are ways of connecting to others and to other situations. They are ways of 'participating in processes larger than ourselves' (p. 6). So affect is a kind of force of existing, and an openness to the immediacy, and to the world through being involved and being a participator. Deleuze (1988) argues that when Spinoza writes about the body he does not differentiate between the organic and the non-organic body; rather he states that a 'body can be anything; it can be an animal, a body of sounds, a mind or an idea; it can be *a linguistic corpus*, a social body, a collectivity' (p. 127).

In line with this, Manning's (2013) philosophy of bodies and movement rejects the unified subject and turns to non-unitary subjectivities, suggesting that we are more than one. Following Deleuze (1988), she gives attention to what is in the making, and this opens for a way to move out of/ beyond a dualistic thinking of subject/object, human/non-human, nature/culture and discourse/matter. Here we return to Deleuze's ontology of becoming in which he writes Life with a capital L and points out that Life is carried by events and forces that can be seen as a form of pre-personal singularities, that exist before a stable and intersubjective 'self' emerges (Rajchman, 2001).

These intensities and forces open up for movement, *for becoming*, and for affects and potentiality, for what is immanent in the present-moment of experience (Massumi, 2002; Stern, 1985). To open for possibilities and processual and event-centred subjectivity, Manning continuously raises the question of how singular experiences and life situations can escape dominant codings, criteria and judgments. She does this by inviting us to pay attention and to be sensitive to the dynamic, subtle and fragile modes of existence and to assemblages of a life, although they may pass almost unperceived. For Manning, these modes of existence are minor gestures or a process of becoming, towards the more-than-currently-human potential that can arise from the encounter between bodies. The encounter has the capacity and power to open new modes of experience, manners of expression and new relations. This process, that always is in movement are creative co-compositions, and transformations of the field of relations that requires that we attend *to things in-the-making*. Ontologically, Manning moves here from talking about bodies to talking about *bodying*, from talking about the world to *worlding* (Manning, 2016, p. 2). Because of this move, and with inspiration from Stengers (2005), she understands our sensibility to affect other beings as an *ecology of practices*. It follows that affect, intensities and vitality are the basis for our connection and interdependency with other human beings as well as with other bodies. Thus, the early childhood pedagogue may be seen in the same way as Manning describes the child: '*There is no inner child. What there is … is an indeterminate tendency for resonating with what else moves across it*' (2020, p. 6). For her this is the becoming-child, and we argue that the same holds for the early childhood pedagogue: there is no inner pedagogue. What there is, is an indeterminate tendency for resonating what else moves across. This is the becoming-pedagogue.

These descriptions of three feminist philosophers are invitations to grasp the importance of philosophies searching for complexities that avoid thresholds to categorizations and essentialism. In many ways, this philosophical thinking has influenced our current feminist standpoint embedded in values based on interrelated critical theories on discourse, feminist ethics, new materialism, affirmative critique, process-ontology and solidarity.

Where to Go

In our introduction to this chapter, we wondered why the term 'feminism' has not been actively addressed by us during our professional lives in ECEC. In one Zoom meeting, we challenged each other to express what feminism in early childhood education and care (and life) can become for us. Our shared knowledge finds support with feminist new materialism built on past historical and onto-epistemological philosophical theories, some of which we briefly examined earlier. A key question we ask in this section is: What if we rethink the individual child and pedagogue from a feminist new materialism perspective? What might occur and how could this thinking bring forward a becoming-child and a becoming-pedagogue? Our thinking/writings bring together descriptions of feminist thresholds that inspire us and are from our own experiences, locations and thinking, and that propose affirmative ethics as potentialities (Manning, 2014) that can affirm and give rise to new becomings.

We have been concerned with how an *affirmative ethics of an encounter and care* (Dahlberg & Moss, 2005) could move the early childhood pedagogue's engagement with difference beyond theories that privilege the fixed, singular and autonomous individual. From a feminist new materialism perspective, becoming-pedagogue, in and of the world today, stresses the importance of collective relations with human and more-than-human entities within immanence. Ethics, as a threshold, always happens in the middle, in-betweenness, through being attuned, and involved in a relational field of potentiality (Manning, 2014; Dahlberg & Moss, 2005; Olsson, 2009). In accordance with this ethics, instead of opposing and being reactive, the early childhood pedagogue seeks to be active and ethically affirmative, by creating networks, feminist alliances and solidarities.

In summary, feminist new materialism from the above perspective does not assume an overarching concept of life, just practices and flows of becoming, complex assemblages and heterogeneous relations. As such, feminisms can become filled with transversal alliances, allowing early childhood pedagogues as critical thinkers to re-unite different transdisciplinary knowledge beyond essentialism, discrimination and ignorance.

Even so, the formation of alternative early childhood pedagogue subjectivities and their actualizations can be risky work so it must be done diligently. The question is how to make alternative subjectivities endure. This question has been particularly important since neoliberalism swept through the Scandinavian countries, like the rest of the Western world. As Braidotti (2008) argues, neoliberalism dangerously 're-territorializes desires through a gravitational pull of established values bent on short-term profit' (p. 20). In turn, this 'achieves a disastrous double effect, as it re-asserts individualism as the norm, while reducing it to consumerism' (p. 20). In Norway and Sweden, early childhood pedagogues, like in many other countries in the world, are now increasingly seen as executers and deliverers of a service, serving parents and children seen as customers or clients. We have insistently resisted this neoliberal fact through our books, articles and talks and through networking with pedagogues, parents, politicians, municipalities and government officials (Dahlberg & Åsén, 1994; Dahlberg & Moss, 1999/2013; Otterstad & Braathe, 2016).

We end this chapter returning with the becoming of the early childhood pedagogue emphasizing 'a more than' to the individual. Individuals are always connected in a web of relationalities. Both Ann Merete and Gunilla, and their colleagues, have, for many years, been concerned with a question, can early childhood settings be seen as a relational space of potentiality and as an ecology of practices? Here, an affirmative ethics of an encounter and care (Dahlberg & Moss, 2005) could move the early childhood pedagogue's engagement with difference beyond individual systems and towards change. Becoming-pedagogue, from a feminist relational ethics, in and of the complex world today, stresses the importance of our own relations with human and more-than-human entities within a politics of immanence. The becoming-pedagogue always happen in the middle, in-betweenness, through being attuned, involved as participator(s) in a relational field of potentiality (Dahlberg & Moss, 2005; Olsson, 2009). Instead of opposing and being reactive as feminist academics we need to be active and ethically affirmative, by creating networks and collective alliances with pedagogues in early childhood education. Otherwise, with inspiration from Manning (2019) (see also Novosel & Dahlberg, 2021), we are 'stealing from' the pedagogue the power of knowing and the power of acting. Instead of 'worlding', and an ecology of practices we, hence, open up for processes of 'unworlding'. Manning (2019) talks about attunement as a different way of feeling the threshold, which can open for a collective way of being. So our timely challenge as feminist researchers in Scandinavia, as well as for a future to come, is to call forth *an affirmative ethics* by developing sensitivities and by embracing an ecological politics of collective individuation through shaping a feminism in early childhood education and care that we have not yet encountered.

Notes

1 In Norway, the first Children's Act Law came in 1975, directly influenced by the Swedish Barnstugutredning.
2 See also other researchers who have contributed to this field (e.g. Birkeland, 2012; Boden, 2017; Lenz Taguchi, 2010, 2017; Murris & Bozalek, 2019; Olsson, 2009; Olsson, Dahlberg & Theorell, 2015; Osgood & Robinson, 2019; Otterstad, 2018a, b; Rautio, 2013; Rossholt, 2006, 2012; Sandvik, 2013; Waterhouse, 2021).
3 In Scandinavia, we mostly use the term pedagogy for teaching, since teaching can be associated with a formal teaching and a learning paradigm related to schooling.

References

Barad, K. (2014). Diffracting diffractions: Cutting together-apart. *Parallax, 20*, 168–87.
Birkeland, I. (2012). Rom, sted og kjønn: begrepsavklaringer og bruksanvisninger. In A. Krogstad, G. Karsten Hansen, K. Høyland and T. Moser (Eds.), *Flerfaglige perspektiver på barnehagens fysiske miljø* (pp. 47–63). Fagbokforlaget.
Bloch, M. N. (1991). Critical science and the history of child development's influence on early education research. *Early Education and Development, 2*, 95–108.
Bloch, M. N. (1992). Critical perspectives on the historical relationship between child development and early childhood education research. In S. Kessler & B. B. Swadener (Eds.), *Reconceptualizing the early childhood curriculum: Beginning the dialogue* (pp. 3–20). Teachers College Press.
Boden, L. (2017). *Present absent. Exploring the posthumanist entanglements of school's absenteeism*. Ph.D. Linköping Universitet.
Braidotti, R. (2008). The politics of radical immanence: May 1968 as an event. file:///C:/Users/annmo/Downloads/273.-The-Politics-of-Radical-Immanence-May-1968-as-an-Event.pdf
Butler, J. (1990). *Gender trouble: Feminism and the subversion of identity*. Routledge.
Butler, J. (2004). *Undoing gender*. London: Routledge.
Burman, E. (1994/2008). *Deconstructing developmental psychology*. Routledge.
Cannella, G. (1997). *Deconstructing early childhood education: Social justice and revolution*. Peter Lang Publishing.
Dahlberg, G. & Lenz Taguchi, H. (1994). *Förskola och skola: om två skilda traditioner och visionen om en mötesplats*. Liber.
Dahlberg, G., Moss, P., & Pence, A. (1999/2013). *Beyond quality in early childhood education and care: Languages of evaluation* (3rd ed.). Routledge.

Dahlberg, G. & Moss, P. (2005). *Ethics and politics in early childhood education*. Routledge.

Dahlberg, G. & Åsén, G. (1994). Evaluation and regulation. A question of empowerment? In P. Moss & A. Pence (Eds.), *Valuing quality in early childhood services. New approaches to defining quality* (pp. 157–72). Paul Chapman Press.

De Lair, H. A & Erwin, E. (2000). Working perspectives within feminism and early childhood education. *Contemporary Issues in Early Childhood, 1*(2), 153–70.

Deleuze, G. (1988). *Spinoza: Practical philosophy*. City Lights Books.

Elfström, I. (2013). *Uppföljning och utvärdering – pedagogisk dokumentation som grund för kontinuerlig verksamhetsutveckling och systematiskt kvalitetsarbete i förskolan*. PhD., Stockholms universitet.

Fendler, L. (2001). Educating flexible souls. The construction of subjectivity through developmentality and interaction. In K. Hultqvist & G. Dahlberg (Eds.), *Governing the child in the new millennium* (pp. 119–42). Routledge Falmer.

Foucault, M. (1997). *Ethics: Subjectivity and truth. The essential work of Michel Foucault 1954-1984*. Penguin Press.

Grosz, E. (2010). The untimeliness of feminist theory. *NORA: Nordic Journal of Feminist and Gender Research, 18*, 48–51.

Halvars-Franzén, B. (2010). *Barn och etik – möten och möjlighetsvillkor i två förskoleklassers vardag*. Doktorsavhandling, Stockholms universitet.

Hammarström Lewenhagen, B. (2013). *Den unika möjligheten – en studie om den svenska förskolemodellen 1968-1998*. Doktorsavhandling, Stockholms Universitet.

Haraway, D. (2016). *Staying with the trouble: Making kin in the Chthulucene*. Duke University Press.

Hekman, S. (2014). *The feminine subject*. Polity Press.

Lenz Taguchi, H. (2010). *Going beyond the theory/practice divide in early childhood education: Introducing an intra-active pedagogy*. Routledge.

Lenz Taguchi, H. (2017). Using concept as method in educational and social science inquiry. *Qualitative Inquiry, 23*(9), 643–8.

Lind, U. (2010). *Blickens ordning: Bildspråk och estetiska lärprocesser som kulturform och kunskapsform*. Doktorsavhandling. Stockholms universitet.

Manning, E. (2013). *Always more than one. Individuations dance*. Duke University Press.

Manning, E. (2016). *The minor gesture*. Duke University Press.

Manning, E. (2019). Radical pedagogies and metamodelings of knowledge in the making, Keynote. 10th Annual New Materialisms Conference on Reconfiguring Higher Education, 2–4 December. University of the Western Cape. https://www.ajol.info/index.php/cristal/article/view/200707

Manning, E. (2020). Radical pedagogies and metamodelings of knowledge in the making. *Christal, 8*, 1–16.

Manning, E. & Massumi, B. (2014). *Thought in the act: Passages in the ecology of experience*. University of Minnesota Press.

Massumi, B. (2002). *Parables of the virtual. Movement, affect, sensation. (Post-Contemporary Intervention)*. Duke Polity Press.

Massumi, B. (2015). *Politics of affect*. Polity Press.

Murris, K. & Bozalek, V. (2019). Diffracting diffractive readings of texts as methodology: Some propositions. *Educational Philosophy and Theory*, *51*(14), 1504–17.

Nordin-Hultman, E. (2004). *Pedagogiska miljöer och barns subjektskapande*. Doktorsavhandling. Liber.

Novosel, Y. & Dahlberg, G. (2021). Translanguaging. An expanded notion involving affect and vitality. *International Childhood Policy Studies*, *8*(1).

Olsson, L. (2009). *Movement and experimentation in young children's learning: Gilles Deleuze and Felix Guattari in early childhood education*. Routledge.

Olsson, L. M. & Dahlberg, G. & Theorell, E. (2015). Displacing identity – placing aesthetics: Early childhood literacy in a globalized world. *Discourse Studies in the Cultural Politics of Education*, *37*(5), 717–38.

Osgood, J. & Robinson, K. H. (2019). *Feminists researching gendered childhoods*. Bloomsbury Academic.

Otterstad, A. M. & Braathe, H. J. (2016). Travelling inscriptions of neo-liberalism in Nordic early childhood: Repositioning professionals for teaching and learnability. *Global Studies of Childhoods*, *6*(1), 80–97.

Otterstad, A. M. (2018a). What might a feminist relational new materialist and affirmative critique generate in/with early childhood research. *Qualitative Inquiry*, *25*(7), 641–51.

Otterstad, A. M. (2018b). *Å stå i trøbbelet1 Kartograferinger av barnehageforskningens metodologier Postkvalitative passasjer og (ny)empiriske brytninger*. Dr. Philos. Det utdanningsvitenskaplige fakultet. Universitetet i Oslo.

Popkewitz, T. (1984). *Paradigm and ideology in educational research: The social functions of the intellectual*. Routledge.

Rajchman, J. (2001). Introduction. In G. Deleuze (Ed.), *Pure immanence. essays on a life*. Princeton University Press.

Rautio, P. (2013). Children who carry stones in their pockets: On autotelic material practices in everyday life. *Children's Geographies*, *11*(4), 394–40.

Rossholt, N. (2006). *Temahefte om likestilling i det pedagogiske arbeidet i barnehagen*. Oslo: Kunnskapsdepartementet.

Rossholt, N. (2012). *Kroppens tilblivelse i tid og rom – analyser av materielle-diskursive hendelser i barnehagen*. Doktorgradsavhandling. Norges teknisk – naturvitenskapelige universitet.

Sandvik, N. (2013). *Medvirkning og handlingskraft i småbarns pedagogiske praksiser. Horisontalt fremforhandlet innflytelse*. Doktorgradsavhandling. Norges teknisk-naturvitenskapelige universitet.

Simondon, G. (1992). The genesis of the individual. In J. Crary & S. Kwinter (Eds.), *Zone 6: Incorporations* (pp. 296–319). Zone Books.

Stengers, I. (2005). Introductory notes on an ecology of practices. *Dissertation*, *11*(1).

Stengers, I. (2018). *Another science is possible. A manifesto for slow sciences*. Polity Press.

Stern, D. (1985). *The interpersonal world of the infant. The view from psychoanalysis and development*. Basic Books.

Tuana, N. (1992). *Woman and the history of philosophy (ed)*. Paragon Press.

Tuana, N. (2001). Material locations: An interactionist alternative to realism/social constructivism. In Tuana, N. & Morgen, S. (Eds.), *Engendering rationalities* (pp. 221–44). Indiana University Press.

Unga, J. (2013). *Det är en spricka i allt, det är så ljuset kommer in: Matematik och förskolebarns experimenterande och potentialitet*. Licentiatsavhandling. Stockholms universitet.

Walkerdine, V. (1993). Beyond developmentalism? *Theory and psychology*, 3(4), 451–69.

Waterhouse, A-H. L. (2021). *Materialpoetiske øyeblikk. En a-r-t-ografisk studie av små barns eksperimentelle materialprosesser i barnehagen*. Phd. avhandling. Universitetet i Sør-Øst Norge.

11

Femme-inist Approaches to Early Childhood Education and Care: Cultivating Pedagogies of Care via Femme Theory

Adam W.J. Davies and Rhea Ashley Hoskin

In 2019, the American blog website *New America* published an article titled 'Celebrating Women in Early Childhood Education'. The author described how 'early childhood education has been a *feminine fortress* throughout the history of the United States and continues to be so today' (Franchino, 2019, para. 1, emphasis added). Yet, despite the historical connections between femininity and care work that are implicit within early childhood education, recent conversations in care theory have attempted to shift care away from being an explicitly *feminine* moral stance (e.g. Noddings, 2013). However, since caring is relational, and relationality *is* feminine, we will argue that efforts to eschew connecting care with femininity are femmephobic; that is, a form of systemic devaluation and regulation of femininity (Hoskin, 2017a).

As we will further argue, questions of femininity are critical to the field of early childhood education and care (ECEC), particularly questions regarding the early childhood educator (ECE), because care, femininity and education are intricately bound (Davies & Hoskin, 2021a; Langford et al., 2017). Care is a feminine *and* feminist moral ethical stance towards relationality (Noddings, 1984) that involves an affective and reciprocal relationship between care-providers and care-recipients (Nodding, 1984; Sander-Staudt, 2018). Despite the long-held associations between young children and care (Varga, 1997), increased attempts to privatize and schoolify ECEC have resulted in discourses of professionalization that devalue care and femininity by seeking to focus on children's development through masculinist values of economic investment and outcomes (Davies & Hoskin, 2021a; Langford et al., 2017; Moss & Dahlberg, 2008). Centring ECEC conversations in logics of economics, management and child development (Moss & Dahlberg, 2008) results in efforts to separate the field from femininity, thereby perpetuating femmephobia in ECEC (Davies & Hoskin, 2021a).

Research in ECEC that focuses on outcomes, standardization and professionalization reproduces femmephobia through attempts to distance from femininity and feminization, with writing in care ethics seeking to disavow femininity (Davies & Hoskin, 2021a; Hoskin, 2021b). Despite conversations about femininity and the feminization of ECEC (i.e. the notion that ECEC is a feminized field given that it is disproportionately made up of women), scholars have yet to centralize *femininity* within ECEC, nor use Femme Theory in the analysis of ECE subjectivity (see Davies & Hoskin, 2021a for an exception). Limited work within ECEC that centralizes issues of gender has examined femininity explicitly independent of its socially constructed relationship to women (i.e. examined femininity distinctly from cisgender heterosexual girls or women). It is important to consider how normative ideas of ECE subjectivity regulate femininity and who is expected to enact feminine care (Davies, 2021a; Davies & Hoskin, 2021a). Interrogations of the inherent gender essentialism in situating care as women's work have taken shape, highlighting the tendency to see feminization as negative and femininity (and care) as exclusively the domains of white heterosexual cisgender women (Davies, 2021a; Davies & Hoskin, 2021b). Applying Femme Theory and making the role of femmephobia in ECEC salient can bolster analyses that use care ethics and theories to understand the gendered discourses that regulate early childhood educators' (ECEs) subjectivities (Davies & Hoskin, 2021a; Langford, 2007, 2010).

Following critical femininities scholars and femme theorists (Hoskin & Blair, 2021; Davies & Hoskin, 2021a), in this chapter we examine how the consideration of femmephobia via Femme Theory can cultivate new understandings of *femme-inist* theorizing in ECEC by fostering new questions and generating novel theorizations of femininity, care and ECE subjectivity. First, we describe our own positionalities and what brought us to femme theorizing. Then, we define Femme Theory and summarize previous literature in both ECEC and pedagogy that have integrated femme analyses. We then move to delineating how Femme Theory can be applied to analyse the subjectivities of ECEs. In doing so, we draw explicit links between Femme Theory, feminist care ethics and feminist poststructuralism, and explicate how Femme Theory can contribute to continued goals of examining and dismantling gendered hierarchies within ECEC. We conclude with some final thoughts and next steps for thinking with Femme Theory in ECEC.

Our Positionalities: What Brought us to Femme

As two femme identified academics, femme became a space of reclamation, emancipation and self-expression in a world that belittles femininity and feminine people (Davies & Hoskin, 2021a, b). Serano (2012) describes how reclaiming femininity involves 'challenging [those] negative assumptions that are routinely projected onto feminine gender expression' (p. 171). We were both brought to Femme Theory through our lived experiences of being devalued as queer people due to our feminine gender expressions, as well as a curiosity for how the subjugation of our respective feminine gender expressions is intricately linked to societal processes (i.e. femmephobia; Hoskin, 2021b). For Adam (he/they), it was their experience of having their male femininity watched by others (Davies, 2021a; Davies & Neustifter, 2021). Growing up, Adam experienced continual gender policing due to their male femininity as other children and adult figures taunted them. As a queer man who works with young children and teaches in pre-service early childhood education, Adam's femininity marked him as queer in heteronormative childcare work settings (Davies, 2021a). As well, Adam experienced femmephobia within queer men's communities, which has become a central part of his research programme (see Davies, 2020, 2021a, b, c; Davies et al., 2021). From a young age, Rhea Ashley (she/her) felt deeply tied to femininity while also feeling that her understandings of femininity ran counter to dominant narratives that positioned femininity as subordinate, oppressive and apolitical. As a femme lesbian and feminist, Rhea Ashley felt excluded by lesbian/queer communities as well as within many feminist spaces (Hoskin, 2021a). For Rhea Ashley, discovering femme writings and communities helped to make sense of her own femininity – and, more specifically, her queer femininity. Turning to femme scholarship helped Rhea Ashley to reconcile what felt to be fractured pieces of selfhood, while also connecting these pieces and experiences to broader systems of feminine devaluation and regulation via Femme Theory (Hoskin, 2021a; 2022).

Femme Theory: An Introduction

The term 'femme' originates from 1940s working class lesbian communities (Brightwell & Taylor, 2019; Hoskin, 2021a; Levitt et al., 2003). Since the 1940s, femme has not only expanded in its use as an identity category (Blair & Hoskin, 2015, 2016; Davies, 2020), but also in its use as a theoretical framework (Hoskin,

2021c). Femme Theory is an emergent theoretical tool used to analyse feminine multiplicities, centralize femininity within intersectional analyses, and, most importantly, address the systematic and societal devaluation and subjugation of femininity (i.e. femmephobia; Hoskin, 2017a, b, 2019, 2020, 2021a, b, c). In addition, Femme Theory offers a framework through which to interrupt the ubiquity with which many feminist theorists dismiss femininity as artifice, without agency, inherently white, heterosexual or deceptive (Hoskin, 2017b; Volcano & Dahl, 2008), offering instead new ways of conceptualizing femininity outside of deeply ingrained assumptions (Hoskin, 2021a). In this sense, Femme Theory is invested in interrogating femmephobia; or, the process through which femininity – and feminine people – are made subordinate and tightly regulated (Hoskin, 2017a).

Through Femme Theory, femmephobia is investigated both within LGBTQ+ communities (Blair & Hoskin, 2015; 2016; Davies, 2020; Serano, 2007, 2013), as well as by society at large (Hoskin & Taylor, 2019; Matheson et al., 2021; Serano, 2012). Thus, Femme Theory focuses on both the societal subjugation of femininity, as well as lived experiences and knowledge production from femme individuals – a gender identity distinct in its reclaiming of femininity by those for whom femininity has been denied and who have been excluded or marginalized from normative feminine ideals (Blair & Hoskin, 2015, 2016; Davies, 2020; Davies & Hoskin, 2021b; Hoskin, 2021b; Serano, 2012). Femme Theory is about writing femmes into existence in places where they have been overlooked (Davies, 2020; Hoskin, 2021a; Lewis, 2012) and authoring the self into an epistemological and methodological commitment to de-centring masculinist objectivist notions of truth (Hoskin, 2021a; Schwartz, 2018). What would it look like to write femininity into existence as both empowering and a source of knowledge within ECEC? Such a question can tackle deeply held femmephobic discourses and assumptions circulating within the field of ECEC.

Situated squarely within the growing field of critical femininities (Hoskin & Blair, 2021; Scott, 2021a, b), Femme Theory is an intersectional analytic that considers how feminine expressions that fail to approximate requisite feminine norms are policed, which effectively calcifies 'patriarchal femininity' as being characteristically the designation of white, cisgender, heterosexual, able-bodied women who are assigned female at birth – to name a few (Hoskin, 2017a, b, 2021a). This is important in the context of ECEC where femininity and care are linked to cisgender women (though, not necessarily valued in this capacity) while men who are educators are treated with suspicion if they embody femininity (see Davies, 2021a). Therefore, analysing how femininity and care are regulated within the subjectivities of ECE's through a Femme Theory lens is critical. Femme Theory postulates that reclaiming feminized attributes that are typically denigrated within masculinist patriarchal regimes (e.g. vulnerability, softness, nurturance, etc.) is necessary to ensure better futures, and to achieve feminist goals such as cultivating more societal inclusivity for marginalized individuals (Davies, 2021a, b, c; Davies & Hoskin, 2021a; Middleton, 2019; Schwartz, 2020a). Reclaiming femininity can also bolster new forms of gender inclusivity in ECEC by embracing vulnerability and interconnectedness. Femme Theory focuses on the dialectical relationship between passivity and agency for feminists to negotiate both feminine and feminist forms of self-expression (Schwartz, 2020a, b; Scott, 2021a, b). In this sense, approaches to femininity that employ Femme Theory move beyond a hierarchical top-down or dualistic analysis to examine how relationships *between* femininities and gendered dynamics emerge in a hierarchical, intersectional manner (Dahl, 2015; Hoskin & Blair, 2021).

Given the historical mistreatment of femmes and femininity within feminism (see Hoskin, 2017b for an overview), many femmes opt for the term 'femme-inist' as a means of signalling a deliberate alignment of femininity with feminism, and to push back against the stereotypes that feminists must disavow femininity (Dahl, 2010b, 2015). Femme-inist perspectives can queer 'the relationship between gender and sexuality, between aesthetics and positionality, and between activity and passivity' (Dahl, 2010b, p. 173). In addition, many femme scholars problematize how femininity is defined in order to mobilize femininity and dismantle masculinist notions of objectivity and authority (Dahl, 2010b; Scott, 2021b; see also Hoskin, 2021a). In this sense, a *femme-inist* critique is one that sees femininity as central to feminist politics and aims to dislodge forms of exclusion that currently construct femininity as only repressive and denying the agency of femme individuals (Hoskin, 2017b; Scott, 2021a, b; Serano, 2013). Notably, Inayatulla and Robinson (2020) articulate how feminized labour (e.g. administration) is placed upon femme individuals within academic settings, which facilitates our interrogation of how femmephobia is at the crux of the treatment of feminized labour within the academy. Care can be considered a form of feminine labour – one that is undervalued and denigrated in current society (Davies & Hoskin, 2021a). Femme Theory emphasizes how femininity, as a gendered construct and relation, is embodied and enacted by diverse individuals (not just cisgender heterosexual women; Dahl, 2015; Hoskin & Taylor, 2019). This is useful for analysing how diverse early childhood educators embody both care and femininity and the differing reactions and responses to these individuals based on gendered norms and hierarchies (i.e. how care is inherently associated with cisgender heterosexual women; Davies, 2021a; Davies & Hoskin, 2021a). Care work can be directly linked to femmephobia, such that it is both devalued (i.e. women may be expected to take on feminized labour, but are not necessarily valued for it) and regulated (i.e. who is expected to care; Davies, 2021a; Davies & Hoskin, 2021a).

Femme Theory and Early Childhood Education and Care

Within a Canadian context, ECEC originates from the nineteenth century, inspired by the foundation of kindergartens in Canadian regions and day nurseries to provide working mothers with places for their children to learn (Johnston et al., 2020; Varga, 1997). Day nurseries and kindergartens were heavily influenced by missionary work (Johnston et al., 2020) in that day nurseries and kindergartens were established as places for children to learn societal values and norms (and for women to reinforce such values and norms) and to ensure that working-class children were exposed to middle-class values (Kelly et al., 2021; Varga, 1997).

Traditionally, ECEC has been associated with feminized emotions, such as care, nurturing and, in particular, maternalism (Ailwood, 2007). Yet, despite this historical association, little to no work has analysed ECEC via Femme Theory. Davies and Hoskin (2021a), however, begin such work by connecting Femme Theory to care ethics and theories in ECEC. Davies and Hoskin also note how the common devaluation of care work, particularly in ECEC, is symptomatic of the larger structural issue of femmephobia. Analysing ECE subjectivities through Femme Theory can offer opportunities for valuing feminized ideas of care and relationality and disrupting notions of 'normative development' that bolster emphases on academic performance, professional regulation and standardized assessment in the early years. This can allow creative space for ECEs to consider their work – and subjectivities – beyond output and performance-oriented measures.

In the context of professionalization discourses within ECEC that seek to both distinctly separate education from care and focus on traditionally 'masculinized' traits and forms of self-expression, Davies and Hoskin (2021a) ask, 'If femininity is not taken seriously, is not seen as genuine but only as fake, deceptive, or unintelligent, how can we ever begin to see femininity as something of value, or even as a professional virtue?' (p. 110). We continue to explain how professionalization discourses in ECEC focus on the schoolification of ECEC, with an emphasis on the highly masculinized connotations of standardized education and developmental trajectories. The focus on child development in ECEC means that independence is seen as the ultimate goal for children through developmental milestones, with 'too much' care and assistance a hindrance to the development of children towards independence (Karmiris, 2021; Langford et al., 2017). Applying Femme Theory to the feminization of 'needs' and ideas of emotional dependency can provide an avenue for the revaluation of care, dependency, and relationality (Davies, 2017, 2021b; Davies & Hoskin, 2021a). Equally, Femme Theory can assist in centralizing the typically devalued realm of care while bringing forward how care and femininity do not have to be associated with any specific bodies or genders (Davies, 2021a; Davies & Hoskin, 2021a).

Care ethics have been critiqued for being gender essentialist and for equating caring with femininity, and femininity as synonymous with women (Davies & Hoskin, 2021a; Powell et al., 2021; Robinson, 2020). Robinson (2020) describes how it is actually patriarchy that reinforces the perspective that 'these conditions [relationality, vulnerability] are simply the pathologies of "some" – the weak, not fully mature, the "feminine"' (p. 13). Similarly, Powell et al. (2021) describe how care ethics are 'only a "feminine practice" under patriarchal conditions, in which women and racialized groups are expected to do invisible and devalued care work' (p. 68). Care ethics challenge liberal legal constructions of independence and see the world and human beings as contextually situated and relational (Langford, 2019; Powell et al., 2021). This is because care ethics create 'space for seeing how everybody and everything is in relation to and dependent on someone and something else' (Powell et al., 2021, p. 66). Care ethics offer a moral and political theory that focuses on the relational subject as an ontological condition of being (Robinson, 2020); that is, all humans being constituted relationally, thereby dismantling any ontological notion of complete independence (Davies & Kenneally, 2020; Lugones, 2008).

Arguments for the importance of acknowledging the care work of ECEs have surfaced within the context of Covid-19, during which the necessity and importance of continuing this work during pandemic-based lockdowns and closures were made clear. In 2021, Ontario childcare centres continued operating despite massive provincial shutdowns and K-12 schools closed temporarily and shifted to an online learning model (Boisvert, 2021). The maintaining of childcare operations became considered a central component of the continuation of the Ontario economy; yet childcare staff remain underpaid and arguments intended to support childcare and early childhood education often rely on economic logics and advancing support for the labour market (Connolly, 2020). In this sense, care becomes important only through economic means and requires a rationalization through profits and gains instead of holding an inherent worth outside of neoliberal capitalism (Davies & Hoskin, 2021a).

Both femininity and care are commonly considered to be inherently interlinked through patriarchal femininity and the regulation thereof (Davies & Hoskin, 2021a). As described by Davies and Hoskin (2021a) care is associated with the patriarchal construction of womanhood (i.e. white heterosexual cisgender womanhood) through gender essentialism, which means that other communities and individuals (especially racialized men) are often not associated with stereotypical images of ECEs (Bryan & Millton Williams, 2017). Femininity is typically associated with maternalism (e.g. Kristeva, 1982), while Eurocentric notions of motherhood and white femininity are often universalized in different geopolitical contexts (Lugones, 2008). This is important to note in relationship with the regulation of ECE subjectivities whereby ECEs are typically expected to perform notions of care, maternalism and nurturance (Taggart, 2011). As noted by Prochner (2000), Canadian ECEC developed specifically as a project of assimilation, with the idea of white female educators caring for the development of children who were to assimilate to Judeo-Christian norms and values. Moreover, ECEC forwarded an approach to early intervention that used early intervention to ensure the 'normative' development of children outside of their primary family (Prochner, 2000). In this sense, how care is deployed is not neutral and is politically fuelled and even harmful – functioning as a regulatory tool in the reinforcement of white cis-heteropatriarchal ableist values (Langford, 2019).

ECEs are trained to observe and assess children by employing positivist and developmentalist standards and ideals, thereby reinforcing the hierarchization of education over care (Davies & Hoskin, 2021a; Karmiris, 2021). Such positivist ideals reinscribe the ECE as the gatekeeper for 'normative development', while promoting the valuing of training pre-service educators in assessment and observation instead of postmodern pedagogical approaches (Karmiris, 2021). The valuing of assessment over care and ideas of 'typical development' moves forward the ideas that hierarchize children and reinforce notions of knowledge as decontextualized, objective and neutral (Karmiris, 2021). By valuing emotionality, interdependence and nurturance (instead of objectivity and independence), a femme approach to knowledge production in ECEC might encourage educators and students to challenge the seeming objectivity and neutrality of developmental knowledge and imagine how to incorporate their own subjectivities into their learning and teaching. Femme Theory specifically brings questions to ECE subjectivity that challenge ideas of ECEs as 'technicians' (Johnson, 2019) and centralize caring relations and femininity as central components of ECE subjectivity.

Femme Theory and ECE Subjectivities

Femme Theory is a useful tool for interrupting binaries and dualisms between passivity and activity whereby femininity is associated with the less valued qualities of docility and relationality and masculinity is associated with valued qualities of agency and independence (Scott, 2021a). The value-laden dichotomization of qualities is especially prominent in child-centred pedagogies (Langford, 2007, 2010). We wonder how interactions between children and educators can become a 'space of vulnerability' (Walcott, 1994, p. 64) where ideas of autonomous subjectivity are decentred, particularly in ECE pedagogical practices. Such spaces of femininity, relationality, vulnerability and decentred subjectivities are ripe for analyses using Femme Theory. Walcott's perspectives are echoed by Langford's (2010) incisive critique of child-centred pedagogy and the traditional decentring of female educators' expertise and knowledge in approaches that centralize (male) children. How can femininity be considered when conceptualizing ECE subjectivities? Langford asks important and related questions, particularly regarding the place of young girls in representations of children in ECEC, as well as the necessity of 'the female teacher to relinquish her expertise, power and authority within child-centred pedagogy' (p. 122). Does femininity always equal relinquishing power and how can femininity, itself, be considered a source of power and agency within ECEC's subjectivities? Femme Theory, importantly, asks how notions of passivity, as well as femininity itself, can be revalued without having to resort to traditionally masculinized notions of agency and individuality (Davies & Hoskin, 2021a; Scott, 2021a, b). These two lines of questioning – Langford's and that of femme theorists' – dovetail in their interest in questions of agency, individuality and selfhood. And, of course, questions of agency and individuality also reflect broader patterns of liberal humanism as a masculinist endeavour. Who is the normative ECE subject if they are decentred? How can we consider the educator in the child/educator relationship if both are destabilized? And where does femininity factor into such a destabilization? Might the decentred subject merely reproduce the masculinist epistemological centre that not only masquerades as value-neutral but also gender-neutral?

While liberal humanism is a broad philosophical branch to completely cover here, what is important to note is its focus on universality, human agency, internal essences and Enlightenment values of inner identity and political liberalism (Butler, 1990; Davies, 2020; Walcott, 1994; Weedon, 1999). Liberal humanist traditions have been heavily critiqued by poststructural feminism for holding patriarchal onto-epistemological foundations and universalizing notions of subjectivity (Butler, 1990; Weedon, 1999). Femme Theory applies a both/and logic that considers femme both a place of epistemological knowledge – a subversion of femmephobic and masculinist logics that reduce femininity to a signifier of oppression (Hoskin, 2019, 2020; Hoskin & Taylor, 2019) – and an identity location that provides community, relationality and identification for those who identify with queer femininity (Hoskin, 2021a, b). This both/and logic can be applied to considering the subjectivities of ECEs in that ECE can be *both* an identity marker and a place of knowledge formation and community building. In this sense, Femme Theory holds forms of knowing and political activism that can help to challenge the entrenchment of dualisms throughout liberal humanist notions of subjectivity that are constructed between children and adults (Davies & Kenneally, 2020; MacNaughton, 2005; see also Butler, 1990). Following Weedon (1999), this can address the 'failure to challenge that normative dualism which defines the essence of humanity solely in terms of rationality [...] at the expense of bodies and emotions' (p. 16). Building on femme's continued history of supporting 'the dissolution of binary systems of classification based on sex, gender, or sexuality' (Hoskin, 2021a, p. 8), Femme Theory interrupts masculinist theorizing that draws from epistemologies (such as liberal humanism) that silence and denigrate femininity.

Poststructural feminist critiques of liberal humanism are not new to ECEC (e.g. MacNaughton, 2005), particularly those that seek to better understand power relations. Smith et al. (2017) edited collection brings together scholars from a diverse range of feminisms. However, despite common conversations about femininity in the literature on gender and ECEC, Femme Theory (or 'femme-inism') is notably absent. Femininity is often excluded from political conversations unless it is taken up as a tool of patriarchal oppression (Hoskin, 2020; Serano, 2007, 2012, 2013; Scott, 2021b). As such, 'femininity as a social and cultural signifier is maintained as ultimately signifying subordination and inferiority' (Hoskin, 2020, p. 2327). Femininity is devalued and regulated (in wider society and ECEC), a likely product of its historical associations with womanhood, and the related enforcement of a normative white heterosexual cisgender model of patriarchal feminine subjectivity (Hoskin, 2017a, b).

Patriarchal discourses of maternal subjectivity inherently associate women with motherhood and care, while regulating the subjectivities of those assigned female at birth through associations between heterosexual cisgender women and children (Ailwood, 2007; Schmied & Lupton, 2001). This means that women have been historically oppressed through their (often) forced feminization and subsequent free/invisible labour. It also means that those who are not heterosexual cisgender white women are not as easily associated with care or relationality (Davies, 2017; 2020, 2021a; Davies & Hoskin, 2021a). This impacts which educators are inherently associated with care and nurturance, and who is seen as properly and appropriately caring (i.e. feminine) – the interpretation of which cuts across a wide range of intersectional identities. For example, queer men who are ECEs experience femmephobia and the regulation of their subjectivities in the field when they present in a more feminine manner and as deviating from the heteronormative masculinity expected from men who are educators, or from the archetypical 'male role model' (Davies, 2021a; Martino, 2009). Analysing how gender and sexuality intersect in the regulation and surveillance of ECE subjectivities is an important task (Davies, 2021a; Davies et al., 2021), particularly through a Femme Theory lens (Davies & Neustifter, 2021).

Feminine labour is another area where Femme Theory can provide new avenues for analysing educators' subjectivities in ECEC. Whiley et al. (2020) describe the 'tainting' of breastfeeding in public as a form of embodied femininity and feminine labour. Whiley et al. work focuses on how women who breastfeed publicly – and find enjoyment in public breastfeeding – speak back to notions that femininity is only for patriarchal consumption. Whiley et al. (2020) describe this by stating how '[f]emme is about defiance; it is about challenging and renouncing the (socially constructed) idea that femininity is for men and that masculine right of access is woven in its very fabric' (pp. 2–3). Breastfeeding is a form of feminine labour that, of course, does not have to be inherently associated with those who identify as women, but is typically seen as feminine and privatized within the home (Schmied & Lupton, 2001; Whiley et al., 2020). Social theorists, such as Kristeva (1982), theorize how the eventual repudiation of feminine relational care/labour is necessary for children's growth and development to maturity. The repudiation of femininity and feminine labour is taken-for-granted as a societal necessity for maturation whereby femininity must be eschewed to authenticate the (presumably male) child's development into independence and the symbolic order (Kristeva, 1982). In this sense, breastfeeding for individual pleasure and feminine labour that is both for the self and other is a disruption to the normative patriarchal order that demands femininity only be consumed by men (Whiley et al., 2020).

Bringing this argument into the context of ECE subjectivities, caring for children becomes a repudiated form of feminine labour that is required but simultaneously reviled and denigrated (see Kristeva, 1982). How can feminine labour and femininity be valued when considering the subjectivities of ECEs through a Femme Theory lens? As described by Hoskin and Blair (2021), 'femininity tends to be stereotyped, reductive, and taken-for-granted as being synonymous with womanhood and experienced as pressure to conform to patriarchal norms' (p. 3). White women and white femininity became associated with teaching in the twentieth century as institutions violently taught eugenics-based content to future female educators to reproduce normativity within the larger population (Kelly et al., 2021; Varga, 1997). Femme Theory, and Black femme theorizing (Keeling, 2007; Story, 2017) in particular, can disrupt inherent associations between white patriarchal femininity and teaching. Femmes turn assumptions about femininity 'on their head' (Hoskin, 2021a; Volcano & Dahl, 2008) – be they about sexuality, ability, race or feminine signifiers. For instance, femmes mobilize feminine signifiers to reject ableist shame (Erickson, 2007; Hoskin, 2022). Likewise, Keeling (2007) argues that the paradoxical visibility of the Black femme (i.e. simultaneously hyper visible and invisible) functions to reveal our deeply imbedded assumptions that maintain femininity as white. In other words, though they are often invisible/erased, when the Black femme 'appears' they simultaneously make visible the taken-for-granted notions attached to femininity (Keeling, 2007). Black femme-inist thought also highlights how the designation of femininity as frail, innocent and soft furthers 'femininity as White', given that femininities of colour have historically been denied softness, innocence and the vulnerability that comes with being seen as human. These critiques are important for disrupting normative images of white patriarchal femininity that are frequently reproduced within ECEC and centralized when considering ECE subjectivities.

By bringing Black Femme theorizing (Keeling, 2007; Story, 2017) that addresses issues pertaining to femininity and racialization, the hierarchical privileging of white patriarchal femininity within ECEC and its historical and current link to ECE subjectivity can begin to be disrupted.

Conclusion

Crip femme Loree Erickson (2007) notes how sites of shame rooted in normativity harbour the seeds of liberation. So too, we argue, does that which is abjected teach us how to recalibrate economies of worth (Davies, 2021a, b, c; Hoskin & Taylor, 2019), and thus harbour the seeds for a more inclusive, femme-inist approach to ECEC (Davies & Hoskin, 2021a). Femme theorizations, or femme-inist approaches, have the ability to destabilize normative notions of ECE subjectivity and ideas of belonging that regulate individual subjectivities (Dahl, 2010a, b, 2015; Davies, 2021a, b, c). By applying a femme-inist approach to ECEC, further analytics can be crafted that emphasize the dialects between passivity and activity and relationality and independence (Davies & Hoskin, 2021a; Scott, 2021a, b). Like poststructural feminism and care ethics, Femme Theory seeks to emphasize relationality and care while still bringing attention to locating femininity outside of its normative attachment to white cisgender heterosexual womanhood. By disrupting and dislodging femininity from white cis-heteropatriarchal connotations, femme-ininity and femme-inism becomes an intersectional analytic of labour, subjectivities and care in ECEC.

References

Ailwood, J. (2007). Mothers, teachers, maternalism and early childhood education and care: Some historical connections. *Contemporary Issues in Early Childhood*, 8(2), 157–65.

Blair, K. L., & Hoskin, R. A. (2015). Experiences of femme identity: Coming out, invisibility and femmephobia. *Psychology & Sexuality*, 6(3), 229–44.

Blair, K. L., & Hoskin, R. A. (2016). Contemporary understandings of femme identities and related experiences of discrimination. *Psychology & Sexuality*, 7(2), 101–15.

Boisvert, N. (2021, April 13th). Ontario daycares are still open but some say a shutdown may only be a matter of time. *CBC News*. https://www.cbc.ca/news/canada/toronto/ontario-child-care-staying-open-1.5984563

Brightwell, L. & Taylor, A. (2019). Why femme stories matter: Constructing femme theory through historical femme life writing. *Journal of Lesbian Studies*, 1–18.

Bryan, N. & Milton Williams, T. (2017). We need more than just male bodies in classrooms: Recruiting and retaining culturally relevant Black male teachers in early childhood education. *Journal of Early Childhood Teacher Education*, 38(3), 209–22.

Butler, J. (1990). *Gender trouble*. Routledge.

Connolly, A. (2020). Want a full economic recovery? Childcare is critical, report says. *Global News*. https://globalnews.ca/news/7230073/child-care-coronavirus-recovery-canada

Dahl, U. (2010a). Femme on femme: Reflections on collaborative methods and queer femme-inist ethnography. In C. J. Nash & K. Browne (Eds.), *Queer methods and methodologies: Intersecting queer theories and social science research* (pp. 143–66). Farnham: Ashgate.

Dahl, U. (2010b). *Notes on femme-inist agency*. Routledge.

Dahl, U. (2015). Sexism: A femme-inist perspective. *New Formations, 86*(86), 54–73.

Davies, A. W. J. (2017, May). Gay nationhood and masculinist belonging: The biopolitics of inclusion and the rational national man. Presented at *Canadian Disability Studies Conference* at Ryerson University, Toronto, Ontario.

Davies, A. W. (2020). 'Authentically' effeminate? Bialystok's theorization of authenticity, Gay Male Femmephobia, and Personal Identity. *Canadian Journal of Family and Youth/Le Journal Canadien de Famille et de la Jeunesse, 12*(1), 104–23.

Davies, A.W.J. (2021a). Queering masculinities in early childhood and higher education classrooms: Gendered regulation and the 'double bind' of queer masculinities. In S. Hillock (Ed.), *Teaching about sex and sexualities in higher education* (pp. 148–63). University of Toronto Press.

Davies, A. W. J. (2021b). Gay fat femininities! A call for fat femininities in research on gay socio-sexual applications. *Fat Studies*, 1–14. Advance Online.

Davies, A. W. (2021c). *Queering app-propriate behaviours: The affective politics of gay social-sexual applications in Toronto, Canada* (Doctoral dissertation, University of Toronto, Toronto, ON).

Davies, A., & Hoskin, R.A. (2021a). Using Femme Theory to foster a feminine-inclusive early childhood education and care practice. In Abawi, Z, Eizadirad, A & Berman R., (Eds.), *Equity as praxis in early childhood education and care* (pp. 107–23). Canadian Scholar's Press.

Davies, A. & Hoskin, R. A. (2021b). Gender/Gender identity/Gender expression. In K. K. Strunk & S. A. Shelton (Eds.), *Encyclopedia of queer studies in education* (pp. 181–7). Brill.

Davies, A. W. & Kenneally, N. (2020). Cripping the controversies: Ontario rights-based debates in sexuality education. *Sex Education, 20*(4), 366–82.

Davies, A. W. & Neustifter, R. (2021). Heteroprofessionalism in the academy: The surveillance and regulation of queer faculty in higher education. *Journal of homosexuality*, 1–25.

Davies, A. W., Balter, A. S., & van Rhijn, T. (2021). Sexuality education and early childhood educators in Ontario, Canada: A Foucauldian exploration of constraints and possibilities. *Contemporary Issues in Early Childhood*, Vol. 0(0), 1–17. https://doi.org/10.1177%2F14639491211060787

Davies, A., Maich, K., Belcher, C., Cagulada, E., DeWelles, M., & van Rhijn, T. (2021). A critical examination of the intersection of sexuality and disability in Special, a Netflix series. In M. Jeffress (Ed.), *Disability representation in film, tv, and print media* (pp. 44–64). Routledge.

Erickson, L. (2007). Revealing femmegimp: A sex-positive reflection on sites of shame as sites of resistance for people with disabilities. *Atlantis: Critical Studies in Gender, Culture & Social Justice, 31*(2), 42–52.

Franchino, E. (2019, March 25). Celebrating women in early childhood education. *New America*. https://www.newamerica.org/education-policy/edcentral/celebrating-women-early-childhood-education/

Hoskin, R. A. (2017a). Femme theory: Refocusing the intersectional lens. *Atlantis: Critical Studies in Gender, Culture & Social Justice, 38*(1), 95–109.

Hoskin, R. A. (2017b). Femme interventions and the proper feminist subject: Critical approaches to decolonizing western feminist pedagogies. *Cogent Social Sciences, 3*(1), 1276819.

Hoskin, R. A. (2019). Femmephobia: The role of anti-femininity and gender policing in LGBTQ+ people's experiences of discrimination. *Sex Roles, 81*(11), 686–703.

Hoskin, R. A. (2020). 'Femininity? It's the aesthetic of subordination': Examining femmephobia, the gender binary, and experiences of oppression among sexual and gender minorities. *Archives of Sexual Behavior, 49*(7), 2319–339. https://doi.org/10.1007/s10508-020-01641-x

Hoskin, R. A. (2021a). Can femme be theory? Exploring the epistemological and methodological possibilities of femme. *Journal of Lesbian Studies, 25*(1), 1–17. https://doi.org/10.1080/10894160.2019.1702288

Hoskin, R. A. (2021b). Femmephobia. In A. E. Goldberg & G. Beemyn (Eds.), *The SAGE Encyclopedia of Trans Studies* (pp. 258–9). SAGE.

Hoskin, R. A. (2021c). *Feminizing theory: Making space for femme theory*. Routledge.

Hoskin, R. A. (2022). The complexities of passing: Dual realities of a queer, crip white femme of lost Jewish descent. *Journal of Autoethnography, 3*(2), 207–11. https://doi.org/10.1525/joae.2022.3.2.207

Hoskin, R. A., & Blair, K. L. (2021). Critical femininities: A 'new' approach to gender theory. *Psychology & Sexuality* 1–8. Advance Online.

Hoskin, R. A. & Taylor, A. (2019). Femme resistance: The fem(me)inine art of failure. *Psychology & Sexuality, 10*(4), 281–300.

Inayatulla, S. & Robinson, H. (2020). 'Backwards and in high heels': The invisibility and underrepresentation of femme (inist) administrative labor in academia. *Administrative Theory & Praxis, 42*(2), 212–32.

Johnston, L. (2019). The (Not) good educator: Reconceptualizing the image of the educator. *ECELink, 3*(2), 40–54. https://d3n8a8pro7vhmx.cloudfront.net/aeceo/mailings/1631/attachments/original/eceLINK_Fall2019_Finalweb.pdf?1570820616

Johnston, L., Shoemaker, L., Land, N., Di Santo, A., & Jagger, S. (2020). Early childhood education and care in Canada. In *Oxford Research Encyclopedia of Education*. Oxford Press.

Karmiris, M. (2021). Failure and loss as a methodological, relational, and ethical necessity in teaching and learning in the early years. *Equity as Praxis in Early Childhood Education and Care*, 147–64.

Keeling, K. (2007). *The witch's flight*. Duke University Press.

Kelly, E., Manning, D. T. A., Boye, S., Rice, C., Owen, D., Stonefish, S., & Stonefish, M. (2021). Elements of a counter-exhibition: Excavating and countering a Canadian history and legacy of eugenics. *Journal of the History of the Behavioral Sciences*, 57(1), 12–33.

Kristeva, J. (1982). *Powers of horror*. University Presses of California, Columbia and Princeton.

Langford, R. (2007). Who is a good early childhood educator? A critical study of differences within a universal professional identity in early childhood education preparation programs. *Journal of Early Childhood Teacher Education*, 28(4), 333–52.

Langford, R. (2010). Critiquing child-centred pedagogy to bring children and early childhood educators into the centre of a democratic pedagogy. *Contemporary Issues in Early Childhood*, 11(1), 113–27.

Langford, R. (Ed.). (2019). *Theorizing feminist ethics of care in early childhood practice: Possibilities and dangers*. Bloomsbury Publishing.

Langford, R., Richardson, B., Albanese, P., Bezanson, K., Prentice, S., & White, J. (2017). Caring about care: Reasserting care as integral to early childhood education and care practice, politics and policies in Canada. *Global Studies of Childhood*, 7(4), 311–22.

Levitt, H., Gerrish, E. A., & Hiestand, K. R. (2003). The misunderstood gender: A model of modern femme identity. *Sex Roles*, 48(3–4), 99–113. doi:10.1023/A:1022453304384

Lewis, S. F. (2012). Everything I know about being femme I learned from sula or toward a black femme-inist criticism. *Trans-Scripts*, 2, 100–25. https://cpb-us-e2.wpmucdn.com/sites.uci.edu/dist/f/1861/files/2014/10/2012_02_09.pdf

Lugones, M. (2008). Colonialidad y género. *Tabula rasa* (09), 73–101.

MacNaughton, G. (2005). *Doing Foucault in early childhood studies: Applying post-structural ideas*. Routledge.

Martino, W. (2009). Beyond male role models: Interrogating the role of male teachers in boys' education. In W. Martino, M. D. Kehler, & M. B. Weaver-Hightower (Eds.), *The problem with boys' education: Beyond the backlash* (pp. 284–302). Routledge.

Matheson, L., Ortiz, D. L., Hoskin, R. A., Holmberg, D., & Blair, K. L. (2021). The feminine target: Gender expression in same-sex relationships as a predictor of experiences with public displays of affection. *The Canadian Journal of Human Sexuality*. Online First.

Middleton, M. (2019). Feminine exhibition design. *Exhibition Fall*, 82–91.

Moss, P., & Dahlberg, G. (2008). Beyond quality in early childhood education and care: Languages of evaluation. *New Zealand Journal of Teachers' Work*, 5(1), 3–12.

Noddings, N. (1984). *Caring: A feminine approach to ethics and moral education*. (1st ed.). University of California Press.

Noddings, N. (2013). *Caring: A relational approach to ethics and moral education* (2nd ed.). University of California Press.

Powell, A., Johnston, L., & Langford, R. (2021). Equity enacted: Possibilities for difference in ECEC through a critical ethics of care approach. *Equity as praxis in early childhood education and care*. Canadian Scholars Press.

Prochner, L. (2000). A history of early education and child care in Canada 1820–1966. In L. Prochner & N. Howe, (Eds.), *Early childhood care and education in Canada* (pp. 11–65). University of British Columbia Press.

Robinson, F. (2020). Resisting hierarchies through relationality in the ethics of care. *International Journal of Care and Caring*, 4(1), 11–23.

Sander-Staudt, M. (2018). Care ethics. *Internet Encyclopedia of Philosophy*. https://www.iep.utm.edu/care-eth/

Schmied, V. & Lupton, D. (2001). Blurring the boundaries: Breastfeeding and maternal subjectivity. *Sociology of health & illness*, 23(2), 234–50.

Schwartz, A. (2018). Locating Femme Theory online. *First Monday*, 7(2). doi:10.5210/fm.v23i7.9266

Schwartz, A. (2020a). Radical vulnerability: Selfies as a Femme-inine mode of resistance. *Psychology & Sexuality*, 1–14. Advance Online.

Schwartz, A. (2020b). Low Femme, low theory: Memes and the new bedroom culture. *Feminist Media Studies*, 1–16. Advance Online.

Scott, J. B. (2021a). Negotiating relationships with powerfulness: Using Femme Theory to resist masculinist pressures on feminist femininities. *Psychology & Sexuality*, 1–10. Advance Online.

Scott, J. B. (2021b). What do glitter, pointe shoes, & plastic drumsticks have in common? Using Femme Theory to consider the reclamation of disciplinary beauty/body practices. *Journal of Lesbian Studies*, 25(1), 36–52.

Serano, J. (2007). *Whipping girl: A transsexual woman on sexism and the scapegoating of femininity*. Seal Press.

Serano, J. (2012). Reclaiming femininity. In A. Enke (Ed.), *Transfeminist perspectives in and beyond transgender and gender studies* (pp. 170–84). Temple University Press.

Serano, J. (2013). *Excluded: Making feminist and queer movements more inclusive*. Seal Press.

Smith, K., Alexander, K., & Campbell, S. (Eds.). (2017). *Feminism(s) in early childhood: Using feminist theories in research and practice*. Springer.

Story, K. A. (2017). Fear of a Black femme: The existential conundrum of embodying a Black femme identity while being a professor of Black, queer, and feminist studies. *Journal of Lesbian Studies*, 21(4), 407–19.

Taggart, G. (2011). Don't we care?: The ethics and emotional labour of early years professionalism. *Early years*, 31(1), 85–95.

Varga, D. (1997). *Constructing the child: A history of Canadian day care*. James Lorimer & Company.

Volcano, D. L., & Dahl, U. (2008). *Femmes of power: Exploding queer femininities*. Serpent's Tail.

Walcott, R. (1994). Pedagogical desire and the crisis of knowledge. *Discourse, 15*(1), 64–74.

Whiley, L. A., Stutterheim, S., & Grandy, G. (2020). Breastfeeding, 'tainted' love, and femmephobia: Containing the 'dirty' performances of embodied femininity. *Psychology & Sexuality*, 1–14. Advance Online.

Weedon, C. (1999). *Feminism, theory, and the politics of difference*. Blackwell.

Commentary 3

Rachel Langford and Brooke Richardson

In the first part of this commentary, Chapter 9 (Meagan Monpetit) and Chapter 10 (Gunilla Dahlberg and Ann Merete Otterstad) are discussed by drawing out key themes from feminist new materialism and posthumanism to consider the early childhood educator subject differently. Following this, insights from feminist queer theory in Chapter 8 (Janice Kroeger) and femme theory in Chapter 11 (Adam Davis and Rhea Ashley Hoskin) are summarized and compared.

Feminist new materialism is discussed by Hekman in the final chapter of her 2014 book. While she views this feminism as defining 'a new approach to knowledge, politics, and the subject that deconstructs the categories of modernism' (p. 185), she also sees it as the 'springboard' for the next approach. Like Hekman, we do not think of the final chapters in this anthology as an end point. What the final chapters of the anthology *do* is further complexify our thinking that can open to, as Dahlberg and Otterstad emphasize, the potentialities of feminisms. In contrast to the focus on discourse in poststructuralism, Newberry welcomes the return to the material – though new materialism is more broadly defined. While materialist feminism was primarily focused on women's labour and bodies as sites of exploitation and oppression (still an important material reality to hold), feminist new materialism incorporates a parallel focus on the material realties of physical beings and matter in the more-than-human world. Drawing on Elizabeth Grosz's (2004) and Nancy Tuana's (2001) works, Hekman (2014) suggests that new materialism provides a way to focus on the 'ontology rather than epistemology, the real rather than the production of knowledge' (p. 157). While poststructuralism brought much-needed attention to the discursive production of knowledge – how we come to know what we know – feminist new materialism re-asserted the centrality of bodily/earthly felt/lived material realities – how we come to be what we are. According to Hekman (2014), feminist new materialism also holds space for bridging dualisms (e.g. masculine/feminine, nature/culture, human/non-human) that characterize modernist thinking. Referencing the work of Jane Bennett (2010), Hekman describes one goal of feminist new materialism to 'develop a theory of the self as an impure, human, non-human assemblage' (p. 161) constituted by the intra-actions of the discursive, the material and other elements.

Monpetit draws on earth-based feminist thinking as one mode of enacting this theory of the self to complexify our understanding of early childhood educator subjects. Monpetit asserts that embracing a posthuman lens is necessary to disrupt universalized notions of human exceptionalism that continue to enact systematic violence on human and more-than-human bodies and matter in the world. To illustrate her thinking, Monpetit reflects on her own experiences as an early childhood educator centring the more-than-human world through exploring a cemetery alongside co-educators and children. She describes the necessity of 'uncomfortable tensions' and the possibilities for reconvening the early childhood educator as a posthuman subject brought on through pedagogical explorations (p. 159).

Working and thinking in the Scandinavian context, Dahlberg and Otterstad make an interesting observation: while they have not been explicitly feminist in their academic writings, the ways they have taken up contemporary theorists has been underpinned by an implicit feminist orientation. Drawing on the work of Erin Manning (i.e. 2016), Dahlberg and Otterstad's understanding of feminist new materialism 'does not assume an overarching concept of life, just practices and flows of becoming, complex assemblages and heterogeneous relations' (p. 185). Using different language, both Monpetit and Dahlberg and Otterstad describe the importance of creating networks and alliances with co-educators, though they recognize the barriers to this work amidst a universalized, humanist context that seeks to control and manage rather than creatively and conscientiously become.

The inherent tensions between feminist new materialism, including posthumanism, and the purpose of this anthology must also be recognized. In many ways, we asked authors to centre the educator in their thinking about early childhood education. And, of course, educators are humans. This tension is not lost on us. Indeed, it has pushed our own thinking. As Monpetit and Dahlberg and Otterstad point out, thinking with posthumanism does not negate the human but broadens our understanding of ourselves and our world. As we have come to appreciate in editing this anthology, the challenges of thinking beyond, let alone moving beyond, child-centredness in early childhood education are real – both discursively and materially.

The chapters by Janice Kroeger on queer feminism and by Adam Davies and Rhea Ashley Hoskins on femme theory continue to expand possibilities for early childhood educator subjectivities. Just as the authors in Chapters 5, 6 and 7 engage with aspects of difference related to Indigeneity and race, Kroeger's chapter brings our attention to the complexities of gender and sexuality in the subjective construction of the ECE. What becomes clear throughout the chapter is that in addition to being white, the neoliberal 'good' early childhood educator is a cis-gender female and heterosexual. Much of Kroeger's chapter problematizes how heteronormative pedagogical practices can exclude queer families and early childhood educators from being fully and meaningfully members of an early childhood community.

For queer theorists, queerness is a manifestation of resistance. It is about not conforming to dominant, binary, gendered and/or sexuality norms. As Kroeger suggests to identify as queer is to function outside of the traditional male/female and heterosexual/homosexual binaries that have too long been accepted as 'fact'. While this 'otherness' may not be immediately visible (though it certainly could be too), educators who allow themselves to be known outside of gender/sexuality male/female, gay/straight binaries may be treated with caution and/or suspicion by their colleagues, superiors and the children/families with whom they work. Understanding and expressing oneself as queer is thus a visible act of revolt when working with children.

While Kroeger's chapter discusses queer theory's aims to dismantle the feminine/masculine binary and norms, Davies and Hoskin's chapter draws on femme theory as a theoretical tool to reclaim feminine identities that resist normative feminine ideals. Their exploration of feminine subjectivities emerges out of analyses of 1940s working-class lesbian communities, experiences of gay men in early childhood education who deviate from expectations of heteronormative masculinity, and Black femme theorizing that disrupts 'inherent associations between White patriarchal femininity and teaching' (p. 202). Thus, the femininity that Davies and Hoskin seek to uproot from 'femmephobia' shares similarities with the femininity that queer theorists want to shake out of an entrenched feminine/masculine binary.

However, the two chapters also point to differences between queer and femme theory.[1] Queer theory emerged out of a critique of gay and lesbian studies' focus on promoting positive identities for community members. Queer theory seeks to dismantle identities produced by binaries and norms and to position gender and sexuality as continually fluid, potentially rendering the very notion of the subject as obsolete. Davies and Hoskin, in contrast, are interested in thinking about new forms of femme and relational subjectivities for early childhood educators. As these authors point out in their chapter, identity/subjectivity as completely fluid runs the danger of recentralizing masculinity. Moreover, Davies and Hoskin suggest that queer theory, in destabilizing the subject, also potentially destabilizes relationality *between* subjects. For these authors, being femme is about being relational and about multiple expressions and productions of femininities that are beyond the singular, essentialist and heterosexual. Femininity is seen as generative rather than only a source of oppression. They also reject that being a femme early childhood educator is not transgressive and queer enough. As Davies and Hoskin state, femme theory centralizes feminine multiplicities in order to develop an intersectional framework that can help us understand femininity, gender, power and identity.

Note

1   We are grateful for insights into differences between queer theory and femme theory provided by Adam Davies and Rhea Ashley Hoskin.

References

Bennett, J. (2010). *Vibrant matter: A political ecology of things*. Duke University Press.
Hekman, S. (2014). *The feminine subject*. Polity Press.
Grosz, E. (2004). *The nick of time*. Duke University Press.
Manning, E. (2013). *Always more than one. Individuations dance*. Duke University Press.
Tuana, N. (2001). Material locations. In N. Tuana and S. Morgen (Eds.), *Engendering rationalities* (pp. 221–43). Indiana University Press.

Concluding Remarks

Rachel Langford and Brooke Richardson

This anthology has honoured a long lineage of feminist thinking in the early childhood education field. Inspired by Luce Irigaray, a French feminist who followed Simone Beauvoir, Hekman (2014) argues that feminist theories must 'jam the theoretical machinery' of Western thought and 'move beyond its parameters to redefine woman' (p. 5). The aim of this anthology has been to do this jamming and moving with the ECE subject. While much of early childhood education literature has understandably focused on conceptualizations of the child and/or the child-in-context, this anthology is unique in its push towards bringing explicit attention to how different feminisms can transform our thinking about the early childhood educator herself/themself.

We are aware that thinking differently about the early childhood educator is truly an expansive intellectual endeavour. In this conclusion we offer some final observations about the chapters in relation to the ECE subject and feminist theory.

What becomes clear throughout this book is that there are so many more possibilities than the hyper-individualized, objective, applier-of-knowledge/skills that has come to dominate understandings of the professional early childhood educator. With all the rich alternatives offered in the chapters, it is amazing to us that the hegemonic, neoliberal technician discourse continues to dominate practice and policy settings. Yet we are not surprised. We appreciate, as do the chapter authors, how deeply entrenched neoliberal discourses of the ECE subject continue to systematically occlude and/or devalue the material, embodied and discursively constructed lived experiences of ECEs. This book is a collective attempt, at an academic level, to bring much-needed attention to ECEs' experiences of their work, bodies, minds and spirituality – their subjectivity.

We also observe that a relational ethic (i.e. affirmative ethics, ethics of care, ethics of an encounter) that remains open to the self and the Other is a priority for all authors. In contrast to traditional, liberal ethical frameworks – often captured/furthered through universalized standards of practice guidelines – these chapters highlight the work of ECEs as deeply ethical, contextual, authentic and open. There is no clear 'right' or 'wrong' way of navigating the complex situations ECEs encounter with their own bodies and minds, other's bodies and minds and the more-than-human world (physical and/or spiritual) every day. As Smith articulates in her chapter, what matters is listening, reflecting, dialoguing and making an effort to act in a way that is authentic to oneself, others and the place/space in which we exist. As several authors further insist this ethical commitment is important not only at the interpersonal and local level, but also at the public policy and global level.

We notice, as well, the conceptual thread of thresholds, bridges, movement and becoming in some way in every chapter, particularly the Dahlberg and Otterstad chapter. Consistent with the postfoundational turn, chapters understand ECEs as professionals who have the capacity to learn, grow, think and be in new ways in every moment. There is an encouragement to embrace the inevitably unexpected, the uncomfortable and the unknown. Anzaldúa's concept of nepantla introduced by Ritchie in Chapter 10 and echoing throughout several other chapters, challenges us to embrace the inevitable in-betweenness of being/becoming an early childhood educator. Too many contemporary early childhood settings – childcare centres, home childcare programmes, kindergartens and nursery schools – glorify busyness, structure, predictability and order whereby regulatory requirements enforce this approach. The result is the subjective positioning of the ECE as the planner, manager, supervisor and even entertainer. The chapters in this anthology give educators permission to loosen their grip on some of that control and open to what arises – even if we don't know immediately what to do with it or how to respond.

While this book is primarily concerned with the early childhood educator, it also offers a rich and comprehensive exploration of contemporary feminisms. Though each chapter focuses on a feminism or feminisms as a theoretical tool to rethink possibilities for ECE subjectivities, these insights are useful for all feminine subjects – particularly those in other highly gendered undervalued professions (e.g. social workers, teachers, nurses). The book's inclusion of multiple feminisms is both unique and an act of resistance in itself as it centres the often taken-for-granted intellectual and material work of women. It is our hope that this book can become a source for the possibilities in feminist thinking in early childhood education and beyond.

As the commentaries show, we noticed more affinities than tensions between the feminisms. Chapter authors collectively use the concepts of neoliberalism, discourse, subjectivity, identity, relationality, multiplicity and resistance to work through their particular feminism in relation to the ECE subject. For chapter authors, the starting point for this work is a feminist critique of dominant developmental and technical approaches to understanding who the ECE subject can be. Furthermore, through the stories chapter authors tell, it is clear that engagement with feminisms is an emotional endeavour. Authors describe on-going struggles to find a place in early childhood education, relief at discovering feminism, and the challenges of meeting the demands of resistance and revolt. At the same time, feminism for authors is an emotional space that provides connection with others, hope and solace.

The clearest tension between the various feminisms explored in this book is discussed in Commentary 3 in relation to queer feminism and femme theory. Another tension, discussed in commentary one, exists between authors who assert that ECEs are already doing enough under difficult circumstances (e.g. Bruce and Powell, Harmon, Ritter and Viruru) and authors who ask ECEs to do more. However, all authors call for ECEs – and those who care about ECEs and their work – to create greater space to think critically about and value the work.

Outside of these reflections, we would characterize points of divergence between the feminisms explored in this book as *tensions*, rather than differences. These tensions emerge in relation to how ideas are *emphasized* rather than being categorically different ideas. For example, while many chapters point to the importance of including the more-than-human in theorizing worldly relations, Ritchie's chapter on ecofeminisms and Montpetit's chapter on feminist posthumanism centres it. Taken together the chapters show that when feminist humanism and posthumanism are allied there is greater potential for challenging the dehumanizing and climate devastating social, political and economic structures that continue to dominate. All chapters emphasize the lived and intersectional experiences of ECEs (e.g. Bruce and Powell, Harmon, Ritter and Viruru, and Newberry), taking this as a starting point for what could/should happen next. All authors embrace the idea of the becoming subject, but Tesar and Arndt challenge us to think more deeply about this becoming through acknowledging/incorporating parts of ourselves we may not yet know (the 'foreigner within'). Similarly, Odim, Rideaux and Salazar Pérez ask us to consider mind-body-spirit relations in the process of becoming. These differences in emphasis between the feminisms may reflect bell hooks' declaration, introduced at the beginning of this book, that feminisms diverge not on the goal itself (ending the domination of women) but *how* to realize this common goal.

This insight, combined with the many affinities identified, suggests an opportunity for greater solidarity between feminists in the ECE community. At a time of pronounced political polarity and environmental collapse, solidarity is urgently needed. We wonder what might be possible if ECEs/pedagogues/pedagogists, academics, childcare policy researchers and advocates working in this area act on authors' calls to centre love for our worlds, 'care with' early childhood educators and 'cultivate spaces where childhood and educator multiplicities and relationalities are nourished' (p. 111). We enthusiastically invite anyone reading this book to continue critical conversations about feminisms in relation to the early childhood educator subject, reflect on their own thinking and being, and take action *with* others. It is well past time that early childhood educators take up their/our much-deserved space in worldly relations.

Index

ableism/ableist 158, 198, 202
add-women-and-stir approach 46
affirmative ethics 158–9, 161–3, 166, 168–9, 185–6, 214
Anthropocene 115, 157–8
anthropocentric 157, 159–60, 164, 169
anthropology 45–6, 54, 141
anthropomorphism 164
anti-Blackness 99, 101, 103, 111. *See also* Black people
anti-racism 121–2, 129, 137. *See also* race/racism
Anzaldúa, G. 120, 137, 141
    Borderlands: La Frontera: The New Mestiza 142
    nepantla 120, 137–8, 214
Aotearoa New Zealand 27–34, 36, 38, 118, 120–1, 129 n.1. *See also* Māori people
    monocultural colonial education system in 119
    Te Hurihanganui programme in 129
    Te Whāriki curriculum 27, 117, 121–2
arts of noticing 168
assimilation 198
Australia 3, 16–18, 27–34, 36, 38
    ECEs in 79–80
    EYLF 18–19
authoritarian model 50, 124
autonomous 36, 66–7, 70–1, 185, 199
Awatere, D. 117–18
    Māori Sovereignty 119

Barad, K., re-turning 177
Barthes, R. 31
Bhattacharya, T. 53
    Social Reproduction Theory: Remapping Class, Recentering Oppression 48
biodiversity 115, 124, 128
Black Feminist Theory (BFT) 21, 87–9

Black people 69, 87–8, 99, 101–2, 104–6, 108, 121–2, 125, 136–7, 140. *See also* Brown people
Black feminism/feminist 6, 83, 85, 93, 100–3, 107, 135–6, 178 (*see also* feminism/feminists; *specific feminists*)
Black femme 202, 211
Blaise, M. 19, 140, 145, 164–5
    Decentring the Human in Multispecies Ethnography 164
Braidotti, R. 158, 162, 186
Brown people 99, 102. *See also* Black people
Burman, E. 51, 179
    Deconstructing Developmental Psychology 179
Butler, J. 14, 139, 141, 182–3
    'formation of a gender' 141
    Gender trouble: Feminism and the subversion of identity 142, 183
    heterosexual matrix 142, 144–5, 148
    performativity 14, 142, 183
    Undoing Gender 183

Canada 3, 8
    ECEC in 198
    Ontario 61, 73, 163, 197
Cannella, G. 66, 115, 126, 179–80
    Deconstructing Early Childhood Education: Social Justice and Revolution 12, 179
capital/capitalism 46–56, 81, 88, 107, 128, 143, 160–1, 163, 165, 198. *See also* economy/economics
care/ethics of care 63–4, 71–2, 80, 102, 191–2, 196–8, 203, 214
care receivers 62–3, 68–73, 191
carers/care labour/caregivers 5, 13, 16–18, 23, 48, 51–2, 54, 62, 68–70, 72, 85–6, 93, 191

community-based 122
discourses 18
and femininity 194–5, 197–8 (*see also* feminism/feminists, feminist ethics of care)
Tronto on (phases of care) 62–3, 68–73
care-giving 71–2
care-receiving 72–3
caring about 70
caring for 70–1
caring with 69, 73
categorization 159, 165, 179–81, 184
childcare/childcare policy 5, 50, 52–3, 84–6, 124, 159, 166, 169, 176, 193, 197, 214, 216
child development 5, 50, 65–6, 124, 167, 179, 181, 192, 197
practitioner (*see* early childhood educators (ECEs))
child labour 52
cisgender 85, 192, 194–6, 198, 201, 203, 211
class. *See* social class
climate crisis 116, 162, 165. *See also* ecological crisis
climate emergency 116, 124
climate empowerment 116
Collins, P. H. 6, 88
matrix of domination 135
colonial education system 119–20
colonialism 47–8, 51, 89–90, 93, 99, 111, 123, 127, 158
colonization 33, 53, 102, 116–18, 120–1, 124
commodification 18, 46
Common Worlds Research Collective 160, 163–4
community-based care 122
consciousness 33, 103–5, 110
critical 121, 123, 129
cooperative thinking/writing 176–8
counter-hegemonies 128–9. *See also* hegemony
Covid-19 pandemic 3, 33–4, 36, 73, 86, 116, 124, 197
creativity 29, 55, 81–2, 123, 138
Crenshaw, K. 6, 69, 101, 135
critical race feminism 90
critical theory 20, 62, 181, 185

culture 18, 20, 28, 36–8, 49, 85, 118, 128, 141–2, 157, 167, 176
curriculum 11, 14, 16, 18, 36, 49, 66, 110, 121, 146, 149, 160–1, 169, 176
EYLF in Australia 18–19
Te Whāriki in Aotearoa New Zealand 27, 117, 121–2

Daly, M. 13
Davies, B. 19–21, 124, 137, 145, 196, 198
day nurseries 196
De Beauvoir, S. 213
The Second Sex 45, 182
decolonizing feminism 115–17, 123–8, 137
DeJean, W. 146–8
Deleuze, G. 181, 183–4
democracy 3, 175–6
Derrida, J. 13, 181
devaluation 64–5, 191, 193–4, 196
developmentalism 3, 56, 158, 161, 169
developmental psychology 14, 162, 179–81
discourses 15–19, 21, 23, 46, 66, 79, 101, 115–17, 124–5, 127, 137
dominant 5, 12–14, 16, 21–3, 65, 80, 91, 126, 144–5, 147–9, 158
gendered 6, 125, 127
historical hierarchical 120
human capital discourse 1, 17, 49–50, 52, 56
humanistic 161
neoliberal 6, 22, 27, 213
professionalization 196
discursive practices 4, 19, 125
diversity 36, 93, 139–40, 148–50
domestic labour 45, 65, 87
dominant discourses 5, 12–14, 16, 21–3, 65, 80, 91, 126, 144–5, 147–9, 158
dominant narratives 1–2, 31, 193
Drag Queen Story Hour programme 145
dualism/dualistic thinking 54, 56, 184, 199–200, 210

early childhood education (ECE) 1–6, 17, 30, 34, 38, 45, 52–3, 56, 61, 68–9, 73, 82–5, 87, 89, 91–2, 94, 99, 102, 115–16, 121, 126–7,

138–40, 157, 160–1, 164, 167–8, 175, 177, 191, 197–8, 210–11, 213, 215–16
complexity 68–9, 72, 128
decolonizing feminism 124–7
feminist queer advocacy (challenge and promise) 148–50
identity discourses 64–5
multiplicity 12–13, 61–2, 66–9, 72–3, 80–1, 165, 215
with posthumanism 159–63
queering of 143–6
relationality (*see* relational/relationality)
scholarship 7, 61, 65, 68
subject/subjectivities 3–4, 7–8, 61–2, 64, 66, 68, 70–3, 80–2, 136, 192, 195, 198–9, 203, 213–15
and Femme Theory 199–202
womanism in 108
workforce 83–9, 92–3, 126
early childhood education and care (ECEC) 31, 45–6, 49, 65, 92, 111, 128–9, 175–6, 178, 180, 185, 187, 191, 197, 202
Canadian 198
feminization of 192, 197
femmephobia in 192, 194
gender inclusivity in 195
in Indonesia 49–52, 56, 80, 82
Nordic 181–2
in Scandinavia 176–7, 179
early childhood educators (ECEs) 1–7, 11–12, 14, 16–22, 27–8, 35–7, 54, 61–2, 79–80, 82–3, 87–9, 93, 99, 101–2, 104–6, 110, 121–2, 125–8, 135–7, 140, 151, 158–62, 167–9, 176–7, 179–82, 184–6, 191–2, 195, 198, 210–16
in Australia 79–80
childhood teacher identities 12, 15, 27–35, 38–9
as early childhood educator(s) 62, 73
materializing 55–6
in Ontario 73
as professional 66–8, 214
queer/queer feminism 139, 146–8
relational 68–73, 82
subjectivation of 50

as substitute mother 64–6
as technicians 1, 5, 17–18, 65–6, 199
in uncaring conditions 63–8
in the US 86, 101
earth-based feminist spirituality 164–9, 210. *See also* spiritual/spirituality
eco-feminism/-feminist 116, 128, 165, 167, 215
ecological crisis 128, 159, 164. *See also* climate crisis
ecological devastation 157–8
economy/economics 1, 16, 18, 37, 47–8, 52, 81, 83, 88, 123–4, 140, 191, 197–8, 203. *See also* capital/capitalism
economic oppression 127
political 45–7, 52, 65
education/educational system 15–16, 49–50, 119. *See also* early childhood education (ECE)
colonial 119–20
educational debt 102
educational spaces 103–6, 109
education racial project in the US 102
educator praxis 99, 106, 110–11
environmental 164
neoliberal 160
Reggio-Emilia educational philosophy 5, 180–1
Electoral Act 1893 (New Zealand) 33
embodied natural beings 48, 54
emotions/emotionality 16, 18, 34–5, 52, 65, 80–1, 104–5, 123, 126, 137, 196–8, 200, 215
Enlightenment 116, 200
Equal Rights Amendment (The United States) 45
essentialism 184–5, 192, 198
ethnic/ethnicity 85, 93, 143, 179
Europe/European (Eurocentric) 34, 46, 52, 55, 93, 140, 179, 198
Euro-Western 64, 161, 170 n.2
Evans, R. 117–18

feminine/femininity 2, 13, 18, 29, 48–51, 53, 81, 144, 191–202, 211–12
breastfeeding (in public) 201–2

gender expressions 193
patriarchal 194, 198, 201–2, 211
feminism/feminists 2–3, 6–8, 12, 19, 21–3, 32–3, 54, 79–80, 83–5, 99, 117, 129, 144, 175–7, 185, 187, 195, 209–10, 213, 215–16. *See also* masculine/masculinity
   academic writing 175, 210
   aggressive 29
   assumptions 117, 182, 193–4, 202
   Black (*see* Black people, Black feminism/feminist)
   collective activism 178, 182
   decolonizing 115–17, 123–8, 137
   eco-feminism/-feminist 116, 128, 165, 167, 215
   feminist ethics of care 7, 28, 30, 61–5, 67–9, 73, 79–80, 82, 124, 192 (*see also* care/ethics of care)
   feminist theories (*see specific theories*)
   feminist thinkers/thinking 8, 12, 14, 20, 56, 101, 115, 176–7, 179, 210, 213, 215 (*see also specific persons*)
   feminized labour 195–6, 201–2
   first wave feminism 85
   fourth-wave feminism 83–7, 91–3, 135–7
   lesbian 140–2
   materialism/materialist 5, 45–6, 49, 53, 55, 65, 79–81, 209
   North American Black and Latinx 120–4
   Pākehā 117
   postcolonial 89–93, 136, 144
   posthumanism (*see* posthumanism/posthuman theory)
   poststructuralism 12–16, 19–23, 27–39, 45–6, 79–80, 124, 144–5, 200, 203
   queer (*see* queer/queer theory, queer feminism)
   second wave feminism 85, 135, 140–1
   spirituality (*see* spiritual/spirituality)
   taken-for-granted 5, 12, 169, 202, 214
   third wave feminism 85, 87, 89, 135–7, 140
   transnational 90, 178
   Western 89–90, 117, 120

feminization 192, 197, 201
femme-inist approach 192, 195, 200, 202–3
femmephobia 192–6, 200–1, 211
Femme Theory 192–3, 211–12, 215
   and ECEC 196–9
   and ECE subjectivities 199–202
   overview 193–6
Fendler, L. 180
First World 90–1. *See also* Third World
forced labour 93, 177
Foucault, M. 15, 20, 45, 80, 141, 180–1
   governmentality 45, 49, 66, 80, 180
   on resistance 22–3
Franchino, E., 'Celebrating Women in Early Childhood Education' 191
Fraser, N. 47–8, 54
Freer, A. 106, 108
Freire, P. 20, 122, 128
Freud, S. 141, 144
Friedan, B., *Feminine Mystique* 121

gender 1, 3, 6, 14, 16, 18, 20–1, 23, 32, 34, 36, 38, 46, 56, 64, 85, 89–90, 99, 101–2, 117, 124–5, 139–51, 177, 183, 193, 195, 197, 200–1, 211–12, 214. *See also* race/racism
   diversity 139, 149
   equality 147, 175–6
   essentialism 192, 198
   expressions 143, 145, 193
   identity 141–4, 148–9, 151, 194
   intersectionality (*see* intersectional/intersectionality)
   MacNaughton's gender analysis 125
   nonconformity 148–9
   performative/performativity 141–2, 145, 149, 183
   struggle 2, 13, 56, 87–8, 117, 149
gender and development (GAD) 46
Genesis 116
Gilligan, C. 61–2, 65, 124
   In a different voice 82
Global North/Global South 8, 46, 49, 52, 56, 102
gonadal sex 145
governmentality 45, 49, 66, 80, 180
Great Chain of Being 116
Grosz, E. 54, 209

Halkyard, H. 117, 119
Heckman, J. J. 178, 209
hegemony 34, 82, 123, 128, 136–8, 140, 213. *See also* counter-hegemonies
Hekman, S. 2, 7, 49, 53, 69, 79–82, 135, 177–8, 182–3, 210, 213
Held, V. 62, 65
heteronormative/heteronormativity 47, 55, 140, 142, 144–7, 149, 193, 201, 211
heterosexual/heterosexuality 141, 143–8, 150–1, 158, 192, 196, 211–12
  cisgender white womanhood 198, 201, 203
  heterosexual matrix 142, 144–5, 148
hierarchies 17, 63, 69, 102, 115–16, 124, 126, 162, 195–6, 198, 202
homo economicus 66
homophobia/homophobic 85, 139, 144, 149
homosexual/homosexuality 147, 211
hooks, b. 2, 88, 109, 120–3, 135, 137, 216
  community-based childcare 122
  Feminist Theory: From margin to center 121
human/human beings 54, 63–4, 93, 99, 116, 125–6, 128, 137–8, 158–60, 165, 170 n.3, 178, 184, 197, 202, 210. *See also* non-human
  exceptionalism 163–4, 166, 210
  human capital discourse 1, 17, 49–50, 52, 56
  humanism 22, 90–1, 199–200, 215
  humanity 100, 103, 115, 200
  more-than-human 4–5, 27, 54, 63, 72, 99, 102, 105–6, 108, 128, 137–8, 157–65, 167–9, 178, 182–6, 209–10, 214–15
  subject/subjectivity 48, 158–60, 162–3, 167, 169

identity/identities 4–5, 12–14, 19–23, 36–8, 63–8, 73, 89, 136, 141–2, 193, 200, 212
  childhood teacher identities 12, 15, 27–35, 38–9
  constructions 28, 35, 62, 64, 67–8, 73
  discourses 64–5

of ECEs 63–4
  as professional 66–8, 214
  as substitute mother 64–5
  as technician 1, 5, 17–18, 65–6, 199
  gender 141–4, 148–9, 151, 194
  identity politics 15, 20
  professional 15, 17–18, 21, 62, 67, 80
  sexual 141, 145
Indigeneity 211
Indigenous people 21, 28, 32–4, 55, 101, 115–16, 122, 124, 167. *See also* non-Indigenous people
individuality 62, 199
Indonesia 45, 47–8, 81
  ECEC programmes in 49–52, 56, 80–1
  global assemblage 51
  modernization 47
  natural disasters and financial crisis 49
  neoliberal democratization (democratic transformation) 49–51
  womenandchildren 51–5, 82
  women in (*see* women (in Indonesia))
Innate Divinity 99
Intergovernmental Panel on Climate Change (United Nations) 116
inter-relationality 120–3
intersectional/intersectionality 6, 32, 36, 51, 55–6, 69, 85, 89, 101, 121, 135, 178, 194, 201, 212, 215
intersex 139, 142–3

Jenkins, K. 117

kindergarten 16, 48, 119, 196, 214
knowledge 5, 11–15, 17, 19–20, 23, 49, 128, 138, 144, 165–6, 170 n.2, 180–1, 194, 198–200, 209
  ancestral 106–8, 122
Kristeva, J. 27–30, 80–1, 201
  Barthes on 31
  foreigner/foreignness 27–31, 35, 37, 81
  more radical approach 29, 38
  Oliver on 28–9
  poststructural feminism 27–39, 79–80
  revolt 35–9
  subject formation 27–31, 35
K12 sector 88, 197

Langford, R. 63–6, 69–70, 72, 199
language 14–20, 22–3, 52, 181, 210
 Māori 117, 119 (*see also* Māori people)
Latina/Latino 101, 140
LGBTQ/LGBTQ+ 139, 143, 146–7, 149–50, 194
 bisexual 139, 143, 148–9
 gay 139–44, 148–50, 211
 lesbian 139–44, 148–9, 193, 211
 queer (*see* queer/queer theory)
 trans/transgender 139–40, 142–3, 145–6, 149
liberal humanism/humanist 90–1, 125, 199–200
location 90–1, 175, 185, 200
long day care services 16, 18
Lorde, A. 107, 120, 123, 135, 137
 Poetry is not a luxury 123
 visionary feminist collective solidarity 123
love 55, 102
 and human inter-relationships 122–3
 professional love 65

MacNaughton, G. 11–12, 19, 137
 gender analysis 125
Malaguzzi, L. 180–1
Manning, E. 177, 182–6, 210
 Always More-Than- One: Individuations Dance 183
 bodies and movement 183–4
 The Minor Gesture 183–4
 Thought in the act: Passages in the ecology of experience 183
Māori people 117–20. *See also* Aotearoa New Zealand; New Zealand
 death rates of Māori women 129 n.2
 education 119–20
 kōhanga reo movement 117, 119
 mana motuhake and rangatiratanga (authority and self-determination) 118
 Māori Sovereignty (Awatere) 119
 mātauranga (Māori knowledge) 118
 Pākehā 117–19
 taonga (everything of value) 118
 te ao Māori (Māori worldview) 120
 Tiriti o Waitangi (1840) 118, 121
 whakapapa (genealogical ties) 117
 whenua (lands) 118
 women activism/activists 117–19
Maparyan, L. 99–100, 110
marginalization 32–3, 37, 69, 85, 127
Marx/Marxist/Marxism 46–7, 53–6, 80–2, 140
masculine/masculinity 13, 82, 143–4, 158, 179, 194–7, 199–201, 211–12. *See also* feminism/feminists
Massumi, B. 177, 183
 Thought in the act: Passages in the ecology of experience 183
materialism
 materialist feminism 5, 45–6, 49, 53, 55, 65, 79–81, 209
 materializing ECEs 55–6
 new materialism 8, 53–6, 82, 176–8, 185, 209–10
material realities 6, 80, 209
maternalism 65, 196, 198, 201
#MeToo movement 85
Mikaere, A. 117–18
mind-body-spirit relations 99, 102, 105, 109–11, 137–8, 213–15
minority group 37, 86, 143, 149, 179
modernism/modernity/modernization 30, 47, 181, 209
Mohanty, C. T. 90–1
monocultural colonial education system 119
morality 62, 92, 164
moral thinking 62, 65
Moss, P. 5, 65
Murray, P. 88

National Te Kōhanga Reo Trust (New Zealand) 117
neoliberal/neoliberalism 5–6, 17–18, 29, 50–1, 61, 65–6, 80, 91, 123, 127, 160–1, 182, 186, 211, 215
 capitalism 53, 198
 discourses 6, 22, 27, 213
 education system 160
neo-pagan 165–6
neuroscience 1, 14, 56
new feminist materialism 8, 53–6, 82, 176–8, 185, 209–10
New Zealand 8, 129 n.1. *See also* Aotearoa New Zealand
 Mana Wāhine 117–20

South African Springbok rugby team to 118
Waitangi Tribunal 118
non-human 158, 160, 170 n.3, 184, 210. *See also* human/human beings
non-Indigenous people 28, 32, 34. *See also* Indigenous people
Nordic countries 6, 175, 181–2
normality 31, 141, 145, 151
normativity 202–3
   normative development 196, 198
   normative dualism 200
Norway 175, 186
   Children's Act Law (1975) 187 n.1
   in 1970s and following years 178–85
nurturing/nurturance 85, 101, 138, 195–6, 198, 201

Oliver, K. 28–9
ontology 3, 54–5, 164, 184–5, 197, 209
   Euro-Western 161
   relational 62, 158
oppression 6, 21, 55, 69, 73, 81, 87–9, 92, 100–1, 103–5, 115, 117, 120–1, 124, 126–7, 135–7, 139, 143, 149, 158, 179, 209, 212
Organization of Economic Co-operation and Development (OECD) 1, 5, 49
Others/Otherness 30, 34–5, 37–8, 81, 103–4, 108, 115–16, 124, 127, 137, 141, 179, 211, 214. *See also* self

Pacini-Ketchabaw, V. 165
   Climate Action Network: Exploring Climate Change Pedagogies with Children 163
   Decentring the Human in Multispecies Ethnography 164
Park, Y. 89–90
Pateman, C., *The Sexual Contract* 46–7
patriarchy 13–14, 23, 47, 51, 61–2, 79, 82, 117, 120, 124, 126–8, 158, 165, 167, 195, 197, 200–2
   patriarchal femininity 194, 198, 201–2, 211
'Pedagogy in a Changing World,' Stockholm Project (1993) 180–2

pedagogy/pedagogies/pedagogues 99, 126, 147, 160–1, 167, 169, 169 n.1. *See also* early childhood educators (ECEs)
   attachment 65
   care-full 65
   child-centred 199, 210
   creative pedagogical practice 2
   dialogical 123
   in Scandinavia 187 n.3
performances 12, 14, 16–17, 21, 23, 46, 144–5, 149, 183
performativity 14, 142, 183
philosophical thinking 182, 184–5
Piaget, J. 124, 144
Piedalue, A. 90–1
Pitman, Mereana 118
Plumwood, V.
   Feminism and the mastery of nature 116–17
   sustainability 128
political economy 45–6, 52, 65
postcolonial feminism 89–93, 136, 144
posthumanism/posthuman theory 8, 137, 157–9, 178, 209–10, 215
   affirmative ethics 158–9, 161–3, 166, 168–9, 185–6, 214
   and ECE 159–63
   subjects/subjectivities 158–9, 161–5, 167–9
postmodern/postmodernism 29–30, 49, 55, 79, 179, 183, 198
post-secondary educational requirements 1, 3
poststructuralism, feminist 12–16, 19–23, 27–39, 45–6, 79–80, 124, 144–5, 200, 203
power 3, 12–13, 17, 19–20, 45, 55, 91, 124, 129, 180, 212
   of capital 46–7, 49
   power relations 13, 15, 23, 64, 69, 72–3, 126, 158, 169, 200
precarity 31, 103
preschool/pre-school educators 50, 83, 86, 178, 180–1
professionalism 2, 15, 17, 22–3, 67
   professional identities 15, 17–18, 21, 62, 66–8, 92
   professional love 65
professionalization 1, 17, 66, 191–2

discourses 196
professionalization gap 67
provocations for womanist praxis 105–10
   childhood relations with water 108–10
   child storytelling 106–8
   storytelling as womanist enactment 105–6

queer/queer theory 21, 139–40, 143–4, 146, 151, 178, 211. *See also* LGBTQ/LGBTQ+
   affective vulnerability through 150–1
   ECEs 146–8
   queer bodies 139–40, 147, 151
   queer feminism 139–40, 144–5, 148, 200, 211, 215
      challenge and promise in ECE 148–50
      rise of 140–3
   queering of early childhood 143–6
   queerness 140, 142, 151, 211
   and third-wave feminism 140

race/racism 13, 18, 21, 33, 38, 51, 73, 85, 88–90, 93, 101–4, 107, 111, 116, 119, 121–2, 125, 135–6, 140–1, 149, 158, 162, 197, 202, 211. *See also* gender
Rajan, R. S. 89–90
rationality 166, 200
Reconceptualizing Early Childhood Education (RECE) community 99, 175
Reggio-Emilia educational philosophy 5, 180–1
Reimers, E. 147–8
relational/relationality 4, 55, 61–2, 64, 66, 73, 82, 111, 138, 164–5, 186, 191, 197, 199–200, 203, 212, 215–16
   ECE 68–73, 82
   relational ethics 186, 214
   relational ontology 62, 158
   relational self 69–70
   relational subjectivity 62–3, 67–9, 82, 197, 212
resistance 4, 12, 29, 62, 73, 79, 81–2, 101, 103, 108, 136–7, 151, 211, 215

Foucault on 22–3
Richardson, E. T. 64, 66
Rishi, S. 90–1
Robinson, F. 62, 69, 197
Robinson, K. H. 16, 19, 145
Rosen, R. 53–4
Rose Pere, R. 119–20
Rousseau, N. 88
Rubin, G. 141

Scandinavia/Scandinavian 175, 178, 186, 210
   ECEC in 176–7, 179
   pedagogy 187 n.3
self 31, 50–1, 56, 63–4, 69–72, 100, 108, 116, 137, 141, 148, 183–4, 194, 202, 210, 214. *See also* Others/Otherness
sex/sexism 32, 85–6, 121–2, 142, 144, 151, 158, 200
   gonadal 145
   sexist harassment 125–6, 141
   sexuality 13, 18, 46, 90, 101, 139–41, 143–4, 146, 148–51, 195, 200–2, 211
she-cession 3, 86–7
slavery 116, 127, 136
Smith, L. T. 117
social class 18, 69, 85, 92, 102, 121, 141
   lower-class 48, 51, 92
   middle-class 11, 33, 50, 85, 117, 121, 196
   upper-class 14
social democratic politics 175–6
social justice 19, 32, 87, 175
socially necessary labour 47, 54
social relations 3–4, 46, 52, 141
social reproduction theory (SRT) 45, 47–8, 51–6, 82
social stratification 53, 56, 140
social transformation 127
solidarity 22, 63, 69, 73, 82, 89, 117, 123, 185, 216
species-beings 54–6, 82
Spinoza, B. 183
spiritual/spirituality 102–4, 106, 110, 120, 128, 137, 157, 213
   earth-based feminist 164–9, 210

Starhawk 166–8
  The Earth Path: Grounding Your Spirit in the Rhythms of Nature 167
  ways of observing 168
Stengers, I. 166, 178, 184
storytelling 101, 105–8, 136–7, 177
subject(s) 4, 6, 12, 22, 27–9, 31, 45, 48, 137, 147
  ECE 3–4, 7–8, 18–21, 56, 61–2, 64, 66, 68, 70–2, 80–2, 136, 192, 195, 198–9, 203, 213
  feminine 2, 13, 48–51, 53–4, 81, 201, 211, 214
  formation 4, 28, 30, 33, 35, 72
  subjectification 12, 20, 163
  subjectivation 48, 50–1, 54, 56
  subjectivity/subjectivities 3–7, 12, 16, 23, 30–1, 46–8, 52, 56, 61, 65–8, 72, 79, 101, 106, 136, 141, 160, 162, 166–7, 169, 184, 186, 199, 211, 213–15
    and feminist ethics of care 62–3
    and Femme Theory 199–202
    posthuman 157–9, 161–5, 167–9, 210
    relational 62–3, 67–9, 82, 197, 212
Sullivan, A. L. 146
Sweden 175, 186
  National Commission on Child-Care (Barnstugeutredningen), 1968 176, 187 n.1
  in 1970s and following years 178–85

Tasman, A. 129 n.1
Third World 90, 142. *See also* First World
thresholds 137, 177, 184–6, 214
traditional moral theories 62
transdisciplinary 51, 176, 185
transformations 29, 32–3, 46, 50, 110–11, 120, 127–9, 147, 178, 181, 184
transgression 149, 212
transnational feminism 90, 178
transphobia 85, 149
Tronto, J., on care and moral values 62–3, 68–73
Truth, S. 87
Tsing, A., arts of noticing 168
Tuana, N. 178, 209

UN Convention on the Rights of the Child (1989) 52
unemployment 47
The United States 3, 8, 84, 86, 92, 102, 136, 142, 181, 191
  and Black women labour 88
  childcare workers in 86, 88, 92
  ECEs in 86, 101
  education racial project in 102
  gay/lesbian parents in 144
  pay penalties 86
  prekindergarten teacher in 86
  US Bureau of Labor Statistics 86
  white supremist 102–5
Urraro, L. L. 146

Van Bussel, T. 90, 92
violence 102, 105, 158, 162, 166, 210
Vogel, L. 48, 53
  Marxism and the Oppression of Women: Toward a Unitary Theory 47
vulnerability 51, 63, 146–7, 150–1, 195, 197, 199, 202

Walker, A. 100, 107
Walkerdine, V. 125, 179
Weedon, C. 13, 19, 31, 200
White, J. 69–70, 72
whiteness 103, 125
white supremacy/supremist 102–5, 111, 122, 137
woman 2–3, 6, 12–14, 16, 21, 23, 29, 32, 55–6, 62, 83, 85–6, 135, 182–3
  African-American 88
  of colour 21, 32, 83, 85–8, 93, 103, 140, 178
  Indigenous 32–3, 92
  in Indonesia 46–9
    in agriculture 46–7, 81
    in democratization, role of 50
    dharma wanita (women's duties) 47
    as domestics 46–7
    domination of 48
    government programmes 48
    ibu rumah tangga (housewives) 46–7, 50
    motherhood 198, 201

role of Mother in family 124, 126
societal abuse of 85, 125, 141
white 85, 90, 117, 121, 201–2
womanhood 85, 90, 198, 201–3
womenandchildren 51–6, 82, 135, 137
womanism/womanists 99–100, 107, 110–11, 136
and ancestral knowledges 106–8, 122
womanist mothering 108
womanist praxis 101–5, 109, 136–7
provocations for (*see* provocations for womanist praxis)
womanist spirituality (spiritual guidance) 102–3 (*see also* spiritual/spirituality)
women in development (WID) 46
working-class 56, 85, 175, 178–9, 196, 211
The World Bank 1, 49–50

www.ingramcontent.com/pod-product-compliance
Lightning Source LLC
Chambersburg PA
CBHW062148300426
44115CB00012BA/2048